משנה

ArtScroll Series®

Rabbi Nosson Scherman / Rabbi Meir Zlotowitz
General Editors

MAKE ME

motivating children for success at home and in the classroom

a practical guide for parents and teachers

by Rabbi Moshe Gans

DON'T BREAK ME

Published by
Mesorah Publications, ltd

FIRST EDITION
First Impression . . . August 1994

SECOND EDITION
First Impression . . . October 1994
Second Impression . . . April 1995
Third Impression . . . May 1997
Fourth Impression . . . July 1999

Published and Distributed by
MESORAH PUBLICATIONS, Ltd.
4401 Second Avenue
Brooklyn, New York 11232

Distributed in Europe by
J. LEHMANN HEBREW BOOKSELLERS
20 Cambridge Terrace
Gateshead, Tyne and Wear
England NE8 1RP

Distributed in Israel by
SIFRIATI / A. GITLER – BOOKS
10 Hashomer Street
Bnei Brak 51361

Distributed in Australia & New Zealand by
GOLD'S BOOK & GIFT CO.
36 William Street
Balaclava 3183, Vic., Australia

Distributed in South Africa by
KOLLEL BOOKSHOP
Shop 8A, Norwood Hypermarkert
Norwood 2196, Johannesburg, South Africa

THE ARTSCROLL SERIES
MAKE ME — DON'T BREAK ME

ISBN
0-89906-113-3 (hard cover)
0-89906-114-1 (paperback)

Typography by Compuscribe at ArtScroll Studios, Ltd.

Printed in the United States of America by Noble Book Press
Bound by Sefercraft, Quality Bookbinders, Ltd. Brooklyn, N.Y.

Rabbi CHAIM P. SCHEINBERG
Rosh Hayeshiva "TORAH-ORE"
and Morah Hora'ah of Kiryat Mattersdorf

הרב חיים פינחס שיינברג
ראש ישיבת "תורה-אור"
ומורה הוראה דקרית מטרסדורף

When parents and teachers motivate children to fulfill their responsibilities, they often use coercion and other negative approaches. The adverse effects of this style often stay with children throughout adulthood. In this book, Rabbi Moshe Gans clearly explains how to motivate children with love, respect, kindness and courtesy — the way חז"ל suggest. He shows the reader why positive methods motivate children and have long-lasting favorable effects. This book should be a valuable companion to every parent and teacher.

I extend to Rabbi Moshe Gans my ברכה of continued success in helping parents and teachers raise children to become responsible and productive members of כלל ישראל.

חיים פינחס שיינברג

רחוב פנים מאירות 2, ירושלים, ת. ד. 6979, טל. 371513-(02), ישראל
2, Panim Meirot St., Jerusalem, P. O. B. 6979, Tel (02)-371513, Israel

ישיבה דפילאדעלפיא

בס״ד

Dear Rabbi Gans שליט״א,

It is my pleasure to recommend your book, Make Me — Don't Break Me, which is a valuable guide for parents and teachers.

The eminent Horav Moshe Chaim Luzzato זצ״ל in his classic work מסלת ישרים reveals to us a remarkable phenomenon of human psyche: שכפי רוב פרסומם . . . כך ההעלם מצוי מאד והשכחה רבה. Matters that are very obvious tend to be overlooked and forgotten. When we are presented with solutions to problems we wonder why we didn't think of them ourselves. This book gives good suggestions and practical advice. It is a great benefit having uncomplicated solutions to many difficult problems.

Being a prominent מחנך yourself, I am sure that many of your wonderful ideas have been tried and tested.

May you merit the זכות הרבים from all who will gain from your success.

בברכה מעמקי הלב

Sincerely yours,

S. Kamenetsky

KAMENITZER YESHIVA
"Knesseth Beth Isaac"
THEOLOGICAL SEMINARY
JERUSALEM
P.O.B. 5036

ישיבת קמניץ
כנסת־בית־יצחק
ירושלים
ת.ד. 5036

בס"ד כ"ה סיון תשנ"ב

ראשי הישיבה:
הרב יצחק שיינר – ר"מ ומנהל
הרב אשר ליכטשטיין – ר"מ ומנהל
הרב חיים שלמה ליבוביץ – ר"מ

לכבוד הא' גדול יקירא עוסק
במלאכת שמים, הרה"ג ר' משה גאנס שליט"א

ראיתי את ספרו העוסק בסוגיא
גדולה וחשובה בדרכי החינוך לילדים
להסביר עליהם להוציא כחותיהם
וכשרונותיהם בדרך התורה והמדות
ועל ידי זה יתקיים בהם מאמר שלמה
המלך ע"ה חנוך לנער על פי דרכו
גם כי יזקין לא יסור ממנה, ומצאתי
שזכה להעלות פנינים ורעיונות
בדרכים שונים להגיע אל נפש
הילד שידע איך ורק בדרך התורה
יצליח כל ימי חייו על כן הנני מברכו
שיזכה להפיץ ספרו ברבים וזכות
הרבים יהא תלוי בו.

בעה"ח יום הנ"ל
לכבוד החינוך הטהור
משה אהרן שטרן
מנהל רוחני דישיבת קמניץ
בירושלים עיה"ק תובב"א

משה אהרן שטרן
רח' הגאונים 10
ירושלים עיה"ק ת"ו
מנהל רוחני דישיבת קמניץ

Abraham J. Twerski, M.D.
Gateway Rehabilitation Center
Moffett Run Road
Aliquippa, Pennsylvania 15001

Virtually all my books have been focused on the crucial role of self-esteem in making a proper adjustment to life. Problems of distortion of the self-concept with consequent low self-esteem often begin during childhood. While parents and teachers may not be causative in a low self-esteem problem, this is not enough. These are the important and "significant others" who can help the child overcome these potentially destructive feelings.

Rabbi Gans has made a major contribution by focusing on the issues in child rearing, both in the home and in the school, with important guidelines to both parents and teachers. The problems of low self-esteem are much more prevalent and have far-reaching effects in the complexity of modern life, and it is foolish to believe that our children will simply grow up to be psychologically healthy unless we make a major effort in counteracting the many deleterious influences in modern living.

All parents and educators should familiarize themselves with Rabbi Gans's book, and give serious thought on how to apply these principles to their children and students.

Abraham J. Twerski, M.D.
Founder/Medical Director

Rabbi Moshe Gans has written a brilliant, all-encompassing guide that is a *must* for every teacher and parent. His wise and compassionate advice will create a much more positive atmosphere at home and in the school. He gives hundreds of practical suggestions for creating a healthy relationship with children.

All too often, adults deal with misbehavior in the most cruel and primitive manner, by criticizing, screaming or hitting children, all of which only reinforce negative behavior. May this book open the hearts and minds of those who destroy children's spirits in this manner.

If all those who work with children would heed his advice, we would be seeing many more children who feel good about themselves, who are learning with enthusiasm and are responsible and kind to others.

This is a book for all Klal Yisrael, to help us turn our homes and our schools into places of love and understanding.

Miriam Adahan, Founder

EMETT: Emotional Maturity Established Through Torah

Acknowledgments

There are many people who must be recognized for helping make this book possible. To these people I owe a debt of gratitude.

To my parents, Mr. and Mrs. J. Gans, and my parents-in-law, Mr. and Mrs. M. Rosenberg, for their support and appreciation of this project. May they have many healthy years and merit to have great nachas from their children and grandchildren.

To Rabbi Chaim Pinchos Scheinberg, Rabbi Shmuel Kamenetsky, Rabbi Moshe Aharon Stern and Rabbi Abraham Twerski, for taking time from their busy schedules to review the manuscript and write letters of endorsement.

To Rabbi Matisyahu Solomon, *Menahel Ruchni* of the Gateshead Yeshiva, who also reviewed the manuscript and approved its contents.

To Rabbi Avrohom Turin, *Menahel Ruchni* of the Scranton Yeshiva, for his meticulous review of the manuscript. Rabbi Turin believed in the project, and spent many hours analyzing the manuscript and sharing his thoughts. Many of his wise insights are found in these pages.

To Rabbi Chaim Bressler, *Rosh HaYeshiva* of the Scranton Yeshiva, and Rabbi Aryeh Rottman, *Menahel Ruchni* of Yeshiva Mercaz HaTorah, for their untiring support and advice.

To Rabbi Zelig Pliskin, whose books are a constant source of inspiration in my personal and professional life. He believed in me and encouraged me to use my skills for the good of the *klal.* He said, "You can do it," and I listened to him.

To Miriam Adahan, whose books have influenced my views on parenting. She assisted me in my counseling and was a constant source of support and enlightenment. Mrs. Adahan reviewed the manuscript and, knowing her, I am sure she derived nachas from the ideas presented.

To Rabbi Meir Zlotowitz, Rabbi Nosson Scherman and Rabbi Sheah Brander, who accepted the manuscript for publication. They are caring professionals and have always been available for suggestions and solutions. The books they publish are a special contribution to contemporary Jewry, and I am proud to be part of it.

To Rabbi Moshe Leiber of the ArtScroll staff, whose support and persistence initiated the publishing process and kept things running smoothly. To Avrohom Biderman, who supervised the final stages of the project and helped assure a high standard of quality. To Fayge Silverman, whose expert editing greatly enhanced the book. To Mrs. Mindy Stern for her meticulous proofreading, Mrs. Bassie Gutman for typesetting and pagination, and Devory Glatzer and Bas-Siyon Drebin for typesetting.

To my brother-in-law and sister-in-law, Nechemiah and Esti Rosenberg, for making the contacts and technical arrangements in Israel.

To the participants of my teacher training institute, whose questions, answers and insights clarified many ideas on motivation.

To people who have used my counseling service. They brought me into their lives by sharing day-to-day challenges and experimenting with my suggestions. Our sessions were mutually rewarding; we all learned and matured. Without mentioning any names, their stories are found throughout these pages.

To the hundreds of children with whom I have come in contact. They inspired me to begin this project and complete it. They are our future, and we owe it to them to be the best parents and teachers we can be.

Rabbi Akiva once pointed to his wife and told his students, "What is mine and what is yours is hers." He recognized that his success and the success of his students were a product of his wife's support. This book, too, is a product of my wife's support. She was my biggest critic and strongest ally. This book would never have been completed without her unrelenting encouragement and, yes, motivation.

Rabbi Moshe Gans

Tammuz, 5754 / June, 1994

MAKE ME DON'T BREAK ME

Table of Contents

Introduction

Parents and teachers have the task of motivating children to succeed in life. The purpose of this book is to help them improve their skills.

This book answers questions such as:

"How can I motivate my son to be more responsible?"

"How can I inspire my daughter to improve her grades?"

"How can I influence my student to behave better in the classroom?"

It suggests ways of enhancing cooperation and instilling an inner drive to succeed. It offers methods that can motivate children to achieve success in their lives, as youngsters and adults, in school and out.

While the ideas in this book are for parents and teachers alike, the focus is mainly on parents in family situations. This avoids the confusion of alternating between home and classroom conditions. Since all the ideas are equally applicable to the classroom, teachers can easily derive conclusions and apply them to their own set of circumstances.

Parents and teachers frequently motivate with negative, coercive methods. They yell, criticize, give orders, threaten, punish and hit. They prefer not to resort to these methods but are at a loss to do anything else. They often ask, "What are some good punishments and ways of enforcing them?"

This book does not answer that question. Instead, it presents positive ways — call them "techniques" — of motivating children to cooperate and succeed, without punishment or coercion. The techniques presented in this book are carefully planned strategies, with one goal in mind — to motivate the child to *want* to succeed. The examples used are based on the experiences of families

I have counseled and reflect common events that occur in almost every home.

Many of the ideas presented are repeated throughout the book. This is intentional. These ideas have different applications in different situations. Furthermore, some ideas are traditionally overlooked by parents and teachers, yet are so important that they cannot be overemphasized.

The techniques in this book can be used to motivate children of all ages. They can even be used to motivate adults. Employers and employees, husbands and wives, will all find ideas which can help to motivate the people with whom they live and work. When it comes to motivation, adults and children are very much alike.

The techniques are not new or innovative. They are founded on the thoughts of *Chazal* and contemporary Torah authorities, and have been proven to be effective. Parents and teachers who have experimented with these techniques have affirmed that the atmosphere in their homes and classrooms has improved as a result. I am convinced that after you understand and experiment with these ideas you will also agree to their value.

This is more than a quick "how to" book. It is designed to help the reader understand *why* each strategy works. People often ask, "Why is it important to understand why each strategy works? Just give me the idea and let me try it!" They want a "quick fix." But a quick fix is not adequate. Each concept has its basis in human psychology and, when we understand the connection, it becomes part of our modus operandi. We come to believe in the concept and are enthusiastic about implementing it. We have more control of it and we do the things that produce the best results.

Many parents and teachers have told me that they have been waiting for a book like this. Their children are not motivated and they need help. They are eager to learn ways of motivating their children — and the quicker, the better.

This book will provide those ideas. However, to be successful, parents and teachers may have to change, too. They may have to alter old mindsets and habits that are ineffective or counterproductive and develop a new style of relating to their children. They may have to become less critical and punitive, and learn to be more patient, sympathetic, complimentary and consistent. This requires work; and, since they are in the leadership role, parents and teachers may have to work even harder than their children to bring about the desired change. There is no magic wand. We cannot expect to change children without changing ourselves, too.

How to Use This Book:

To get the most out of this book, first read it from cover to cover. Then, return to the chapters in which you have special interest. I suggest this approach for several reasons:

First, the techniques in this book share common elements. As you progress through the book, you will see how those elements are used in various circumstances. This will enhance your understanding and level of application.

The second reason is also practical. Suppose you hire a repairman to do a home repair. Even though he may only use two or three tools, he comes with a full tool box. Why? Because when he has a variety of tools at his disposal, he can quickly choose the most appropriate one without returning to his shop. You, too, may use only two or three of the motivational techniques presented here. But after reading the entire book and getting an overall perspective of each technique, you will have a variety of "tools" at your disposal. You will then be able to choose the appropriate one for each event.

After reading the entire book, commit yourself to just one technique at first. Don't use several at once and don't improvise by combining bits and pieces of different techniques. Wait until you become skilled in one technique before combining and adapting.

After committing yourself to one technique, use it several times. If it is not effective, go back to the book to check if you have been using it properly. If you have, the technique may not be appropriate for your particular set of circumstances; not all methods are appropriate for all children and all situations. You will have to use another.

If you use a technique and find that it is not bringing about *dramatic* improvement, don't become discouraged. Even if it brings about a 20% improvement, your situation is 20% better than it was before. Relatively speaking, this is significant progress.

If you view your child as "hopelessly" lazy or unmotivated, don't assume it is too late to change. On the contrary, make up your mind to help the child improve — today. Choose a technique you think has promise and follow it through.

If the child cooperates at home and performs well in school but can still do better, use the ideas in this book to help him improve. For example, the child may be capable of attaining grades of 98% but is attaining 92%. He can do better — and should do better — and with your influence, he can improve.

A physician would not dream of performing surgery before extensive training in the skills of surgery. A chef would not cook in a large restaurant and a tailor would not make garments before learning the skills of their trades. But, as life has it, parents begin practicing their profession before learning parenting skills, and there are teachers entering classrooms with minimal professional training. It is my hope that this book will provide some of the essential knowledge and skills which parents and teachers can use to become the successful professionals their children rightfully deserve.

Chapter One
Motivation and Parenting

We all want our children to succeed. We want them to develop skills, both as youngsters and as adults, in all arenas of life: social, emotional, academic, religious, familial and professional. The question is — what can we do to help? One part of the answer is that we must motivate them.

But how do we motivate? A variety of approaches, negative and positive, are commonly and instinctively used. Because negative approaches are so prevalent in our society, we will discuss them first. Hopefully, the reader will see the disadvantages of the negative approaches and have a greater appreciation for the positive ones.

Negative Motivational Methods

Picture this scene:

A parent wants her child to perform a task. It may be an immediate directive such as "Clean your room" or a long-term goal such as "Improve your grades in school." The child looks at the parent, shrugs his shoulders, and does not comply. How do parents typically deal with this?

At one extreme, there are parents who allow their children to "get away with murder" rather than prod them or fight with them. They believe that children eventually become motivated on their own, so they allow a great deal of independence in the hope that their children will one day mature naturally and become cooperative, responsible and dependable.

The problem with this mode of thought is that the parents are teaching their children to disregard them. With every episode, they send the unspoken message, "Neither we nor our goals are worthwhile." The children do not learn to respect their parents or to value responsibility. Instead, they learn to be arrogant, defiant and careless — traits incompatible with a healthy Torah lifestyle.

At the other extreme, there are parents who take on the fight. With a strong sense of custodial duty, they attempt to "beat some sense" into their children. As horse trainers break untamed horses, they break their children with an array of physical and/or mental pressures. They believe that with enough coercion their children will eventually become compliant. They persist in their forceful, sometimes brutal, ways with the conviction that they are being true to Torah principles by enforcing obedience and respect.

"Breaking" a child is a form of child abuse. It can cause a variety of problems — tears, hurt feelings, injured bodies, broken relationships, reduced self-confidence, stuttering, bed wetting and an array of other nervous habits.

"Breaking" motivates a child to perform out of fear, not desire. It is like holding a gun to his head and ordering him to relax; the pressure is too high and he cannot relax. Furthermore, when he performs out of fear, he will probably not develop a positive attitude toward the goal.

Even if the coercive parents win the battle and are successful in getting cooperation, they have not won the war. Coercion creates power struggles and causes children to rebel.[1] Additionally, the child will not value the goal or adopt a healthy pattern of

---

1. Rabbi Shamshon Raphael Hirsch, *Yesodos HaChinuch*, Netzach Publishers, 1957, pp. 65-66.

obedience, and once the parental pressure is removed he will revert to his original behavior.[1]

Between the two extremes, there are other approaches, incorporating varying degrees of authoritarianism and independence. Ideally, one of these approaches should be used; however, many parents fail to select the particular approach that fits the individual nature of the child. The result can be just as devastating.

Our well-intended methods can be counterproductive. People often operate with erroneous assumptions thinking they are correct. Take, for example, the parents who use force to imbue their children with respect. Why do they conduct themselves this way? Because they believe that applying physical and mental pressure will bring about the desired result.

As we have mentioned earlier, they are not instilling respect; they are really instilling fear. The child who cooperates does so out of fear, not respect. Secondly, a child receiving harsh parental treatment may eventually learn to scorn his parents. And thirdly, he may learn to treat other people with the same disrespect that has been shown to him. This is hardly the result his parents are hoping for.

One very typical scenario is the parents who want their child to develop good *middos*. Each time the child displays any type of poor *middah* or a lack of consideration for others, they offer a sharp reprimand. The parents believe that the child will improve only if they call attention, in a sharp way, to each and every mistake.

Although the parents think they are being productive, they may be creating more problems. With constant criticism, the child feels attacked and put down. Like a person with a loaded gun pointed at him, he never knows when the next shot will come or where it will strike. The child also feels violated and may protect himself by rebelling and doing the opposite of what his parents want him to do. Or he may feel so isolated and lonely that he builds a protective shell around himself. He becomes self-centered and develops a strong drive to preserve his pride and identity. This attitude is hardly conducive to developing good *middos.*

Furthermore, parents who degrade a child teach him an important lesson: if you disapprove of another person's actions, you may

---

1. Vilna Gaon, *Mishlei* 22:6.

put him down without regard for his feelings. By example, his parents teach him to be intolerant and inconsiderate — the opposite of what they want him to learn.

These examples illustrate that human nature does not always work the way we would like it to. Sometimes, parents think they are doing the proper thing but instead cause damage that lasts a lifetime. Their well-intended methods can be counterproductive.

Over time, astute parents may begin to realize that their methods are not bringing about the kind of response they want. They notice that the defiant child continues to disobey, the forgetful child still forgets, the lazy child is still lax in his work, and the obstinate child remains set in his ways. Yet they repeat their pattern.

Why? Because they saw their parents and teachers doing the same thing — or because they are simply using the approach that comes naturally to them. They surmise that since their elders used the approach and/or it sounds right it must be proper, even if it is negative. Besides, they do not know any other way.

But there *are* other ways. There are positive ways of motivating children to cooperate and achieve success. These approaches foster in the child a desire to excel. Cooperation is enhanced, the parent/child relationship is enriched and the child's emotional stability is reinforced.

Positive Motivational Methods

The definition of the word "motivate" is to *provide with a motive.* "Motive" is defined as *something that causes a person to act.* It implies an emotion or desire operating on the will and causing it to act.[1]

When we motivate, we influence the *will* of the other person. After being motivated, the other person has a *desire* to perform the act. His drive is from within, because he *wants* to do it. With this understanding, negative methods cannot be called "motivational" at all because they result in the desire to abandon the goal as soon as the parents are no longer in the picture. Positive

---

1. *Webster's Ninth New Collegiate Dictionary*, 1984, p. 774.

methods, however, can be called "motivational" because they create an *inner desire* to perform.

The importance of inner drive. *Chazal* tell us that a drive from within has the most enduring effects:

> "If I am not for myself, who will be?" [This means:] If I do not push myself to motivate myself to do *mitzvos*, who will motivate me? Motivation from others is beneficial on a temporary basis but when a person motivates himself every day, he will continue to think about serving Hashem and he will not become forgetful, as his heart desires. This is the proper way for a person to live (Rabbeinu Yonah, *Avos* 1:14).

Because inner drive is so important, *Chazal* instruct us to prepare ourselves to live free of external motivation. Then we can reach our goals on our own:

> "When there is no man, try to be a man." [This means:] When there are no people to help you do *mitzvos* and to chastise you, try to be a man and correct yourself, to do only the good and straight in the eyes of Hashem (Rabbeinu Yonah, *Avos* 2:5).

The objective in using positive motivational methods is to foster an inner drive to perform. The child will then be able to call on his own drive to propel himself forward.

If you take the word "motivation" and divide it in half, you have MOTIV / ATION. Using your imagination, you can discern two words — "motive" and "action." People with motivation have a motive; that is, they have a purpose, a reason and a cause. As a result of their *motive*, they take *action*.

Positive motivational methods share common elements. The motivational techniques presented in the forthcoming chapters share some common elements. They are positive and capitalize on the child's strengths. They give respect to the child and show concern for his welfare. They preserve the child's pride, build his sense of responsibility and independence, and create an atmosphere conducive to success.

Using positive motivational methods is preventive. Using positive motivational methods precludes a variety of negative outcomes. For example, when a child is motivated to accept responsibility, his parents do not have to pressure him to perform. This averts the potentially explosive confrontations which so often result from coaxing and cajoling.

Because motivation considers the needs and sensitivities of the child, his self-esteem and self-confidence remain intact. Cooperation is enhanced and the relationship he has with his parents is enriched. Numerous problems, familiar to all of us, are prevented.

Using a positive method, the forceful parents can relax their pressure without fearing that their children will never learn respect or responsibility. Children develop these traits more quickly when they are treated with respect and motivated properly.

With a positive method, the parents who allow too much independence can intensify their interventionary efforts without fearing that their children will rebel. With a positive method, resistance is minimized and cooperation is maximized.

The Motivation / Self-Confidence Connection

Using a positive approach to motivate a child results in high self-confidence. A negative approach results in low self-confidence. Why is self-confidence so important? Rabbi Moshe Feinstein explained:

> Many people do not reach their potential and also become sinners because they degrade themselves or the matter at hand. For example, a person thinks he cannot do great things such as learn Talmud with all its commentaries. He therefore does not learn because, according to his opinion, it will not help to know anything anyway. The result is that he is unable to learn and he becomes an ignoramus (*Darash Moshe*, p. 111).

The high self-confidence that we are referring to is not conceit, haughtiness or an artificial sense of greatness. Rather, it is one's sense of security in his own general worthiness and in his capability of achieving particular goals. Low self-confidence, on the other hand, refers to the negative sense of security one carries about himself. A person with low self-confidence may be very capable; the problem is his self-perception. And, as Rabbi Feinstein explained, this feeling of inferiority inhibits success.

The degree of a person's self-confidence often determines the degree of his success in life. A person with high self-confidence has an "I-can" attitude and believes he can succeed at his tasks. He performs enthusiastically and accepts full responsibility for completing a job. Mistakes or obstacles do not weaken his drive; rather, his faith in himself motivates him to persevere. Just as the wings of a bird enable it to stay airborne and fly, high self-confidence enables a person to soar and reach his goals.

Self-confidence is the engine that powers the machine of achievement. A self-confident person is more creative, more imaginative and more solution oriented. He speaks more effectively and has less fear and self-doubt. He has more of a positive attitude toward himself and others. A self-confident person can define his life more clearly and has greater control in choosing its direction. He has a sense of inner security and is less resistant to the motivational efforts of others. With his strong engine of self-confidence, he is empowered to achieve.

In contrast, the individual with low self-confidence believes he cannot succeed. He often resists the motivational attempts of others, for he has little respect for himself and believes he is not worthy of success. He performs unenthusiastically and below his real level of capability. When confronted with a challenge, he is more concerned with the problem and the fear of failure than with the solution and the rewards of success. Instead of *making* things happen, he *lets* things happen. His weak engine of self-confidence does not deliver much power to his machine of achievement.

Low self-confidence does not only express itself in relation to Talmud study. It influences many other areas of a child's life as well. We can observe its effects in a child who feels he is incapable of making friends and does not exert himself to do the things that will attract people to him. He says to himself, "Nobody will like me, so why should I bother trying to make them like me?" Another example is the child who thinks he is not athletic. Because of his conviction, he will not even try to excel at sports. When faced with a decision to do something that requires courage and commitment —

and we all have to make such decisions — the child with low self-confidence will back off and take the path of least resistance, even if it is not the most beneficial path for him. He has the capability to succeed, but his feelings of inadequacy hold him back from succeeding.

You may say, "Everything is in Hashem's hand.[1] The degree of success a person attains is determined by Hashem, so what difference does it make if he has high or low self-confidence?"

The answer is that we *can* control our future, to some degree, through our self-confidence. Let us explain.

Hashem took Adam around Gan Eden and told him, "See how beautiful My works are. All that I created is for you. Take care not to destroy My world."[2] Adam was given a tremendous opportunity — life in Gan Eden, along with all its benefits. He was also given some control over his destiny; by choosing to conduct himself properly or improperly, Adam had the power to perpetuate his opportunity of life in Gan Eden or destroy it.

Similarly, Hashem provides all of us with many opportunities. Like Adam, we can neglect them or capitalize on them. And like Adam, we do have some control over our future.[3]

For example, Hashem blesses a man with the opportunity to learn Torah in a yeshiva. He supplies this person with tools: a study hall, teachers, and people with whom he can study. The man can neglect those tools and fail, or use them as a means to grow. The choice is his. He has control.

Hashem blesses a person with the opportunity to earn an income. He provides him with a job as a tool to attain it. The person can neglect the tool by performing poorly and missing work, resulting in the termination of his employment. Or he can secure his future by performing responsibly. He has the control.

Similarly, a carpenter can use modern, accurate, professional tools to become a successful builder, or he can use old, less accurate tools and produce items of inferior quality. The choice is his.

As we have mentioned, high self-confidence and positive attitudes produce better results than low self-confidence and negative

---

1. Talmud *Berachos* 33b.

2. *Koheles Rabbah* 7:28.

3. Inferred from *Mesilas Yesharim*, ch. 1.

attitudes. In other words, self-confidence is also a tool — a tool for success. Hashem gives the tool of self-confidence to every human being. We can develop *high* self-confidence and utilize it to derive benefit from the opportunities that Hashem provides. Or we can live with *low* self-confidence and use it to produce failure and unhappiness. We all have talents and abilities, and to the degree that we frustrate and inhibit them through self-condemnation, we turn our backs on the wonderful opportunities that Hashem provides.

All this talk about self-confidence is not just theoretical. In reality, we *can* control how much self-confidence we have. We can actually imbue ourselves with it. There is a great deal of literature on this topic, enough to fill a separate book.

For our purposes, however, it is enough to say that parents are in a unique position to offer their children the tool of high self-confidence. By relating to them positively and motivating them properly, they can help their children develop high self-confidence, helping to secure a brighter future for their children.

The Motivation / Obedience Connection

Obedience is the essence of Torah life. Every Jew must have unfailing obedience to Torah requirements. Even if a person does not understand the value of a *mitzvah* or disagrees with it, he must perform it out of sheer obedience.

Similarly, children should have unfailing obedience to parents. Parents should be able to make demands and expect their children to yield to their authority, even if the children do not appreciate the value of the demand.[1]

How, then, can we reconcile 'motivation' with 'obedience'? 'Motivation' tells us to help the child understand the value of the goal and develop a desire to reach it. 'Obedience' tells us to expect the child to comply even if he does not appreciate the value of the goal. When does 'motivation' apply and when does 'obedience' apply?

Indeed, obedience is the ideal that every parent should strive to instill. *Halachah* requires children to treat their parents regally.

---

1. Rabbi S. R. Hirsch, *Judaism Eternal*, Soncino Press, 1976, vol. 1, pp. 229-231.

Children are supposed to follow every order and even serve their parents' personal needs.[1]

However, some children are incapable of obedience. They are lazy, forgetful, independent, obstinate or defiant. They respond to parents' requests and demands when they are nagged, threatened, screamed at, punished or physically forced. From these children, parents should not demand obedience. Let us explain:

King Shlomo said, "Train a child according to his way."[2] He was telling us that with every instructional interaction, parents must consider the child's nature. Why? Because a child's nature cannot be broken; it remains with him an entire lifetime. Even if parents prevail through coercion, the child will revert to his natural tendencies when his parents are no longer near him. The only rational thing to do, therefore, is to work with the child according to his nature.[3]

Rabbi Simcha Zisel Ziv of Kelm used this principle to help his daughter correct a character flaw. He observed that she had a liking for money which he felt was inappropriate. He did not coerce her to give up whatever little she had, nor did he rebuke or spank her. Rather, he gave her a few coins every day and walked her to the charity box so that she could deposit them for poor people. He helped her refine her character by working *with* her and aligning himself with her nature.[4]

If a child is incapable of obedience, how can parents "train him according to his way"? By *motivating* him to perform the desired act, not by demanding obedience. Although parents are in the position of authority, they should not force their goals on such a child; rather, they should find more agreeable ways of influencing him to reach his goal. Positive motivational methods, with the intent of creating inner drive, serve this purpose.

Parents can also use positive methods to motivate children to develop the trait of obedience. Like any other goal, parents can motivate a child to become obedient by using rewards, praise and persuasion. Once a child learns to be obedient, the parents can begin to rely more on the principles of obedience instead of

---

1. See *Yoreh Deah* 260.
2. *Mishlei* 22:6.
3. Vilna Gaon, *Mishlei* ad loc.
4. *Tenuas HaMussar*, vol. 2, p. 92.

motivation. But before that happens — and it may take a long time — they have to rely on principles of motivation.

And then we have the children who can be obedient but respond negatively to demands of obedience. Even obedient children disobey from time to time. Positive motivational methods are the way of getting these children to do the things they must do.

Some children are obedient but for some reason do not seem to be developing an inner drive to do the things their parents want them to do. If they never develop an appreciation for the goal, they will cease performing once their parents are not there to make the demand. Here, too, parents should not demand obedience; rather, they should foster in the child an appreciation for the goal and a desire to reach it.

Obedience occurs when the child feels he *has* to do the action. Motivation occurs when the child *wants* to do the action. Both have a place and, as we said earlier, obedience is the ideal. But when it is ineffective or counterproductive — especially if parents do not know how to bring about obedience — it becomes an inappropriate policy. In these instances, helping the child to understand the value of the goal fosters a willingness to reach it.

Some parents think that if they shift from obedience to motivation they will lose control and will no longer be in charge. On the contrary, when their expectation of obedience is ineffective, they do not have meaningful control anyway. But when they use motivation, they are taking charge of the situation in a mutually agreeable way and, at the same time, nurturing the child for future obedience.

Treating Children as Individuals

No two children are alike. Every child has his or her own character, abilities and sensitivities. One child may find a particular task difficult or uninviting while another finds it easy or stimulating. And, depending on mood, a single child may respond differently to similar situations.

Because no two people are alike, parents cannot expect their children to be carbon copies of themselves. Parents are who they are because of their distinct personalities and conditioning. Children also have distinct personalities which are invariably different from their parents' and which, for the most part, cannot be changed.

King Shlomo's directive that we "train the child according to his way" suggests that when we ask a child to perform an action, our approach should blend with his or her temperament, as well as the atmosphere of the occasion. We have to decide if we will motivate the child, demand obedience or withdraw from the issue altogether. Whatever our decision is, the plan must blend with the child's individual nature.

> The passage ["Train a child according to his way"] requires unequivocal individualized training. A life of Torah and *mitzvos* is the general aim, but the approaches that bring one to the purest level of fulfilling Torah and *mitzvos* alternate according to a child's character, abilities, tendencies, and intellectual and emotional strengths; therefore, every method is not suitable for every child. We want our son who is like Esav to become as proper and trustworthy as a son who is like Yaakov; therefore, we must plan our training and raise each of our children according to his personal character, because this determines the difference between future lifestyles (Rabbi S. R. Hirsch, *Yesodos HaChinuch,* Netzach Publishers, pp. 55-56).

Effective leaders will tell you that they reached their position because they have made a habit of paying careful attention to the individual needs of each personality with whom they come in contact. Parents are leaders, too — they are leaders of their children and should employ the same principle. Rabbi Chaim Shmulevitz discussed this point:

> The man who has the spirit in him [i.e., a true leader] is able to work with each and every person, and he deals with all people according to their intellect. This is a most important skill for a father to have — that he does not deal with his children in a single way but deals with each child according to his or her individual spirit. He also works with each child as if he or she were an only child (*Sichos Mussar* 5733:21).

Chazal presented a variety of motivational methods in their writings. Obviously, they believed that there is no single way of motivating every child and that parents should have a repertoire of approaches.

Now the question is — even after developing a repertoire, how does one choose the appropriate approach for each child? First, you have to know your child. Know what stimulates him or her. Become acquainted with his or her strengths and weaknesses. Then, make the appropriate match between the child and the motivational method.[1]

The Role of Parents

Train children while they are young. During the first years of life, whenever a child gives a cry, the parents are there to satisfy his or her every need. The child can be demanding, even rebellious, and the parents respond in a very agreeable manner. How, then, at the age of four or five, can we expect a child to suddenly become cooperative? Indeed, we cannot expect sudden improvement, but we can expect gradual improvement. The child must be reshaped and retrained gradually, and the time to begin is while he or she is still young.[2]

The principle "Train a child (in Hebrew, *na'ar,* meaning young boy) according to his way" tells us openly that parents should train their children during *childhood.* The time to teach life skills and imbue success-oriented attitudes is while the child is young. After years of practice, the youngster will be able to carry those skills and attitudes into adulthood.[3]

Prepare children for adulthood. The principle "Train a child according to his way" has a purpose found at the end of the passage — so that "it will not depart from him when he becomes old."[4] In other words, training a child has a long-term objective — responsible adulthood. Parents have the custodial duty

---

1. See Rabbi Yeruchom Levovitz, *Daas Torah, Shemos* 19:3; see Vilna Gaon on *Mishlei* 16:4 and 22:6; see *Midrash Rabbah, Bamidbar* 21:15.

2. Rabbi S. R. Hirsch, *Judaism Eternal,* vol. 1, pp. 229-231.

3. Rabbeinu Yonah, *Mishlei* 22:6 and *Avos* 1:14.

4. *Mishlei* 22:6.

of preparing their children for responsible and successful adult living.

If a child has an impediment that will inhibit future success, his parents should help him conquer it. If it is low self-confidence, parents should offer encouragement and provide opportunities for success. If he is lacking motivation to excel in school, parents should motivate him to excel. Children need successes now in order to propel them toward the future.

Be proactive. Create an atmosphere conducive to growth. The way to help children succeed is to be more than active; it is to be proactive. *Take steps* to enrich their lives and the relationship you have with them. *Look* for ways to help them grow, then *motivate* them to follow through.

It is easier to do this with children who are naturally lovable. Their pleasing personality, sense of humor and cute appearance make them more appealing. The real challenge, though, is dealing with children who are not so lovable. It is with these children that parents have to make a special effort to provide love and motivation.[1]

Take the initiative in resolving conflicts. Families are rarely formed by choice. Husbands and wives can choose each other, but they cannot choose the character or personalities of their children. Interests and personalities are diverse, and this often results in family quarrels. Conflicts must be resolved, and the question is, who is to take the first step in that process — the parents or the child?

The parents should take the initiative. Why? Because preparation for responsible adult living — the long-term goal of childhood — can only be accomplished in an atmosphere conducive to growth. An atmosphere which is conflict-free is most conducive to growth. And if parents fail to create an appropriate atmosphere, they have not done their full job. Therefore, it is the parents' responsibility to take the necessary steps to bring about a resolution in any conflict.

Besides, children do not have the maturity, experience or skill to initiate compromise and create mutual understanding. Parents have the intellectual and experiential advantage.

Be a friend to your child. Parents who use positive motivational techniques have better relationships with their children than

---

1. Rabbi S. R. Hirsch, *Judaism Eternal*, vol. 1, pp. 249-251.

those who use negative techniques. This is important, because the extent of success parents have with children is dependent on the relationship they have with them.

The parent-child relationship is certainly important while children are young, but its impact is much more far-reaching. Rabbi Shamshon Raphael Hirsch put it beautifully:

> In those years, parents, become friends to your children; let the son and daughter have no greater or closer friend than father and mother — parents, too, have no greater or more natural friend than their children when grown up. They must pour their hearts into yours, and should heaven and earth abandon them they must ever find loyal support, at once kindly and stern, in father and mother ... It will certainly blossom for you if you yourselves do not crush it out of sheer ignorance, if you do not insist on seeing in the young man and young woman nothing more than a mere boy and girl, if you do not forget that as they grow older they must be treated differently, and you must become friends to them in order that they may become friends to you. Then, when you have firmly linked their hearts to yours in this way, you may confidently allow them to leave you and wander abroad. Over mountains and valleys, over land and sea they carry your picture at once smiling and stern in their hearts, and in the hour of temptation it will with warming mien appear to them as Jacob's picture did to Joseph, and will become their guardian angel to keep them worthy of you and save them from sinking (*Horeb*, translated by Dayan Grunfeld, Soncino Press, N.Y., 1981, p. 414).

All parents want to have this kind of relationship with their children. Using the techniques presented in this book can help.

Improving Your Own Character

Positive motivational techniques such as rewards, persuasion or constructive criticism may seem foreign and time-consuming to many parents. They may defend their familiar approaches to motivation with comments like these:

"If I yell at him, I know my message will get across."

"If I ignore the problem, she will grow up to be a brat."

"If I hit him just once, he will change his ways quickly."

These parents rely on their natural impulses. But the principles of effective motivation dictate that we oppose those natural impulses. They tell parents to understand why the child is not performing, then to generate a willingness to perform — all the while preserving the child's pride and his relationship with his parents.

Yes, developing a positive motivational approach takes more effort and is more time-consuming; however, in the long run it has an enduring positive effect. The child becomes a more cooperative individual, and the parent/child relationship is enriched.

The Vilna Gaon said, "The purpose of life is to break the *middos* that have not yet been broken."[1] Rabbi Shlomo Wolbe writes that the demands of raising children create the strongest necessity to improve one's *middos.*[2] If motivating children requires parents to change themselves, they will reap a double benefit — their own character improvement and their children's success.

---

1. Vilna Gaon, *Mishlei* 4:13.

2. *Alai Shur,* p. 260.

Chapter Two
Motivate With Praise

Take a moment to recall a time when you were praised. After hearing it, how did you feel about yourself? How did you feel about your abilities? As a result of the praise, did you become motivated?

If you are like most people, receiving praise causes you to feel better about yourself and your abilities. It motivates you and boosts your enthusiasm. Frequently, praise makes such a lasting impression that you vividly recall the person who gave it, the place and time it happened, and the exact words used.

If you have a weak spot for praise, you are not a weak person. You are normal. Praise penetrates a person's very emotions. This is human nature.

Why does praise make such an impact?

People Have a Need to Feel Important

People consider themselves important and every person has a need to be recognized as important. In fact, this need is the strongest force within a person's psyche.

When people see group photographs, whose faces do they look for first? That's right — their own!

Rabbi Eliyahu Dessler said, "To most people, there is no word more beloved than 'I' and there is nothing more beautiful than their own name."[1]

Many years ago, the New York Telephone Company conducted a study to discover which words people use most frequently. They found that people use the word "I" most frequently. Is it any wonder? As one expert put it — people think about themselves before breakfast, during lunch and after dinner.

> The desire for honor is greater than the desire for wealth ... Honor is the driving force because one cannot endure being and seeing oneself lower than another ... Honor drives the heart of a person more than all the yearnings and desires in the world (*Mesilas Yesharim*, ch. 19).

Throughout history, famous leaders have illustrated this basic drive of human nature — sometimes with fatal consequences.

> Many stumbled and were destroyed in their pursuit of honor. Yeravam ben Nevat lost his share in the next world because of his pursuit of honor ... Honor caused Korach and his group to be destroyed ... The spies spoke negatively about the land of Israel and brought death to themselves and their entire generation because they feared that their honor would be reduced after entering the land and that others would replace them. Shaul began to chase Dovid because of honor ... (ibid.).

All these leaders were driven by a need to feel important. King Shaul launched a campaign to kill Dovid because Dovid was given more honor after they both returned from war. The spies tried to prevent the Jewish people from entering Israel because they did not want to lose their distinguished level of importance. Korach and his band of rebels sought Moshe Rabbeinu's position; they were warned of the danger but persisted anyway. Hashem offered Yeravam ben Nevat a spectacular reward if he would repent — a walk in Gan Eden together with King Dovid and Hashem. When he learned that

---

1. *Michtav M'Eliyahu*, vol. 4, p. 244.

he would walk behind King Dovid, he rejected the offer and continued in his evil ways.

Because people feel important they have difficulty seeing their personal faults. They even justify their mistakes.[1] King Shaul illustrated this tendency when he allowed Agag, the king of Amalek, to live. He acted in direct violation of Hashem's mandate, yet he did not accept full responsibility for his action afterward. He blamed the people for encouraging him to spare Agag's life.[2]

The need to be important causes jealousy and hatred. We see this from the fact that skilled craftsmen dislike the other members of their trade. Each craftsman wants to be recognized as the most skilled in his trade but the existence of competitors reduces that possibility.[3]

This need for importance explains why praise has such a strong impact on people. Praise satisfies the need to be recognized and affirms a person's importance. Praise is to the soul what air is to the lungs and blood is to the heart.

A wise person once said, "There are four billion people in the world who go to sleep every night starving for a decent meal. But there are five billion people who go to sleep every night starving for a few words of sincere praise and appreciation."

Rabbi Yeruchom Levovitz said that every person wants recognition. It is as if every person "stands and yells loudly, in all forms of announcements, 'Consider me and make me important,' 'Don't embarrass me or degrade me,' 'Recognize my words.' "[4]

Make People Feel Important

The truth is, all people have innate value and importance.[5] We should not wait until they seek recognition from us; instead, we are

---

1. Talmud *Kesubos* 105b, explained by Rabbi Yoel Schwartz, *The Eternal Jewish Home*, Jerusalem Academy Publications, 1982, p. 43.

2. *1 Shmuel* 15:9, explained by ibid.

3. *Bereishis Rabbah*, ch. 19, explained by ibid., p. 42.

4. *Daas Chochmah U'Mussar*, vol. 3, p. 68.

5. Mishnah *Sanhedrin* 4:5: A person should always say, "The world was created for me." Also, *Avos* 3:14: Hashem went out of His way to inform us that man is so dear that he was created in His image. Also, *Bereishis* 1:27: Man was created in the image of Hashem.

instructed to honor people and make them feel important. *Chazal* tell us:

> Honor others the way you honor yourself (*Avos* 2:10).
>
> The one who honors others is honored (*Avos* 4:1).
>
> The honor you have for others should be the same as the fear you have of your Rebbe (*Avos* 4:12).
>
> Having a "good eye" [means] that one is not jealous of his friend, and that his friend's honor is as dear to him as his own (Rashi, *Avos* 5:19).

Making people feel important is a major component in making friends and influencing people. It is so crucial that one successful business manager visualizes all her employees with a sign on their foreheads stating, "Make me feel important." One psychologist advises parents to imagine their children wearing badges that state, "Catch me doing something good." A children's advocate group once produced bumper stickers with the slogan "Have you hugged your child today?" reminding parents to make their children feel loved and important.[1]

Successful educators, business managers, camp counselors, athletic coaches and military leaders use this principle to influence and build effective relationships with the people they manage. By making your children feel important, you can manage them better, too.

Praise Lifts Spirits

When people are praised they feel important. They become more confident and take pride in their performance. Their state of mind is transformed and their spirits are lifted. Try praising someone. Be sincere. Make it meaningful. Then, watch that person's spirits soar.

High Spirits Lead to High Achievement

When do you do your best — when your spirits are up or down? If you are like most people, you feel your best and do your best when your spirits are high. Your mind is open. Your

---

1. See Rabbi Chaim Shmulevitz, *Sichos Mussar*, 5732:29, 36, for a thorough discussion of this point.

imagination and creativity are inspired. You are motivated to succeed and you take pride in the outcome.

Children are the same. When their spirits are high, their chances for success are enhanced, too.

Praise Is a Motivational Technique

As we said, praise lifts spirits, which in turn increases the likelihood of success. This means that praise is a powerful tool which can enhance a person's potential for success.

Seen this way, praise is more than nice words which make people feel good. Praise is a *tool* which *motivates* people to perform successfully and reach goals.[1] Praise reinforces a person's self-confidence. It helps him realize his own worth and strengths, and it encourages him to continue growing and building on his strengths.[2] If you can make children feel good about themselves through praise, you have directly enhanced their ability to succeed in life.

There is a story about a sales manager in the cosmetics industry who used praise to increase the productivity of one of her sales representatives. After several unsuccessful shows, the sales rep made a $35 sale. The manager praised her in a very excited tone of voice, exclaiming, "You had a $35 show ... that's wonderful!"

The manager later explained that, although a $35 sale is nothing to become excited about, this sales rep had sold nothing at all in her first three shows. Through praise, the manager was trying to encourage the rep to keep progressing. As a result, the rep went on to a fifth show, and her sales continued to increase. Had the manager reprimanded her for low productivity, she probably never would have gone on to a fifth or sixth show. Through praise, this manager made lemonade out of a lemon. The point is, if it works for adults it can work for children, too.

When an adult asks a large group of children to be quiet, the children typically ignore the request. However, through praise, a

---

1. Rabbi Shlomo Wolbe, *Alai Shur*, p. 261: "Praise and prizes are more effective than threats and punishments." Also see *The Eternal Jewish Home*, pp. 63-65: according to the Sh'lah, parents should encourage their children by pointing out both large and small achievements.

2. Rabbi Chaim Mordechai Katz, cited by Rabbi Z. Pliskin, *Love Your Neighbor*, Aish HaTorah Publications, 1977, p. 374.

school principal and a camp counselor are able to quiet hundreds of children single-handedly. How do they do it? One way is that when they initially ask for quiet, they take notice of the rare child or group of children who become quiet immediately. They then call attention to it by announcing, "I like the way so-and-so is being quiet." Invariably, others who want to be complimented in public become quiet, too. They continue announcing the names of children with whom they are pleased. Soon, all the children become quiet.

Catch Your Children Doing Things Right

We are all familiar with the tradition of catching other people doing things wrong. It happens between parents and children, husbands and wives, employers and employees, school principals and teachers. Good performances go by unnoticed. But as soon as we make a mistake — POW! We hear it!

There is an old rhyme which aptly captures this idea: "Once I did wrong and about this I heard ever. Twice I did right and about these I heard never."

> Shani was proud of her report card. She received five A's and one C. When she showed it to her parents, their only comment was, "Why did you get the C? Try to do better next time."
>
> Yoni and Avraham do not always get along. When they fight, their father sends them to their rooms. When one complains that the other is not sharing, their father is quick to give a lecture on the merits of sharing. But when they play nicely with each other, their father says nothing.

All too often, parents catch their children doing things wrong. They let ordinary good behavior go by without comment but are quick to recognize, even magnify, poor behavior.

Why do these parents act this way? Some are not aware of the power of praise. Others are lazy — and will admit it. Still others actually believe that children who perform to expectation do not deserve praise. They say, "These children are just doing what they are supposed to do anyway." But when their children make a mistake, they believe that it is their duty as responsible parents to provide immediate and unfaltering correction. They tell their children, "If you don't hear from us, it means everything is okay."

Parents want their children to repeat good performances, but when they do not recognize those performances the children may not be motivated to repeat them. Children who play nicely or get good grades are encouraged to repeat their performances when they are rewarded with praise. Saying "I am so proud of the way you do ..." can motivate a child to continue doing it. To ignore the good performances and/or recognize only the mistakes is to neglect the motivational benefit that praise can provide.

With some children, pointing out a poor behavior may even reinforce that behavior. Psychologists say that children with a need for attention do whatever they can to receive it. For many of these children, the attention itself is rewarding — even if it is in the form of criticism. If parents disregard good behaviors and recognize only the negative ones, the child will repeat the negative behaviors just for the attention. In the process, the parents unknowingly reinforce the behavior they want to eliminate.

Catch your children doing things right. Be liberal; you don't need an excuse to do it. Be on the lookout for the times your children do something praiseworthy and call attention to it. Be like a gold miner who finds gold by digging through the dirt and all the time focuses on the gold. Look past your children's "dirt." Focus on their good points and bring out the best in them.

Catch your children playing peacefully and let them know you are pleased. Catch the A's in the report card and make a party for your child to show how proud you are. See what can be done to bring about improvement in the subject receiving the C, but always emphasize the good performances. This generates more of the same behavior and should carry over to the weak subject.

Some parents believe that praise and success spoil and inflate a child's ego, so they take children who are high and knock them down a few pegs. They put these children down as a protective measure, even if they show no conceit. These parents are making a mistake. Success propels, energizes and encourages growth. Failure, on the other hand, results in bitterness and low self-esteem.

The purpose of any motivational technique is to foster within the child an internal drive to perform well and reach goals.

Praise accomplishes this more effectively than criticism. Criticism debilitates, while praise rehabilitates. With criticism, ability withers; with praise, ability blossoms.

❦ ❦ ❦

Praise can be used, in a more sophisticated way, as a *planned strategy* to enhance a child's performance. Applied at the appropriate times and in the appropriate way, praise has more power than many people think. We will now explain how to get the most out of it.

Praise Every Improvement

Did you ever attend an aquarium sea show? Walruses perform dancing acts and dolphins race around the pool. There are also whales that jump over a rope, ten feet in the air. How are these sea animals trained?

Let's talk about the whales. The whale trainers stretch a rope across the bottom of the pool. Every time the whale crosses the rope, they reward it with a fish. Then they raise the rope a little. When the whale swims over the rope, they reward it; when it swims under the rope, they do not reward it. The trainers continue raising the rope, little by little, giving the whale a fish every time it swims over. It does not take long for the whale to learn that it must swim over the rope to receive the fish. So when the trainers stretch the rope above the water line, the whale leaps over it to receive its reward. The trainers continue raising the rope into the air until the whale reaches the ten-foot goal.[1]

Let's analyze this training program.

> 1) The trainers set a goal for the whale — to jump ten feet in the air.
>
> 2) They structure a program of progressive, achievable steps by raising the rope incrementally.
>
> 3) They reward every good performance even before the final goal is reached.

---

1. Information provided by Guenther Skammel, Senior Marine Mammal Trainer, New York Aquarium for Wildlife Conservation.

This training program illustrates an important principle — behavior that is rewarded is repeated. The trainers do not wait for the final goal to be reached before providing the rewards; rather, they reward the whale every time it shows a small improvement in the right direction.

Parents, without realizing it, use the same idea when teaching a child to walk. After the child takes the first step, they become excited. They hug and kiss the child. They telephone their friends and relatives. The child feels the excitement and appreciates the recognition. The child is probably thinking, "You think I did well *this* time? You just wait and see what I'll do the *next* time!"

Each day, the parents urge the child to take one more step. They reward each small improvement with more recognition, and the child responds by repeating more of the same behavior. This continues until the child becomes a proficient walker. Once the child is able to walk independently, parents no longer have to give recognition because the newly acquired independence is self-rewarding.

Parents teach a child to talk using the same principle. When the child wants milk and says "mih" for the first time, the parents become excited. They praise the child and call all their friends. The child feels good about this reward and is motivated to continue saying "mih."

The parents, however, are not satisfied with their child's baby talk and after a short time encourage her to say "milk," "please" and "thank you." They reward each small success — even if she says "mil" or "plis" — with praise. The child is motivated to add more words to her vocabulary and, little by little, develops language proficiency. Once the child is able to communicate well, parents no longer have to give recognition because the ability itself is self-rewarding.

These examples illustrate the first element in using praise as a motivational strategy. Parents set a goal and recognize every small success in the direction of the goal. They do not wait for the child to walk and talk proficiently — an *exactly* correct performance. Rather, they praise the child when she says a word or takes a step — a small improvement in the right direction.

Praise success. Don't reprimand failure. If the whale swam under the rope and the trainer whipped it, how would the whale respond? It may sense a hostile environment and avoid the situation entirely by staying in one corner of the pool.

How would children react if parents were to spank them for not taking five steps or not saying "milk, please" right away? They might become less cooperative. They may learn to walk and talk in spite of their parents' harsh treatment, but progress would likely be at a slower rate and they might be left with the scars of nervous tension.

Whale trainers do not penalize the whale for swimming under the rope; rather, they focus on good performance, even if it is not perfect. Parents easily relate to this approach when they teach their children to walk and talk. However, when it comes to other kinds of performances, they sometimes abandon the approach. Let's look at a familiar scenario.

> Sarah's chore is to clear the dinner table and stack all the dishes in the sink. After dinner, on the first day of her new assignment, she clears fifteen of the twenty dishes on the table.
>
> Sarah's mother tries to remain calm and says, "Your job is to clear all the dishes. Please remove the other five from the table." Sarah rolls her eyes, as children often do, and finishes the job.
>
> The next night, Sarah clears all but two dishes and one fork. Her mother becomes irritated and says, "This is the second night in a row you did not complete your chore. Now please clear the table properly." Once again, Sarah complies.
>
> The third night, Sarah clears the entire table but doesn't stack the dishes properly in the sink. Her mother is becoming frustrated and reprimands her once again.

Does it sound familiar? After three nights, Sarah is still amiss in her duties and her mother is becoming increasingly frustrated. She feels that Sarah does not deserve to be praised because she has not yet performed her job properly. So she ignores the parts that Sarah performed properly and calls attention to the parts she neglected.

Instead, Sarah's mother should recall how she motivated her daughter to walk and talk. She praised every small improvement and disregarded her shortcomings. When using praise as a motivational technique, she should give Sarah the same treatment. This means that as long as there is improvement, her mother should look for the things Sarah does right, praise her for them and disregard her mistakes. How would she do this?

On the first night, she should call attention to the fifteen dishes that were cleared and say, "You did a good job clearing those fifteen dishes. I am very proud of your willingness to share household responsibilities."

What child would not appreciate this response! Sarah made an effort to reach the goal and did succeed, to some degree — just as the child who takes only a few steps in the beginning and succeeds to some degree.

This is the second time Sarah is hearing about the chore; before dinner her mother first told her about it and she is now reminding her. She knows what she is supposed to do and will probably do better next time. Why? Because the behavior that is rewarded is repeated. Sarah may be so impressed by the praise that the next day she will clear all the dishes and even wash the tabletop. This is the ideal response.

But what if the next day comes and Sarah clears all but two dishes? Shouldn't her mother become frustrated? Two days have passed and she still can't do a simple chore!

Whether Sarah is being neglectful or not, think of it this way: only two days have passed and she has made so much progress. Before the assignment she cleared nothing. The first night she cleared fifteen dishes. The second night she cleared eighteen dishes. This is real progress and she should be recognized for it, not reprimanded. Her mother should focus on the accomplishment, not the problem — just as she did when Sarah was learning to walk and talk. Sarah appreciates the praise and will probably perform better the third day.

But what if several more days pass and Sarah is still not clearing all the dishes? Obviously, she needs another reminder. Following the guideline of no criticism, her mother should say in a gentle, respectful tone, "You have been clearing most of the dishes from the dinner table. I am happy with the progress you have made. Let's see if you can clear *all* the dishes from now on." She is not reprimanding Sarah or focusing on the negative. She is focusing on the positive by praising Sarah for her good performances and encouraging her to do better. Hopefully, her daughter will do better the next day.

A parent once shared with me her difficulty in using praise: "Whenever I criticize or threaten my child, I make it a point to praise," she told me. "But I still get no response. I guess praise does not really work." Her problem was that although she was criticizing properly, she was not using praise — as a motivational strategy — properly. Her constant criticism and threats detracted from the impact of the praise.

This is not to say that there is no place for criticism or threats of penalty. These methods have their place.[1] However, when using praise as a *motivational technique,* they are conflicting approaches.

Additionally, demanding obedience and/or using criticism and threats are acceptable if parents can use them *properly.* All too often, though, there are negative side effects. In those cases praise is a viable alternative.

Dealing with a resistant child. Let's continue Sarah's story. Suppose her mother gave her the first gentle reminder and, after several more days, Sarah is still not performing properly. Her mother has been following all the rules: she has been praising improvements, disregarding mistakes and giving gentle reminders. But it just isn't working. She senses that Sarah is resisting. What should she do?

Since praise alone is not effective, it is time to reprimand Sarah for her neglect.[2] Then, as she improves, her mother should continue praising her. It is true that admonishment dilutes the purity of the praising technique, but in this case it must be done.

What if Sarah still does not improve? Her mother will have to use her judgment to decide if Sarah will respond to another reprimand. If she thinks that Sarah will not respond, she should change her approach and use a different motivational technique.

---

1. See Rabbi Eliyahu Dessler, *Michtav M'Eliyahu,* vol. 4, p. 228: Fear of penalty can be an appropriate motivator.

2. See Chapter Seven for a discussion on how to reprimand.

All along, as Sarah resists her responsibilities, her mother should examine their relationship. Why? Because if a parent does not have a loving, trusting relationship with a child, praise will not be effective.[1]

Sarah's mother should ask herself these questions:

1. Do my daughter and I struggle for power?

2. Does either of us have a need to assert control or be independent?

3. Do I satisfy Sarah's needs or fight them?

If the answers to these questions point to a troubled relationship, the mother should take steps to restore it. She may find that as the relationship grows, her praise will become more effective. But until that time, she should use another technique better suited to the relationship and the occasion.

Perhaps the relationship is healthy, but Sarah simply does not respond to praise the way most children do. She may have very low self-esteem or she may be impervious to praise. In this case, Sarah's mother should use another technique better suited to her personality.

Even if Sarah's mother fails to motivate her through praise, she should not walk away thinking that she wasted her time. Her praise probably enhanced their relationship and injected a good feeling into the general household atmosphere. The stage is now set for Sarah to respond more satisfactorily to the next motivational attempt.

Dealing with a long-time violator. A parent once asked me, "How can I motivate my daughter to clear the dinner table properly? She knows exactly what to do, but after ten weeks, she still doesn't do it right." The parent added that for the past ten weeks she has been trying to motivate her daughter by reprimanding and punishing her for her mistakes.

We talked about praise as a motivational technique. I suggested that she begin that day to praise her daughter's successes and to disregard her mistakes.

She then asked an interesting question: "If she clears twelve of twenty-five dishes tonight, why should I disregard her mistake? She was assigned the chore ten weeks ago. She is not new at it. She is

---

1. *Mishlei* 27:6. Also, see Chapter Seven for a discussion on this point.

already at the more advanced stage of difficulty and shouldn't be dealt with as a beginner."

I explained that, while her daughter is not new at the chore, the motivational technique is new. Therefore, she should consider today the first day of the assignment. She should praise whatever her daughter does right and disregard mistakes. She should proceed just as Sarah's mother did, beginning to offer reminders only after several days have passed. Unlike Sarah's mother, though, she should expect the improvement process to take longer. Sarah was new at the chore but this little girl is a veteran and has already developed a habit of doing it wrong. Sarah's mother had to be patient, but this mother has to be even more patient.

Summing up. You can use praise to motivate children to perform household chores, improve school grades, accept more responsibility and behave in a more socially acceptable manner.

Don't wait for your children to reach the final goal before recognizing their accomplishments and don't catch them doing things improperly — that is, anything short of the desired performance. If you do, they may never reach the final goal, or they may reach it slower and with more mistakes. Rather, set the goal and openly recognize each small achievement the child makes in that direction.

Set Clear Goals

Praise can motivate only when the child has a clear idea of the expectation. Obviously, if a child does not know exactly what her job is, all the praise in the world will not motivate her to perform well. So, before anything, set clear goals for the child.

> Chavi, eight years old, was assigned the household chore of clearing the dinner table. Her mother said to her, "Your new job is to clear the dinner table nicely."
>
> That night, Chavi started her chore thirty minutes after dinner. She stacked the dishes on a kitchen counter, not in the sink, and she left a few items on the table.
>
> Chavi's mother was upset and asked her why she had performed so poorly. Chavi said that she did not see anything wrong with stacking the dishes on the counter and leaving a few items on the table. Nor did she see a

problem in starting thirty minutes after dinner. She thought she had done a "nice" job.

Her mother then explained what a "nice" job means: "Clear *every* dish from the table and pile them in the *sink*, with the larger dishes on the bottom. It should be completed by *seven o'clock.*"

The next day Chavi followed all the instructions, and her mother was pleased.

A child can reach desired goals only if she knows what they are. At first, Chavi's goal was to do a "nice" job, and so she innocently did what she thought was a "nice" job. When her mother clarified the goal, Chavi performed to the new specifications. Had her mother been clear in the beginning, Chavi may have performed properly the first time, too.

Now that Chavi knows the goal and is performing well, her mother has to praise every improvement, keeping several other principles in mind: praise specifics, offer praise immediately and deliver the praise in an effective manner. We will now discuss these points.

Praise Specifics

Calling attention to specifics reinforces the desired behavior. If Chavi's mother would say, "You did a nice job," what might Chavi think? "I performed meticulously and the only feedback I get is that I did a nice job"? What does 'nice' mean, anyway? Maybe I didn't have to do *all* that work! Maybe tomorrow I'll do less."

By saying only that Chavi did a nice job, her mother does not emphasize the kind of performance she wants her daughter to repeat. And Chavi does not feel rewarded for all her efforts. As a result, she may not repeat the performance the next day.

Instead, her mother should say, "You did a good job clearing every dish from the table before seven o'clock. You also piled them in the sink, with the largest ones on the bottom. I am very pleased." Chavi now knows which behavior to repeat and she feels rewarded for each individual action. The probability of repeating the performance is enhanced.

The rule of praising specifics also applies to times when the child does *not* perform well. This means that if Chavi understood the goal and still left a few items behind, her mother would say, "I am pleased that you cleared fifteen dishes and piled them in the sink, and that you did it by seven o'clock." This is the truth. She cleared fifteen dishes. Her mother does not have to say how many were *not* cleared; she only has to praise Chavi for her progress. As mentioned earlier, criticism clashes with praise, and they should not be used together when using praise as a planned motivational strategy. Hopefully, Chavi will do better the following day.

Be specific with your child's school work, too. Set clear goals and praise specifics. Don't tell your child, "Do better in school." Don't praise by saying, "You did nicely." Be specific about the goal and the performance. Say, "I expect you to study every night from five to six o'clock, and to score five points higher on the next test." When the child improves, say, "Your test score is five points higher, and I noticed that you studied every day from five to six o'clock. I am very proud of you."

Use the same approach for every expectation. Clarify the goal so the child knows what to do, and reinforce it by praising specifics.

Specificity conveys sincerity. Some children, especially those who often hear insincere praise, may wonder if you really mean it when you say, "You did a good job." They have heard this line many times before, and they may think you are trying to make them feel good, manipulate or flatter them.

When you praise generalities, the child may doubt your sincerity. For example, a child draws a picture and asks your opinion. You respond, "It is beautiful." The child may think, "Does he/she really mean it?" But if you say, "You used six different colors and they match beautifully. The lines are straight and the circles are round. The expression on that face is so real!"; the child then knows exactly what she did right and will feel proud of herself. There is no doubt as to your sincerity.

When you are specific, you and your words are more credible. Instead of saying, "You are such a good boy," say, "You took your sister to the park and did a very responsible job supervising her." The child knows that those are the facts and he will believe that you are sincere.

Another advantage of praising specifics is that you can never take back those particulars. When you call a child "a good boy," you can take it away tomorrow by calling him a "bad boy." But you can never take back the praise of supervising a sibling in the park. He already did it, and he did it well — and he knows you have acknowledged that.

Praise Immediately

The child feels most proud right after a performance, and that is when he has the greatest need for affirmation. For this reason, praise is most beneficial when provided immediately after a performance. Praise given at the right time has the strongest impact.

Delivering the Praise

Some experts recommend that you also tell the child how good you feel about the performance. Say, "Your grades have improved by five points, and I am *very pleased.*" Say it with feeling. Saying how good you feel conveys sincerity and creates a strong impression.[1]

These experts then recommend that you stop for several moments of silence. Let the child get a sense of how good you feel. This reinforces the impression.

Next, encourage the child to repeat the behavior. After telling the child how pleased you are with the performance, say, "I know you can do well again next time."

Finally, make physical contact with a handshake, a caring touch, an arm around the shoulder or the like. This reinforces your sincerity. One word of caution: some children dislike physical contact, in which case you should not do it.

There is no need to prolong the delivery. The entire message can be conveyed in a minute or less.

These experts also recommend that you do not deliver praise in this manner every time the child does something right. In the beginning it is necessary, but as the child becomes accustomed to performing well, parents can curtail and abbreviate the delivery.

---

1. Adapted from *The One Minute Manager*, Blanchard and Johnson, William Morrow & Co., Inc., 1982.

As the Child Improves, Use Less Praise

While a child is in the development stage — that is, learning new habits and becoming proficient at them — things come harder, and he needs support and encouragement to persist. Praise satisfies this need. Once the child becomes proficient in the task and acclimated to the routine, however, things come more easily and he needs less support and encouragement.

At this point, he should learn to depend more on his inner drive and less on external motivation. Why? Because inner drive has the most enduring effects. With inner drive, the child is motivated to succeed whether or not other people are there to offer support. And since the goal is constantly on the child's mind, he will perform as often as necessary without the encouragement of others.[1]

Once the child is proficient, continuous praising can be detrimental. If he depends constantly on someone else's praise for motivation, he will not learn to activate his inner drive and will not benefit from its value.

Some Benefits of Receiving Praise

Praise promotes successes by creating images of past success. When a parent praises a child's performance, an image of success is left in the child's mind. The next time he has to perform, he unconsciously recalls that image. He does not say, "I can't," because he already proved that he can. His high self-confidence enables him to perform better than he otherwise would have. Let's illustrate.

> Simcha was not a good ball player. He did not catch well and "felt" that he would *never* catch well. He had such a poor image of himself that he didn't even try to succeed.
>
> His father began to practice with him, praising every small improvement. After several weeks, Simcha finally learned to catch a ball.

---

1. Rabbeinu Yonah, *Avos* 1:14 and *Mishlei* 22:6. See the first chapter for a discussion on this point.

> His father gave him a suggestion: "Before every game, recall the successful catches you made the day before. Think to yourself, 'I can.' "
>
> Simcha used the suggestion and became a successful ball player.

Praise, as a visualization tool, promotes future successes. Visualization is the technique of seeing yourself, in your mind's eye, performing well in an upcoming event. Visualization goes one step further than recalling past images of success; it takes you into the future. It is a mental rehearsal of an upcoming event. The better and more often you visualize future success, the greater your chance of succeeding. Why? Because you have already been there many times in your mind.

Rabbi Eliyahu Dessler said that our forefathers reached their greatness by using visualization.[1] He said that creating images in the mind can generate success:

> A wonderful suggestion for a person who wants to withstand tests is to do this: frequently, before the experience, he should create images of the experience and the success he will have in it. He should think of all the reasons and arguments he will use to conquer his evil inclination, and how he will be happy with his success. Then, when he comes to the experience, it will be easier for him to succeed. This is a proven and tested method (*Michtav M'Eliyahu*, vol. 4, p. 253).

While Rabbi Dessler discussed visualization as a technique to conquer the evil inclination, it can also be applied to any life experience.

Children appreciate praise and want to be praised again and again. They look forward to more successful performances so that they will receive more praise. While looking forward to the praise, they rehearse a successful performance in their minds. This is visualization, on a lower level of consciousness.

Parents can help their children visualize success at a higher level of consciousness, too. They can do this by adding a prophecy of

1. *Michtav M'Eliyahu*, vol. 4, p. 252.

success to their praise, saying, "You did great. You are going to do great next time, too. Just think about it." This induces the child to look forward to success and to consciously rehearse a successful performance. Let's illustrate:

> Dov, four years old, constantly fought with his playmates. On a normal day, he would start fighting after thirty minutes of play.
>
> His parents had an idea. They let him play for approximately twenty minutes. Before the fighting began, they praised him for his performance and removed him from the scene. They said, "Dov, you played so nicely with your friend, and we are very proud of you. We are sure that you will play nicely next time, too. But now we have to go home. You will be able to come back tomorrow." Dov departed with images of success, looking forward to another pleasant play session.
>
> Between sessions, his parents told him how confident they were that he would have another peaceful play session. They talked about it and brought Dov into the discussion.
>
> Dov gradually improved and was able to play for longer periods of time without fighting.

Dov's parents helped him visualize future success by creating images of peaceful play sessions. By the time each session came, Dov had already rehearsed several successful play sessions — some real, others in his mind. Through visualization he was able to develop good social habits.

Praise creates a positive atmosphere. Some parents have an instinctive routine of reacting to their children's undesired behaviors by criticizing, reprimanding and enforcing penalties. Such behavior strains the relationship and reduces mutual trust. Every day presents another ordeal that both parents and children would rather avoid. They forget — or perhaps never even knew — what it is like to have a peaceful family life where all the members enjoy each other's company.

It does not have to be this way. Parents *can* create an atmosphere of peace, mutual trust and respect.

There are many factors that contribute to this kind of atmosphere. Praise is one. When children are praised, they feel better about themselves and their parents. Praise makes children proud of their performances and happy about the support they receive. And when parents give praise, they learn to be proud of their children's growth. They focus on the positive and, almost magically, find it. They appreciate their children more and look forward to spending time with them.

Praise puts control in the hands of the child. Parents who consistently praise create an environment in which children *expect* to be praised when they do things right. The children want to be praised, so they make an effort to behave and perform well in all their activities. The control to perform well is now in the hands of the children — where it belongs.

Praise creates an "I-want-to" attitude. You probably have had days when you felt you *had* to go to work and other days when you actually *wanted* to go. Did your attitude affect the day's productivity or the outlook you had on your work? You probably had a brighter outlook and were more productive on the days you wanted to be there. When people *want* to do something, they are more enthusiastic and productive than when they feel they *have* to do it.

Two of the most important factors that contribute to the satisfaction you have at work are the atmosphere and the support you receive. Praise contributes significantly to both factors, resulting in an "I-want-to" attitude. Children are the same. When they are supported with praise, they feel good about their responsibilities and perform better. Why? Because they *want* to.

More Praise Suggestions

Deliver the praise in a way the child will appreciate. Some people conclude their praise with a congenial tickle, a friendly swat on the back, a loving poke in the stomach or an affectionate pinch on the cheek. However, the child may not appreciate the gesture. Although the praiser's intent is to be supportive, some children may not find it rewarding to be pinched, tickled or poked.

Before you praise, ask yourself if the child will appreciate your gesture and choice of words. He may not. Each child is different, and you should match your words and gestures to his individual personality.[1] For example:

> "You are learning so well. You are going to be a big *Rosh Yeshiva* one day."

A parent or teacher may think that this is the biggest compliment. And it is — for the child who aspires to become a big *Rosh Yeshiva.* But if the child does not have such inclinations, it is not praise. Here is another example:

> "You are one cool dude."

A parent or teacher may think that this remark is cute and affectionate. But if the child does not appreciate being called such a name, it is not appropriate praise.

Make it a 100% praise. Praise motivates because it affirms a child's sense of importance. Don't diminish its impact by attaching negative comments. For example:

> "You did poorly on your last test, but you did very well on this one."

Here, the praiser highlights a good performance by comparing it to a poor one. The intent may be sincere, but the praise contains a touch of criticism.

> "You got a 98% on the test. You are so smart that you could run a company ... maybe a high priced garbage-collecting company."

Here, the praiser tries to boost the child's spirit with something "cute." The intent may be sincere, but the praise contains a touch of sarcasm.

Avoid comparisons. First, let's give an example of a comparison.

> Chaim's mother was training him to straighten his room. When he finally succeeded, she said, "I am so proud

---

1. See Rabbi Yeruchom Levovitz, *Daas Torah, Shemos* 19:3; also see Vilna Gaon on *Mishlei* 16:4 and 22:6; also see *Midrash Rabbah, Bamidbar* 21:15; also see Rabbi S.R. Hirsch, *Yesodos HaChinuch,* pp. 55-56.

> of you. You cleaned up your room as nicely as your sister cleaned hers."

Chaim succeeded and wants recognition. So what does his mother do? She recognizes him along with his sister. He feels gypped because it is *his* success and he wants all the honor. Now he has to share it. And if Chaim is already jealous of his sister or does not like her, the comparison will be especially irritating.

Chaim's mother should praise him — him alone — for his good performance. If she wants to illustrate the significance of his achievement, she may do so in a way that does not detract from the recognition he deserves.

Don't make light of the difficulty of the task. Sometimes parents try to minimize the difficulty of a task. They think this motivates the child to persevere but in reality they may be putting him down. Let us illustrate.

> One morning, Menachem came from his room dressed neatly. This was a great accomplishment because Menachem had a problem with organization and was ordinarily unkempt.
>
> His father wanted to encourage him to continue dressing neatly. He said, "Your shirt is buttoned and tucked into your pants. Your shoes are tied and your hair brushed. I am so proud of you. You see, it's so simple. Let's see if you can do it all the time."

Menachem's father implied that dressing neatly is easy and can be done with minimal effort. For whom? Not for Menachem. Organization does not come easily to him. Hearing that dressing neatly is such a simple task may cause Menachem to feel incapable of something other people find easy. Instead of encouraging Menachem, his father may have put him down.

Tell why you like the performance. When praising a particular performance, give the reason you are pleased. Give a general reason which can be applied to an assortment of events. For example:

> Elana often comes home from school long after dismissal. She also comes home from visiting friends long

after the designated time. Her mother constantly talks to her about it and reminds her that she has to be more responsible.

One day, Elana came home on time. Her mother wanted to encourage her to continue being punctual, so she praised her by saying, "I asked you to come home today by five o'clock, and you did. This shows responsibility, and I am very proud of that."

Elana's mother was not only specific about the performance, she gave a reason for being pleased: Elana's sense of responsibility. The message is that responsibility is a virtue worthy of pursuit — a virtue so important that it transcends the significance of the performance itself.

Elana now has an appreciation for this higher ideal, and she is motivated to apply it and become more responsible in other matters, too — so that she will be praised again.

Praise effort. *Chazal* tell us, "Your duty is not to complete the task, but you do not have the freedom not to try."[1] Although they said this regarding Torah study, it can be extended to all matters consistent with Torah ideals.

Chazal are telling us that effort is a goal in itself. It is the key to success, whether the goal has been reached or not. Praising effort transmits this ideal to the child. It tells the child, "Whether you perform excellently or not, it is more important to make a genuine effort to do your best."

If the child studies for a test and does poorly, recognize the effort and emphasize its importance. Say, "I saw you studying and I am very proud of your effort. This indicates that you are a serious student. I know you will score better next time."

Even if the child does well, you can still praise the effort. Say, "I see you scored 95%. Because you studied, you did well." This reinforces the significance of effort.

If a child makes a genuine effort to succeed, whether or not he reaches the goal of excellent performance, he has reached another important goal — making a genuine effort. With praise, his chances of performing well the next time are better.

---

1. *Avos* 2:16.

You can praise with a gesture. Another way of acknowledging success is to make meaningful non-verbal gestures. Smiling, clapping, cheering, shaking hands, a thumbs-up sign, nodding the head and patting the back are all gestures that convey the message, "You did a good job. I am proud of you."

Gesturing can be an effective approach with children who have already learned to perform properly. However, it is not as effective with children who are still learning to perform; they need specific verbal praise to motivate them to keep progressing.

Don't praise the child for a task you did. Sometimes parents complete a task that is difficult for the child, and then praise the child for doing a nice job.

> Yocheved, five years old, was having trouble drawing a picture for the *succah*. Her mother did not want her to fail, so she took a crayon and completed the drawing herself.
>
> Then she held up the drawing, showed it to Yocheved and exclaimed, "Look at the beautiful picture you drew!"

How did Yocheved feel about her mother's praise? She knew who had really drawn the picture. She was not fooled. Yocheved may even have thought, "My mother didn't let me complete the drawing because I am not capable. I can't draw nicely." The intent was to boost Yocheved; instead, it put her down.

Had the mother offered suggestions and encouragement, Yocheved may have completed the drawing on her own. Then her mother would have been able to give her genuine praise for her work.

Praise publicly. People like praise no matter where it is given, but most people appreciate public praise more. Public praise is especially rewarding because it announces to others that this person is important. Thus, the motivational effect is stronger.

Tell the truth and be positive. Some parents and teachers lead children to think that they are doing better than they really are. They think they are being helpful, but they are really creating other problems. We will illustrate this with a classroom example, which parents can easily apply at home.

Zahava's attitude in school is not good. She has been failing tests and has not been paying attention in class. The teacher thinks that Zahava has low self-esteem and that she will improve when she feels better about herself.

The teacher decides to strengthen Zahava's self-esteem by making her performances look better than they really are. When Zahava cannot answer a question because she is not paying attention in class, the teacher says, "I'm glad you tried. Just keep paying attention and you will get the answer." When Zahava gives a partially correct answer, the teacher exclaims, "Excellent. You did a fine job!"

The teacher is confident that this plan will help Zahava improve. But Zahava continues her poor performances and shows no sign of improvement.

Zahava's teacher is misleading her into thinking that she is performing well. How does Zahava react? She believes her teacher and surmises that there is little room, if any, for improvement. As a result, she may never put effort into *really* performing well.

Again, the rule is that the behavior that is rewarded will be repeated. Here, the teacher is rewarding Zahava for poor behavior. The result will be a repetition of poor behavior.

Instead of distorting or inflating the truth, Zahava's teacher should be honest. She does not have to mention the negative aspects of her performance, but she should recognize the positive aspects. For example, when Zahava cannot answer a question due to lack of attention, the teacher can say, "I see you are sitting in your seat nicely. That makes me think you are making an effort to pay attention. I am very happy about this."

Indeed, Zahava may deserve a reprimand; she has neglected her duties and needs to change. However, when using praise as a motivational strategy, Zahava's teacher should not criticize. As we mentioned earlier, this dilutes the impact of the praise.

Similarly, when Zahava gives a partially correct answer, the teacher should find something positive to recognize. She can say, "You are partially right. That means you are thinking. Keep it up. I am proud of your progress." She is truthful, yet positive.

When Zahava gives a completely wrong answer and is not even sitting properly in her seat, what should the teacher say? Many teachers might become perturbed in such a situation and say, "No! You are wrong! Now sit straight and pay attention!" Zahava did neglect her responsibility and deserves criticism but, as we mentioned, criticism and praise are not compatible when using praise as a planned motivational strategy. Consistent with this guideline, the teacher can say, "No, that's not correct. But I'm going to call on you again soon and when I do, I know you'll have the answer." She is truthful, yet positive.

There is no need either to distort the truth or to emphasize its negative aspect. Parents and teachers can recognize the truth and look for the good in it. There is good in everything, and recognizing it is the key to using praise as a motivational technique.

Sometimes, parents and teachers have no intent of misleading a child, yet they choose misleading words. For example:

> Ahuva is trying to improve her handwriting. Her father is proud of her progress and in a cute, affectionate tone says, "Ahuva, you have the best handwriting in the world!"

Ahuva's father is not trying to mislead her. He made the remark to be jovial, but he does not really want Ahuva to believe it. There is no harm done if Ahuva understands her father's intent. But if she believes him, she will think that she has already achieved excellence and that there is no need to improve. Because there is no way of knowing how Ahuva will respond, her father should be careful about the comments he makes.

Be sincere. People appreciate sincere praise but detest phoniness. When they sense a false compliment, they interpret it as flattery or manipulation and soon learn to distrust the praiser.

Children can sense immediately if you are sincere or not. They detect it in your tone of voice, facial expressions and show of interest. And if they sense that you do not mean what you say, the effect is no different than if you had openly declared your insincerity.

Be enthusiastic. Why do people reprimand others with more enthusiasm than when they offer praise? When they criticize, they are often quite verbal and animated, but when they praise they are sparing and dull. There are several psychological reasons for this but one thing is certain — praise deserves at least the same enthusiasm.

You are in control. When your child behaves well or brings home a good school report, don't just say, flatly, "Good job." Say it with enthusiasm. Make the achievement stand out. Imagine how emphatic you would be if you were reprimanding the child for misbehaving. Try to be at least as excited over the achievement.

Show your children how much you really care. Raise your voice. Put on a big smile and let your eyes beam. Drink a *L'Chaim* over a glass of orange juice. Write a congratulatory note and attach it to the refrigerator door. Demonstrating your feelings, even in a slightly exaggerated fashion, works. Your children really want to feel that you care and are proud of them.

Keep a journal of praises. Create a journal of every meaningful compliment you give your children. After each incidence of praise, you or the children can enter a note into the journal about the performance and the praise. Periodically, review the journal entries with your children.

Reviewing good performances and praises reinforces their positive effect. Once again, it strengthens self-esteem and motivates the children to perform well in the future, so that they can enter more praises into the journal. And you may find that the journal not only lifts your children's spirits, but yours, too.

When Praising Is Against Your Nature

There is a story of a little girl who misbehaved quite frequently. One day she made a special effort to cooperate but her mother did not call attention to it. That night in bed, she began crying. Her mother came and asked why she was crying. The little girl slowly looked up and asked, "Wasn't I a *little* better today?" This small question made a big impact on the mother. She realized that she was always quick to criticize, but slow to offer a word of appreciation.

Some people have a difficult time praising. They say, "It's just not in me to praise" or "I'm not the flowery type" or "I don't have the time." There are some who simply do not notice good behavior; their "antennae" are always focused on negative behaviors.

If you are one of these people, you don't have to let a personality quirk get in your way. Here are some strategies you can use to help bring the praise out.

Follow a formula. When you notice a good performance, think of this two-part formula:

What action do I see?___________________

Why am I pleased?_______________________

Now, fill in the blanks and repeat the words to your child.

Your child, for example, has just cleaned his room without putting up a fight. Think of the two-part formula and fill in the blanks:

What action do I see? *He cleaned his room.*

Why am I pleased? *He is sharing household duties.*

Now say, "You cleaned your room, and I am pleased that you are sharing household duties."

You may feel like a robot, but that's okay. Doing it mechanically is better than not doing it at all. Eventually, it will become more natural.

Set aside daily praise time. If you think you do not have time to praise, dedicate fifteen minutes a day for praising. At the beginning of each day or week, plan the exact time of day you will offer praise to your children. Mark it in your calendar or daily planner. As a reminder, set your watch or oven alarm for that time.

When it is time to begin praising, don't spend the entire fifteen minutes scurrying around the house looking for behaviors to praise. Rather, just keep your eyes open for opportunities. Be wise and sincere in your routine. You and your children will enjoy these few minutes of positive recognition. It may be so rewarding that you may even find additional time for praising.

Know what to say. Some people do not know what to say when they praise. They want to say more than "Very good" but cannot find the words. Here is a list of eighty ways of saying "Very good." Teachers may find it especially useful.

That's a good boy/girl!
You are unbelievable!
You've got that down pat!

Congratulations!
You are a joy!
Good remembering!

You are really coming along!
I think you have it now!
That's the way!
You're really improving!
You're doing beautifully!
You just about have it!
You're doing a good job!
Now you've figured it out!
You are learning fast!
That's the way!
You haven't missed a thing!
Nothing can stop you now!
You did that very nicely!
Now you have the hang of it!
You're really going to town!
Keep up the good work!
That was first-class work!
You outdid yourself today!
You are very good at that!
That's quite an improvement!
That's better than ever!
That's how to handle it!
You certainly did well today!
You must have been practicing!
You are really learning a lot!
Now, that's what I call a fine job!
I'm glad I'm your *Ima/Abba/*Teacher!
You've just about mastered that!
That kind of work makes me happy!
I'm proud of the way you did that!
Congratulations. You got it right!
Couldn't have done it better myself!
You've got your brain in gear today!
You are doing much better today!
I've never seen anyone do it better!
I'm happy to see you working like that!
Keep working at it. You're improving!

Beautifully done!
Good for you!
Keep on trying!
That's right!
That's good!
That's great!
That's better!
Good thinking!
You remembered!
Exactly right!
Super good!
'Atta boy/girl!
Wonderful!
Superb!
Tremendous!
Right on!
Nice going!
Super!
Great!
Wow!
Fine!
Terrific!
Good job!
Fantastic!
That's it!
Excellent!
Spectacular!
Keep it up!
Remarkable!
Marvelous!
Sensational!
Outstanding!
I like that!
Good going!
Way to go!
Much better!
Good work!

Praise even if you don't feel like it. Below is an article written many years ago about a father who did not praise his son.[1] It is a classic and has been published in the United States and in many foreign countries. Because it illustrates the importance of praise so poignantly, we are presenting it now.

Father Forgets

Listen, son: I am saying this as you lie asleep, one paw crumpled under your cheek and the blond curls stickily wet on your damp forehead. I have stolen into your room alone. Just a few minutes ago, as I sat reading my paper in the library, a stifling wave of remorse swept over me. Guiltily, I came to your bedside.

These are the things I was thinking, son: I had been cross to you. I scolded you as you were dressing for school because you gave your face merely a dab with a towel. I took you to task for not cleaning your shoes. I called out angrily when you threw some of your things on the floor.

At breakfast I found fault, too. You spilled things. You gulped down your food. You put your elbows on the table. You spread butter too thick on your bread. And as you started off to play and I made for my train, you turned and waved a hand and called, "Good-bye, Daddy!" and I frowned, and said in reply, "Hold your shoulders back!"

Then it began all over again in the late afternoon. As I came up the road I spied you, down on your knees, playing marbles. There were holes in your stockings. I humiliated you before your boy friends by marching you ahead of me to the house. Stockings were expensive — and if you had to buy them you would be more careful! Imagine that, son, from a father!

Do you remember, later, when I was reading in the library, how you came in, timidly, with a sort of hurt look in your eyes? When I glanced up over my paper, impatient at the interruption, you hesitated at the door. "What is it you want?" I snapped.

1. Written by W. Livingston Larned, condensed in *Reader's Digest*, May, 1935.

You said nothing, but ran across in one tempestuous plunge and threw your arms around my neck and kissed me, and your small arms tightened with an affection that G-d had set blooming in your heart and which even neglect could not wither. And then you were gone, pattering up the stairs.

Well, son, it was shortly afterwards that my paper slipped from my hands and a terrible sickening fear came over me. What has habit been doing to me? The habit of finding fault, of reprimanding — this was my reward to you for being a boy. It was not that I did not love you; it was that I expected too much of youth. I was measuring you by the yardstick of my own years.

And there was so much that was good and fine and true in your character. The little heart of you was as big as the dawn itself over the wide hills. This was shown by your spontaneous impulse to rush in and kiss me good-night. Nothing else matters tonight, son. I have come to your bedside in the darkness, and I have knelt there, ashamed!

It is a feeble atonement; I know you would not understand these things if I told them to you during your waking hours. But tomorrow I will be a real daddy! I will chum with you, and suffer when you suffer, and laugh when you laugh. I will bite my tongue when impatient words come. I will keep saying as if it were a ritual: "He is nothing but a boy — a little boy!"

I am afraid I have visualized you as a man. Yet as I see you now, son, crumpled and weary in your cot, I see that you are still a baby. Yesterday you were in your mother's arms, your head on her shoulder. I have asked too much, too much.

Make Praise a Lifestyle

Praise is not a thing you pull from a bag of tricks. It is an unremitting attitude toward people and life. It is a lifestyle which acknowledges the human need for appreciation. It is a commitment to see the positive and a conscious effort to recognize it.

Praise helps you bring out the best in children by making them feel important. It shows that you notice and care, and it generates more successful performances. It conveys a message about your standards and expresses appreciation for meeting those standards. Praise creates a cooperative atmosphere, conducive to success, and it will make you and your children feel better about your relationship and the goals that have to be reached. With praise, everyone wins.

Chapter Three

Motivate With Rewards

Picture this scene: You ask your child to share in household responsibilities or to relate well with siblings. The child understands the importance of these behaviors and agrees to a course of action. She values the goals and has an inner drive to reach them. She is obedient and follows through with few reminders.

Obedience, inner drive, commitment to goals — this is the way it *should* be. But all too often, it isn't. Even in the best of families, children are sometimes uncooperative and determined to do just as they please. Parents coax and lecture, but to no avail.

The parents find themselves in a dilemma; they do not want to ignore the uncooperative behavior nor do they want to coerce through unpleasant means. Ignoring the behavior leads to more defiance and promotes arrogance. Forceful, unpleasant measures, on the other hand, reduce a child's self-confidence and impair relationships. How can these children be motivated to reach their goals?

People Are Motivated by Personal Gain

The Rambam explains that the proper motive in *mitzvah* performance is love of Hashem.[1] But what should motivate a person who does not yet have this love? He should consider the reward for compliance and the penalty for defiance.

In his discussion, the Rambam shares some fundamental principles of human motivation.

> A person only does an action to receive a benefit or to avoid a loss and if not for this, the action is meaningless to him ... Therefore, so that people should be comfortable, *Chazal* permit them to perform *mitzvos* for the promise of reward and to refrain from sins for fear of punishment. *Chazal* motivate people with this idea and support them until they fully understand and know the truth and the proper way ... People do not lose anything at all when they perform *mitzvos* for fear of punishment and anticipation of reward, except that they are not perfect. But this approach is good for them until they develop strength, habit and endeavor in following Torah, and from this they will be inspired to know the truth and they will serve Hashem with love. This is what *Chazal* meant by saying, "A person should always be engaged in Torah even if it is not for its own sake, because it leads to doing it for its own sake"[2] (Rambam, *Pirush HaMishnayos, Sanhedrin*, ch. 10).

Whatever people do, their strongest motive is personal gain. People produce more readily and derive meaning and satisfaction from actions which have a personal benefit. This is the foundation of all motivation.[3]

Chazal devised a formula for building proper Jewish attitudes:

---

1. *Pirush HaMishnayos, Sanhedrin*, ch. 10. Also see *Orchos Chaim LeHarash* 52: "Do not do *mitzvos* to get the reward and do not avoid sins because of the punishment, only serve Hashem out of love."
2. Talmud *Pesachim* 50b.
3. See also *Chovos HaLevavos*, beginning of *Avodas Elokim:* All people are motivated by personal gain.

in the beginning, before proper attitudes are developed, one should perform *mitzvos* for an extrinsic benefit. In time, he will correct himself, focusing on the intrinsic value, and will become motivated by love of Hashem.[1]

Yes, a properly motivated person should perform *mitzvos* out of his love of Hashem, not personal gain. But if he does not have this attitude, *Chazal* do not *force* him to have it. They understand that attitudes are formed as a result of habits. This means that frequent performance of *mitzvos* leads to acquisition of proper attitudes, even if the initial motive is personal benefit.[2]

Rewards for Children

Using these principles, the Rambam advised teachers to offer children rewards for Torah study.[3] He structured a reward program which addresses the child's maturity level: food for very young children, nice clothing for older ones and the promise of honor for the oldest. As the child matures and becomes accustomed to Torah study, he learns to appreciate its intrinsic value, and his selfish motivation converts to a selfless one.

Indeed, we are instructed not to do *mitzvos* for the purpose of receiving rewards[4] and not to use Torah to gain honor or any other personal benefit.[5] However, a child is incapable of learning Torah for any other reason. Since this is the nature of children, the Rambam recommended using rewards. Seen this way, a reward is not an end in itself; rather, it is the *means* by which proper attitudes are acquired.

Dealing with the non-compliant child. What makes a child non-compliant? There can be any number of reasons. The child by *nature* may be lazy or forgetful. He may be experiencing anxiety over something that happened in school or a tense relationship with a friend. He may be locked into a power struggle with his parents.

---

1. See *Tosafos, Taanis* 7a: A person will make the shift to proper motivation only if he initially acts without the intent to hurt others or put them down.
2. See also *Sefer HaChinuch, mitzvah* 16: Attitudes follow action.
3. Rambam, *Pirush HaMishnayos,* ibid.
4. *Avos* 1:3.
5. *Avos* 4:5.

He may have an emotional need to express control or act independently. He may have conflicting interests, too compelling to abandon for the sake of conforming to his parents' demands. He may have a strong need for attention, and the only way he knows to get it is through defiance. Yes, he has the mental and physical capacities to meet his parents' expectations, but something else is keeping him from cooperating.

A non-compliant child does not analyze the advantages and disadvantages of cooperation, then make a rational decision to defy; rather, something inside tugs at him and impairs his ability to rationalize altogether. He is like an asthmatic or dyslexic person. The asthmatic's physical deficiency prevents him from breathing properly. The dyslexic's visual deficiency prevents him from reading properly. The non-compliant child's state of mind prevents him from cooperating.

Some parents think that a non-compliant child can be forced to comply. They are correct. Compliance can be forced — at the cost of broken spirits, the acquisition of nervous habits, decreased self-confidence, impaired relationships and reduced parental effectiveness. Even if the child does comply, he will eventually revert to his original behavior because he has not been conditioned with a healthy pattern of obedience or a sense of the importance of the goal.[1] Further, the child may rebel against his parents.[2]

Rabbi Shlomo Wolbe said, "Praise and prizes are more effective than threats and punishments."[3] Parents can effectively motivate a non-compliant child with rewards. Once the child becomes comfortable with the behavior and has an inner drive to perform, the rewards can be eliminated.

Parents who have instituted reward programs in their homes by following the guidelines in this chapter have affirmed that their family life has improved. As their children accept more responsibility, they have less need to coax, persuade, threaten and coerce. The parent/child relationship is more productive and the general home

---

1. Vilna Gaon, *Mishlei* 22:6: Do not try to break a child. Work with his qualities to bring out the best in him.
2. Rabbi S. R. Hirsch, *Yesodos HaChinuch*, p. 66. Also see Rabbi Shlomo Wolbe, *Alai Shur*, p. 261: children who have excessive fear of parents may rebel.
3. *Alai Shur*, p. 261.

atmosphere is more relaxed; there is less friction and fewer power struggles. Daily successes and rewards do cause children to be happier and more motivated.

Initiating a Reward Program

Parents typically launch a reward program by proposing a deal with the child. They say, "If you do ... I will give you ..." It sounds like bribery, doesn't it? The problem is that if the child feels bribed or manipulated, he will oppose the plan. How can parents launch a reward program in an acceptable manner?

First of all, choose a relaxed time to sit and talk with the child. Say, "I've been watching you lately, and I've decided that you are not being rewarded enough for doing nice things. I've decided to give you something that you would appreciate for doing nice things."

Presenting it in this way shows that you are concerned with the child's welfare and consider his feelings. It sets a positive tone and does not sound as manipulative as the other approach.

Manipulation is getting the child to do something for *your* benefit. Motivation is getting him to do something for *his* benefit. As long as the child sees a personal benefit in a reward program, he will not feel manipulated.

Setting the Goals

Any behavior in need of improvement may be contracted. Behaviors may relate to *middos,* conduct, personal grooming, housework, schoolwork, improving sibling and social relationships, or learning a skill such as carpentry, sewing or playing a musical instrument. The first step is to target the desired behavior and set clear, attainable performance standards. We will explain these points now.

Target the desired behavior and get the child's agreement. First, make a list of the behaviors you want the child to develop. Then, prioritize the behaviors. Target those which are important and attainable.

Now that you have targeted the behaviors in *your* mind, it is time to get the child's agreement. There are two ways of doing this:

1) Present the list to the child and ask for his agreement; 2) without showing him your original list, formulate another list together with the child. Include any behavior he thinks is important or needs improvement.

"Why," you may ask, "should you seek the child's agreement?" Because when the child agrees, he feels that he has some control over the matter. He feels part of the decision-making process. He buys into the plan and commits himself to it. For this reason, the second method is most effective. Formulating a list together with the child gives him more of a sense of control. He has helped to create the ideas and will be more committed to making the plan work.[1]

Even if you choose this path, it is a good idea to produce a private list beforehand. It clarifies and prioritizes target behaviors in your mind, and prepares you to sit down "at the negotiation table" to produce a functional list.

A reward program has two components: a goal and a reward. The goal is what the child is supposed to do, and the reward is what he is supposed to get in return. The goal must be attainable and the reward desirable — *in the child's eyes.* Parents cannot coerce a child to accept a reward program.

Set clear performance standards.

> Avigail was a tempestuous ten-year-old girl. Among other faults, she constantly disturbed her class by calling out and having private conversations with classmates. Her parents had discussed the problem with her many times. Finally, Avigail agreed to improve her conduct in return for a special toy.
>
> Over the next three days, Avigail's parents received notes from school indicating that problems still existed: one day, Avigail was up from her seat without permission; the next day, she did not do her homework; the third day, she stayed in the bathroom too long.

---

1. See Talmud *Bava Metziah* 38a: "A person prefers one share of his own possession to nine identical shares of his friend's." Rashi explains that a person cherishes that which he works to get. We are extending this concept to thoughts, ideas and opinions. Also, see *Mishlei* 21:2: "The way of a man is straight in his eyes."

They decided not to give Avigail the reward. She could not understand the reason. This was their conversation:

Parents: We agreed that you would be good. You were not, so we are not giving you the special toy.
Avigail: But I didn't disturb the class, even once.
Parents: Yes, but you were up from your seat without permission.
Avigail: Because I had to get my pencil. Besides, I didn't disturb the class.
Parents: You also didn't do your homework one day.
Avigail: But that didn't disturb the class.
Parents: And one day you stayed in the bathroom too long.
Avigail: But that didn't disturb the class, either.
Parents: All of this is not what we call being good. When you decide to be good, you will get the reward.

Does Avigail deserve the reward? Her parents feel that she does not deserve it because her conduct is still unacceptable. Avigail contends that she does deserve it because she no longer disturbs the class. Who is right?

To answer this question, look at the goal. The goal was to "be good." Well, what does that mean? Avigail interpreted it as not disturbing the class; her parents interpreted it as following all classroom rules. Each agreed to something different. The goal was never outlined with specific performance standards, and the result was frustration and misunderstanding.

This problem could have been avoided. Her parents should have set clear performance standards by saying specifically, "Do all your homework; stay in your seat; talk only with permission; and when you go to the bathroom, return to class quickly." While a parent can never anticipate *every* problem that will arise, it is necessary to structure the agreement as clearly as possible. This means that performance standards that are not clearly stated cannot be part of the agreement.

Here are some more examples of setting clear performance standards:

Don't say: Improve your grades.
Say instead: Improve your *Chumash* grade by five points on the next test. Study every night for thirty minutes, between six and seven o'clock.

Don't say: Straighten your room.
Say instead: Make your bed with the pillow placed at the head of the bed and no wrinkles or lumps in the blankets. Clothes are to be hung in the closet. Toys go in the toy box.

Don't say: Get along nicely with your sister.
Say instead: Share toys with your sister when she asks to use them. Don't fight with your sister or raise your voice to her.

You can only expect a child to do what she thinks she agreed to do. Be one step ahead! You know what you want her to do, so articulate it in specific terms.

Set active, observable goals. Suppose you ask a child to think clearly or listen carefully in return for a reward. Will you ever know if he is doing it? It may appear that he is not being careful, but he really is — or vice versa; there is simply no way of knowing. And if you do not know how well he is performing, you cannot reward him for the performance.

For this reason, set active, observable goals that can be measured and rewarded.

Set attainable goals.

> Ezra, twelve years old, was hyperactive. He did not sit in his seat longer than ten minutes at a time. In school, he constantly squirmed, stood near his seat or took strolls in the back of the classroom.
>
> His father had an idea. For the past six months, Ezra had been asking for a tape recorder. He decided to make a contract with Ezra: if Ezra would sit quietly in his seat for one day, he would receive the tape recorder. Ezra enthusiastically agreed.
>
> The next day, Ezra sat for twenty-five minutes and then began squirming. The teacher noticed and quickly re-

minded him of the deal. This helped, but after another fifteen minutes Ezra was out of his seat. The teacher reminded him again, but after five more minutes Ezra was in the back of the room taking one of his strolls. When she reminded him of the tape recorder, he coolly replied, "Oh, who cares about the tape recorder anyway! I don't need one." After that, Ezra reverted to his regular behavior.

If goals are too difficult or too numerous, the child may decide that he is incapable of reaching them. His psychological defense mechanism becomes activated and expresses this attitude: "It's too hard. Besides, the reward is not so important anyway." His taste for the reward is soured and he quickly loses interest in the entire program. He is no longer motivated. However, if he believes the goal is attainable, he will be motivated to reach it, in anticipation of receiving the reward.[1]

An effective reward program creates a cycle of success; the child reaches the goal, receives a reward and is motivated to repeat the performance. A parent can keep the cycle going by setting goals which are challenging, yet attainable.

First, observe the child when he is involved in the behavior you wish to moderate. Take a careful, objective look at his performance and capabilities.[2] After several minutes, you may realize that you will have to lower your expectations, which is quite common.

Here are some examples of lowering expectations in an appropriate way:

A hyperactive child is incapable of sitting still for a long period of time.

Do not offer: a reward for sitting quietly during an entire period in school.

Offer instead: a reward for sitting quietly during the first twenty minutes of each period.

---

1. See Rabbi Shlomo Wolbe, *Alai Shur*, p. 263: children who are pushed to reach goals at a level unbefitting their age may develop nervousness and phobias, and they will delay becoming independent.
2. Rabbi S. R. Hirsch, *Yesodos HaChinuch*, p. 55.

A carefree child, due to a happy-go-lucky personality, may find certain challenging goals too burdensome.

Do not offer: a reward for receiving test scores of 95%.
Offer instead: a reward for raising the score of the next test by five points.

A severely disorganized child is incapable of perfectly neat performances.

Do not offer: a reward for keeping a perfectly neat room.
Offer instead: a reward for making the bed one day, hanging clothes up another day. Begin the second goal after the child becomes adept at the first.

In the beginning, goals should be easily attainable. What happens when a child reaches a goal and is rewarded for it? She becomes enthusiastic about repeating the performance. As she reaches the goal again and again, she becomes accustomed to it and is in a position to accept additional goals.

What happens if the goal is too challenging and the child does not achieve it right away? She loses interest in the goal and possibly in future goals as well. This may jeopardize the success of the entire program.

Take Avigail, for example, the ten-year-old girl who constantly violates classroom rules. Her parents want her to remain in her seat, return quickly to the classroom after going to the bathroom, remain quiet during the lesson and complete all her homework. This is a large mandate. She cannot be expected to reverse all her behaviors in one sudden effort. She may become overwhelmed and abandon the entire program.

Therefore, in the beginning, Avigail's parents should solicit her agreement on one easy goal. Once she reaches the goal and receives the reward, she will become enthused about the program and more confident of her capabilities.

After Avigail is comfortable with the first goal, they should add another to the program. As their daughter becomes accustomed to each new behavior, the cycle of success builds momentum. The parents can continue gradually to add one goal at a time until all the desired behaviors are incorporated in the program. In time, Avigail will become a disciplined, responsible young lady.

One rule of thumb: you can always tighten up and become stricter but you may not have the opportunity to become lenient. Therefore, make it easy in the beginning. If your standards are too strict when you begin, you may dampen the child's enthusiasm and jeopardize the success of the program.

Choosing the Reward

The child elects the reward.

> Shmuel, seven years old, has trouble getting organized. His mother offers him a trip to the zoo if he keeps his school bag organized the entire week. After she presents the idea, they have this dialogue:
>
> **Shmuel:** I just went to the zoo three weeks ago.
>
> **Mother**: That's right, and you really enjoyed it.
>
> **Shmuel**: I know, but I'm tired of the zoo.
>
> **Mother:** If you enjoyed it then, you'll enjoy it again.
>
> **Shmuel:** I don't know about that. Besides, it's too hard to organize my bag.
>
> **Mother:** Isn't it worth such a nice prize?
>
> **Shmuel:** But ...
>
> **Mother:** So we have a deal! I know you can do it! Good luck!

Shmuel's mother is trying to motivate him with a reward *she* believes is valuable, but one he does not appreciate. Will this motivate him to keep his school bag organized? Probably not.

We mentioned earlier that people are more committed to their own ideas than the ideas of others. Use this principle when contracting rewards. Do not decide unilaterally on a reward you think your child would like. Even if he agrees, he may not be sufficiently committed to the plan. Say to him instead, "Think about what you would like to have as a reward for reaching the goal and tell me what you decide. If I agree, you can have it." The child is put in control and will buy into the plan with greater commitment.

If the child cannot think of a desirable reward, offer suggestions. Think of activities he likes to do, places he likes to go, items he likes to receive, privileges he likes to have and foods he likes to eat. Offer several options from which he can select.

When the child chooses unreasonable rewards.

> Shifra has not been doing her homework. She agrees to do it every night and wants a trip to Disneyland as a reward. There is only one problem: Shifra lives in Toronto.
>
> Avraham has a habit of screaming. He agrees to talk in a normal voice and asks for a motorcycle in return. There is only one problem: Avraham is seven years old.

Shifra and Avraham are serious about their requests. Their parents, however, do not consider them reasonable. When they deny the requests, Shifra and Avraham will feel rejected. Control will once more have been taken away from them and their enthusiasm for the plan will be greatly reduced.

Parents can avoid this problem by staying one step ahead. They know their children and can forecast the kind of rewards they might choose. If they anticipate that a child will make unreasonable requests, they should use the alternate method of choosing rewards: offer several options from which the child may select. While the child does not have total control of the process, he has enough control to assure a viable program.

How large a reward? I once counseled a mother who was having difficulty putting her four strong-minded children to bed at night. After learning about rewards, she decided to try using them. That evening she proposed the plan to her children, offering them a reward in return for going to sleep on time. She then asked what they wanted. To her amazement, the three boys requested rubber bands, cartoon band-aids and stickers. Her daughter requested an elastic bracelet.

Children are often satisfied with surprisingly small rewards. They usually understand the purpose of rewards and do not take advantage.

Some parents apply the "Law of More" to rewards. This law states: "If a small reward motivates, a larger reward will motivate even more. If one reward motivates, two or three will motivate even more." So they offer cassette tape recorders, radios, wristwatches, and hand-held video games for reaching limited goals such as paying attention in class for one day.

Excessive rewards, either in quality or quantity, obscure and diminish the value of the performance. The effect of the reward is short-lived because the child does not repeat the performance the following day. Why should he? No tape recorders or radios are being offered the second time around. Additionally, this practice sets a costly standard for future rewards. Children will begin expecting large rewards and will not accept anything less for good behavior.

Small reward options. Here are some ideas for small rewards:

- ☐ Stickers
- ☐ Crayons
- ☐ Pencils
- ☐ Candy
- ☐ Cookies
- ☐ Extra dessert
- ☐ Later bedtime
- ☐ Another bedtime story
- ☐ Additional computer time
- ☐ Inexpensive carnival trinkets
- ☐ Visits to friends or relatives
- ☐ A trip downtown with a parent
- ☐ The responsibility of taking baby brother for a walk

The reward does not have to relate to the goal. If the goal is to improve *Chumash* grades the reward can be a toy, trip or clothing.

***Mitzvos* as rewards.** Some *mitzvos* — such as *berachos, succah, matzah* — are obligatory. These *mitzvos* are constant and their performance is not dependent on any particular action. Whether the child is good or bad, reaches goals or not, he or she is still obligated to perform them. Therefore, parents should not give children the opportunity to perform these *mitzvos* in return for reaching goals.

However, there are other *mitzvos* that are not obligatory. These include things like helping Mother cook for Shabbos, taking care of a baby sister or attending the *Tehillim* club. People perform these *mitzvos* voluntarily. Because these *mitzvos* are elective, parents may give children the opportunity to perform them in return for achieving certain goals.

Should the Agreement Be Verbal or Written?

A written agreement is preferable to a verbal one. While both types of agreements are effective, a written contract has several advantages. It is official, signed by parents and child, and generates more commitment. It clarifies goals and performance standards.

A clearly written contract can resolve disputes. For example, parents say that a child's chore should be completed by seven o'clock, but the child contends that a deadline was never stipulated. They can settle the dispute by referring to the written terms of the contract.

Parents can even make a written contract with a child who is too young to read by drawing a picture of the contracted activity and the reward.

Adjusting the terms of the agreement. Since goals are continually being evaluated and adjusted, set the terms of the contract for one or two weeks at a time. This will give you the flexibility to make adjustments. After the initial time period, make another contract to include all the adjustments. Once again, both parents and children should agree to the newly adjusted terms.

Reward Immediately After the Performance

The child feels most proud and has the greatest need for affirmation immediately after the performance. Giving a reward at that time has the strongest motivating impact. If the child earns the reward in the morning, give it to him in the morning, if possible. Waiting until the afternoon or evening reduces its motivational effect.

Don't give the reward before the performance. A cunning child may propose this plan: "I'm going to do it tomorrow, just as we agreed. Let me have the reward *now*." Show your appreciation for his positive attitude by complimenting him or even giving him a small tangible item, but never provide the contracted reward before the performance.

Reward Performance, Not Effort

> Baruch, eleven years old, continually arrived home one hour after being dismissed from school. After many discussions with his parents, he finally agreed to arrive home by 4:45, fifteen minutes after school dismissal, in return for extra dessert at dinner.
>
> The next day, Baruch arrived home at 4:55, ten minutes after the contracted time. His parents wanted to reward him for his effort, so they gave him the contracted reward of extra dessert at dinner, thinking this would encourage him to improve.
>
> From then on, Baruch always arrived home sometime between 4:50 and 5:00, and his parents continued to reward him for his effort. They were still not totally satisfied, but no matter what they told him, he never arrived before 4:45.

A recurring theme runs through this book — the idea of impressing children with the importance of effort.[1] However, this theme does not apply to contracts in which rewards are provided in return for specific observable behaviors. If, in these cases, parents reward effort instead of performance, the child will repeat the same effort and never exert himself to perform successfully. The rule is that the behavior that is rewarded will be repeated. If a performance is rewarded, it will be repeated. If effort is rewarded, the effort will be repeated.

This is the problem that faces Baruch's parents. Their son never comes home by the designated time because he is being rewarded for another sort of behavior — effort. He always falls short of the goal because the reward motivates him to continue *trying*, not performing.

A decision has to be made as to which behavior will earn a

1. *Avos* 2:16; *Darash Moshe, Bamidbar* 4:22.

reward for the child: effort or performance. If effort is the targeted behavior, specify that the reward is for effort, not for good performance. But if performance is targeted, provide the contracted reward in return for nothing less than good performance.

This does not mean that parents should not recognize improvement. On the contrary, they should praise the child for every small improvement and may even provide a tangible item as a token of their appreciation. They should also re-examine the goal and decide if it needs adjustment. However, until those adjustments are made, parents must vigilantly observe the terms of the contract. It is "legally binding" and should be treated as such.

A Token System of Rewards

While small rewards are preferable, they may not be the ideal choice for every program. Here are two instances where small rewards are insufficient.

> Zev, twelve years old, has not been fulfilling his responsibilities. He and his parents agree on six attainable goals: getting up on time in the morning, brushing teeth, dressing quickly, making the bed, eating breakfast with reasonable speed and going to school on time. For each successful performance, Zev will receive a small candy. This means that Zev can get six candies every day.
>
> One week and some forty candies later, Zev loses his appreciation for candy. So his parents agree to use other small rewards. Two weeks and eighty rewards later, the novelty has again worn off.

> Chaya, ten years old, has the same six goals. Small rewards such as candy, computer time and visits to friends are not enough to satisfy her sophisticated taste. She wants a bicycle, a pocket calculator, a wristwatch, trips to other cities, and a portable blackboard with chalk and eraser.

Zev has been receiving so many small rewards that he is no longer motivated by them. Chaya wants something too large to be given after each performance. Small rewards are obviously not going to work for these two. How can their parents create an effective reward program?

They should consider larger rewards and agree that the rewards will only be provided after several performances. They can create a reward program that runs like this:

First, they assign a value to each of the six goals. Getting up in the morning may have a value of two points because it is a difficult task. Brushing teeth has a value of one point because it is easier. Or they can simplify the system by assigning a value of one point to each and every goal.

Then they decide on the number of times the child must perform to be eligible for the reward. Chaya and her parents decide that she is eligible for a bicycle after one month's performances. Thirty days multiplied by six goals equals 180, assuming each performance has a value of one point. This means that Chaya must receive 180 points. If her parents wish, they may reduce the requirement to allow for some probable failures.

There is one snag: we mentioned earlier that a reward has its greatest motivating effect when the child receives it immediately after the performance. If Chaya reaches all her goals consistently, she will receive her bicycle after a full month. The problem is that she may lose interest in the program after several days of reaching goals and not receiving rewards. And if she does not reach every goal each day, her waiting period will be even longer and she will become increasingly disenchanted.

The solution is to use tokens. Tokens are items which are given as a reward substitute until the final reward is received. Tokens can be stars, stickers, paper clips, poker chips or any other small item that is given after a good performance and reminds the child that she is on her way to the contracted reward.

When Chaya performs well, her parents give her a token. She places it in a storage box. When she earns 180 tokens, she exchanges them for a bicycle. If her parents suspect that she may lose her tokens or that her siblings will tamper with the box, they should put it in a high place or in a locked cabinet.

The "reward store." The reward store is a variation of the token system. The child receives a token for each good performance. At the end of each month, the parents set up a "store" with a variety of rewards, assigning a value to each item. Using the tokens she earned during the month, the child "purchases" items from the "store."

Combining tokens and rewards. Some children are not motivated by a token system. They do not get the desired reward soon enough and lose interest after several days.

The token system may not be for them. But before abandoning it altogether, try combining tokens with rewards. Give a small reward together with a token after each performance. The child may derive enough satisfaction from this combination to remain motivated.

Weekly Performance Charts

> Avi and his parents have agreed on five daily goals. Avi has requested stars on a chart in return for each performance.
>
> After each good performance, his parents give him a star to attach to the appropriate spot on the chart. They build his enthusiasm by letting him attach the star himself. Avi is proud of his achievements and frequently inspects his collection of hard-earned rewards. His chart is an integral part of the reward.
>
> His sister, Naomi, has four daily goals and has requested a coloring book ($1.50 value) in return for one week's performance. After each good performance, she receives a star or a pencil mark in the appropriate box. Naomi's parents build her enthusiasm by letting her attach the star or make the pencil mark. Her parents use the chart to track her progress, and Naomi frequently inspects it to see how close she is to the coloring book.

A chart can be a tracking device, as in Naomi's case, or an integral part of the reward, as in Avi's case. When it is set in a conspicuous place, it is also a powerful reminder to perform.

Following are the charts made for Avi and Naomi. They list each of the target behaviors for a period of one week. At the beginning of each week, a new chart is begun.

NAME: **Avi** WEEK OF PARASHAS: **Beshalach**

REWARD: **Star** TO BE GIVEN AFTER: **1** POINT

	SUN.	MON.	TUES.	WED.	THURS.	FRI.	SHAB.
MAKE BED							
BRUSH TEETH							——
DRESS QUICKLY							
EAT BREAKFAST QUICKLY							
SCHOOL ON TIME							——

NAME: **Naomi** WEEK OF PARASHAS: **Beshalach**

REWARD: **Coloring Book** TO BE GIVEN AFTER: **18** POINTS

	SUN.	MON.	TUES.	WED.	THURS.	FRI.	SHAB.
WAKE UP ON TIME							
HANG UP CLOTHES							
DO HOMEWORK							——
PRACTICE PIANO							——

Avi and Naomi's parents have more goals for them. But they do not want to contract more than four or five at a time. They feel that too many assignments will be overwhelming and may jeopardize the success of the program. What can they do? They can rotate goals by removing some and adding others every two weeks. This way,

Avi and Naomi will have the opportunity to reach an assortment of goals.

A chart can also be created for a child who does not read. Instead of writing the target behavior, draw a picture of it. For example, draw a picture of a child brushing her teeth,

It is a good idea to create a blank chart and photocopy it many times to avoid the bother of duplicating charts by hand every week. At the beginning of each week, parents and children should agree on goals and fill in the appropriate spaces.

Daily Interval Charts

> Shimon, twelve years old, was constantly getting out of his seat in school. He and his teacher made a contract: after each full day of sitting quietly, he would receive a much-desired privilege as a reward.
>
> After the first hour he began squirming. He decided that sitting quietly for an entire day was too difficult. He lost interest in the plan and reverted to his regular behavior.

The goal of sitting quietly was too much for Shimon. After a short time, he realized that he could not sit for an entire day, so he did what anybody in his position would do — he lost interest and gave up.

In this case, Shimon's teacher can try using a daily interval chart. This is the way it works: first, observe the child to evaluate his capabilities. Next, target the time frame in which the child is expected to sit quietly — for example, nine o'clock to eleven o'clock every morning. Then break that time frame into smaller, *attainable* units of time; for example, one hour is divided into three twenty-minute units. The child receives one credit for each unit he sits quietly. Determine the number of credits the child must earn to receive a reward.

In the beginning, Shimon may only be able to sit quietly for one unit of time. Since this is the reasonable limit for him, the teacher should agree to give him one reward for every credit. As he becomes acclimated to the behavior, the requirements should be modified.

An interesting thing may happen. Shimon's successful performance during one unit may have a domino effect. As he becomes less restless, he may surprise everyone, including himself, and sit quietly for more units than expected.

Why does an interval system have such a positive effect? Because when Shimon contemplates the idea of an entire day of sitting quietly, he immediately assumes, "I cannot possibly do that." But when he considers sitting quietly for twenty minutes, he says, "Twenty minutes is not too long. I think I can do it." After receiving a reward for one unit of successful behavior, he takes on a new attitude and says, "If I can do it once, I can do it for another twenty minutes."

Following is Shimon's daily interval chart. It is divided into six twenty-minute units. For every two units in which Shimon sits quietly, he is eligible for ten minutes extra recess. He can select his own time slots.

NAME: *Shimon*		DATE: *Monday, December 9*
GOAL: *Sit quietly in class*		TIME PERIOD: *9:00-11:00*
REWARD: *10 min. extra recess*		TO BE GIVEN AFTER *2* UNITS
9:00-9:20	9:20-9:40	9:40-10:00
10:00-10:20	10:20-10:40	10:40-11:00

This method is very helpful for any child needing smaller units of time — for example, a child who constantly gets up from the dinner table or who does not complete homework because he does not have the patience to sit for more than fifteen minutes. Breaking a difficult goal into small units makes it attainable.

Family Politics

To illustrate the problem of family politics, we will refer to Avi and Naomi, the recipients of the earlier weekly performance charts.

While Avi and Naomi are enthusiastically using charts and happily being rewarded for good performances, their four brothers and sisters begin to wonder why they are not included in the fun. The parents tell them, "You perform well at all your tasks but Avi and Naomi need special treatment to motivate them to perform."

The four siblings, however, do not accept the explanation and are beginning to think they are being treated unfairly. They demand their own charts, goals and rewards.

This is a very common case of family politics. First, the parents should try to explain their rationale. Children, depending on their age and sensitivity, often understand and accept it. But when they don't, the issue must be resolved in another way.

The solution is to give the siblings charts, too. The parents should find four or five target behaviors for each of the other four siblings and produce weekly charts for them. Not only will this placate the children, it will motivate them to do some of the things they have been neglecting. (And remember the photocopier!)

Should Parents Offer Reminders?

In the morning, Esther brushes her teeth only after several reminders from her mother. To correct this, she and her parents agree on a reward program: Esther will brush her teeth by 8:00 A.M. in return for ten minutes of additional computer time in the evening. Esther is looking forward to spending more time at her favorite activity.

At 7:50 on the first day of the program, Esther has not brushed her teeth yet. Her parents want the program to succeed, so they gently remind her, "You have ten minutes to brush your teeth. You want the extra computer time, don't you?" At 7:57, she still has not begun.

With three minutes to go, should Esther's parents say nothing, remind her again or simply order her to brush her teeth? They can give her an order or a reminder, and Esther may respond. But if they say nothing, all three will derive full benefit from the program. Let's explain.

If the parents say nothing and the deadline passes, the following dialogue may take place:

Parent: It is now 8:15. You did not brush your teeth in time. This means no extra computer time tonight.

Esther: (startled) But you didn't remind me.

Parent: I did remind you once. Besides, reminders are not part of the agreement. It is your responsibility to remember.

Esther is confused. She is not connecting the consequence with her behavior. That night, after her regular twenty-minute computer activity, the discussion resumes:

Parent: Your twenty minutes are up. Please turn off the computer.

Esther: But I brushed my teeth and we agreed to more time.

Parent: You get more time if you brush by eight. You were late this morning.

Esther: (agitated) But you didn't remind me. You always do!

Parent: I reminded you once, and you chose to be late. You will have another chance tomorrow. Please turn off the computer now.

Esther: (grudgingly) That's not fair.

Esther turns off the computer but still has not made the connection between her behavior and losing the reward. She has until tomorrow morning to think about it and make the connection.

Esther will probably meet the eight o'clock deadline the next morning. In fact, she may not even wait for the reminder! But if she is neglectful again, she will lose her reward and suffer disappointment again. She will soon learn that her inaction results in losing the reward and she will be motivated to improve.

It is the nature of children to become involved with activities and lose track of time. For this reason, it is appropriate to provide a reminder. One reminder is sufficient. Afterward, the parents should step to the side and let the children choose their own direction. Parents can make this policy official by including it explicitly in the contract.

Parental interference dilutes the motivational potency of rewards. When they constantly offer reminders, the child learns to rely on the reminders. Rewards are meant to motivate — let them do their job! Parents do not have to play the role of policemen who coax, order, remind, threaten and physically coerce.

Furthermore, a no-reminder policy lets the child learn self-reliance. She learns to rely on her own determination, rather than to depend on an adult.

A reward program encourages responsibility. Parents can teach responsibility by giving children the opportunity to make independent choices. They can choose to perform well or poorly, and then must accept the resulting reward or penalty. They learn that the outcome is a direct result of their behavior; good performance results in a reward, poor performance in none. Once they connect the performance with the outcome, it becomes evident that the result is just as much a part of their decision as the performance itself.

The word "responsibility" can be divided into two words: response / ability. The implication is that people have the *ability* to *respond* as they want, with the understanding that their actions affect the outcome. By not offering continual reminders, parents are giving their children the opportunity to become responsible for their own actions.

The Parent as Provider, Not Judge

Let's return to Esther's story. At first, when Esther was denied additional computer time, she was angry with her mother and accused her of unfair treatment. Her mother, however, deflected the accusation by saying, "You chose to be late." That was very smart. Esther had the opportunity to meet the deadline and she did choose to be late. (In fact, her mother went above the call of duty by reminding her of the time.)

The parent is not a judge who determines if the child deserves a reward. The child can do that on her own by answering this simple question: "Did I perform according to set standards?"

The child is in control and the parent should never let her forget it. When the child points at the parent and says, "You did not give me the reward," the parent should point back and say, "You chose not to *take* the reward." Similarly, a parent should never say, "I am not giving you a star because you did not perform well." Rather, she should say, "You are not getting a star because you *chose* not to get one." The reward is available for the taking; when the child earns it, the parent supplies it.

This attitude reduces a child's negative feelings toward her parents and helps preserve a positive relationship. After all, the child cannot really hold a grievance against a parent when the penalty is her own choice!

Remain Emotionally Detached

Imagine this scene as part of Esther's story:

> It is 7:50 A.M. and Esther has not yet brushed her teeth. In a forceful tone, her mother says, "Esther, you have ten minutes to brush your teeth. Hurry up!" Two minutes later, her mother grits her teeth and gives another reminder. One minute later, she threatens Esther with the loss of the reward. Esther grudgingly brushes her teeth.

In this scenario, Esther's mother expresses an emotional attachment to the performance. She really cares if Esther brushes her teeth, and Esther knows it. If Esther is the spiteful type or if there are power struggles between mother and daughter, she may decide that causing her mother distress is more rewarding than the extra computer time. Causing her mother distress gives her a feeling of control, which is just what she wants in the relationship.

However, if her mother remains emotionally detached, the unspoken message is, "You have a choice ... Whatever you decide is okay." Now that her mother is not distressed by the choice she makes, Esther has nothing to gain by resisting. Instead, she will work for the extra computer time — the next best reward. She will perform well because she wants the reward.

Of course, parents care that their children reach the goals they set for them, but that does not mean that they have to make an emotional investment in the goals. With a little effort, a parent can create a mindset of emotional detachment, keeping in mind the positive effect it has on the reward program.

Be persistent. When I advise parents to begin a reward program, they are sometimes uninterested. They have tried it before and do not want to try it again. This is a common dialogue:

Parent: (rolling her eyes) Oh, rewards. We've done that before.

Counselor: How long did it last?

Parent: One or two weeks.

Counselor: During that time, were your children motivated to reach the goals?

Parent: Yes.

Counselor: So why did it last such a short time?

Parent: (embarrassed) Because it was too difficult for me to keep up.

There you have it: a program whose success is tested and proven, but which is discarded because of the difficulty parents have keeping it going.

To these parents, I offer two questions: 1) How can you expect your children to persevere in their goals if you do not persevere in yours? You can only demand of your children what you demand of yourself; 2) Which is more difficult: fighting with your children or maintaining a reward program? Indeed, maintaining weekly charts and supplying rewards is a small price to pay for a healthy family atmosphere.

If parents do not provide a chart at the beginning of the week, the child will not do it on his own. If parents forget to supply a reward, the child may remind them once or twice; but if they consistently fail to supply rewards, he will surmise that the program is not serious and will return to his original behaviors. Whose fault is it that the program failed? You know the answer.

Yes, maintaining a reward program may be a burden. But by

being consistent and persistent, both parents and children can derive significant benefits.

Eliminating the Reward

The purpose of the reward program is to acclimate the child to new behaviors. Once that is accomplished, it is time to consider how and when to wean the child from the program.

Ideally, a child should be able to perform without the incentive of an external reward. In fact, too much external reward weakens internal motivation. When parents sense that the child has reached that point, they should begin the weaning process and allow internal forces to take over. They can do this by offering fewer rewards for the same goals or the same number of rewards for more goals.

One word of caution: Don't begin the weaning process too soon. If the child thinks you are being disloyal to the program, it is an indication that he is not ready to be weaned.

Uncontracted Rewards

In this chapter, we presented a reward program designed to motivate children to reach planned goals. It is a formal, systematic technique involving parent/child agreements and tracking systems.

A reward can also be informal. It can be a tangible gesture of appreciation that gives weight to a verbal recognition: a nod, a smile, a cheer, a handshake, a thumbs-up sign or an item of some sort. It sends the message that you care and appreciate the child's performance. It is not part of a system; it is uncontracted and unexpected.

The rule, as always, is that the behavior that is rewarded will be repeated. The result of these uncontracted rewards is that it will encourage the child to repeat the desired behavior.

Use uncontracted rewards whenever you want, but don't do it excessively. Just make it a point to catch your children doing good things and praise them for it. Then reward them with gestures or tangible items. They are left with good feelings and will want to repeat those performances.

Chapter Four

Motivate Through Persuasion

Naomi doesn't enjoy learning *dikduk* (Hebrew grammar) and refuses to study for tests in the subject. Her parents coax her to study and threaten her with punishment. She finally yields to the pressure and studies.

Even if Naomi gets a good grade, how will she feel about the subject? How will she feel about her parents? This is hard to predict because every person responds differently; but it is very likely that, since she performed under negative conditions, she has negative feelings toward both her achievement and her parents. This is not the kind of success we want our children to have.

Rabbi Cohen announces to his class that they will stay in for recess to review some important material. The students are unhappy about it and complain. But Rabbi Cohen thinks he knows what is best and keeps them inside.

The students feel forced to learn against their will, and they resent having their recess taken away. Even if they do learn — and many of them won't — it is very likely that they will not be successful in the way we want them to be.

The children in these two scenarios may have reached the goal established for them but if they resent being coerced they may not feel good about the achievement. They will not appreciate its benefits and may even begin to detest it. If they are required to repeat the performance again, they may openly disobey or find a sneaky way of avoiding the task altogether.

Yes, they have *reached the goal,* but it cannot be called a *meaningful success.* They are not successful in the way we want them to be.

Naomi's parents and Rabbi Cohen could try motivating their children with rewards. The problem is that rewards do not foster an immediate appreciation for the goal or an immediate inner drive to reach the goal. And if the children perceive it as a bribe or manipulation, they would probably resent it.

There is another option — persuasion. Persuasion is a motivational technique that creates an immediate, or nearly immediate, inner drive. Children who have been persuaded understand the importance of the goal and may even buy into it. They will also have a stronger drive to reach it. They can succeed — the way we want them to.

Persuasion Is a Sales Strategy

To better understand the fine art of persuasion, let us look at a field which relies heavily on it — professional sales. Through years of trial and error, the sales industry has developed methods of persuasion which have been proven very effective.

Effective sales methods are necessary because it is difficult to sell a product to people. You cannot simply exhibit a product and point out its features, hoping that if the other person needs it, he will buy it. There is a major obstacle to selling which has to be broken down — the fact that people are comfortable with their attitudes and routines.

People are set in their ways. People must be moved to see, let alone, appreciate, another idea. This truth applies to ethical matters as well as physical necessities.

> All the ways of man are pure in his eyes (*Mishlei* 16:2).
> All the ways of man are straight in his eyes (*Mishlei* 21:2).
> It is natural for a person to see all of his traits as pure, whether they are good or bad; therefore, correcting traits is very difficult (Rabbeinu Yonah, *Mishlei* 16:2).

People have a natural tendency to hold on to their opinions and ideas. When you try to persuade a person to accept a new idea, you are working against that force. Professional salespeople know this. They know that persuasion is not a simple procedure, but rather a skill, a craft which has to be learned and applied.

People buy good feelings and solutions. Professional salespeople have a saying: "People buy two things — good feelings and a solution to their problem." In other words, the customer buys from someone he likes, and he only buys items that provide a personal benefit. So before making a sale, a salesperson creates good feelings with customers and shows them how the product is beneficial to them. Parents who want to successfully persuade their children to accept a goal can also apply this method. We will now elaborate.

Create Good Feelings

Receptivity grows out of good feelings. When you go shopping and decide to buy something, do the feelings you have for the salesperson — positive or negative — influence your decision? All things being equal, you would probably buy more quickly from someone you like than from someone you don't like.

Good salespeople know this. They invest time cultivating good will and creating good feelings before making a sales presentation. Once they have made a favorable impression on the prospective customer, they do not stop. They continue maintaining a positive rapport for the duration of the relationship.

You may recall teachers for whom you had good feelings. They may have been tough and demanding, but because you trusted and liked them, you were receptive to their demands. You may also recall teachers for whom you had poor feelings. You had little trust and respect for them, and you were not very receptive to their lessons or demands.

People who enjoy a good relationship tend to be receptive to each other. People who have a poor relationship tend to be less receptive to each other. This works in family relationships, too. You want children to "buy" the goals you are "selling." So do as the professionals do. Create receptivity by creating good feelings.

How to create good feelings. You create good feelings with your children by giving them value and making them feel important. When children know you value them, they feel good about you and are more receptive to your ideas. Respect them and be sensitive to their feelings. Be tough on the issues but easy on the person. Be tactful when saying what they need to hear. Listen carefully when they talk. Address their concerns.

You may say, "Parents need time — weeks, months, even years — to develop a healthy relationship with their children. How can they create good feelings at the time they present a goal?"

Building healthy family relationships does take time. However, parents do not need a fully developed relationship to "sell" a goal. It is possible to create good feelings, *adequate to make the "sale,"* at the time they present the goal. (This is certainly more effective than presenting the new goal and creating bad feelings or no feelings at all.)

Creating good feelings in a tense relationship. Even if the relationship is already tense, you can begin to create good feelings at the time you present the new goal. How? By taking steps *not* to create barriers or negative feelings about the new goal. By valuing the children and making them feel important *now.* By being sensitive to their needs and letting them know you support them *now.* By presenting the idea with a soft tone of voice that reflects warmth and compassion. King Shlomo said:

> A gentle reply turns away wrath, a harsh word creates anger (*Mishlei* 15:1).

Being harsh and unfriendly can generate new feelings of anger. However, a gentle tone of voice and friendly words have the power to placate a person's anger.[1] This approach reduces friction and

1. Vilna Gaon and Rabbeinu Yonah, *Mishlei* 15:1.

creates good feelings. It may even be the beginning of a new, improved relationship!

Find a Benefit or Solve a Problem

People are receptive to ideas that benefit them. Did you ever go shopping and meet a salesperson who tried selling you something you did not need? Did you buy it? Probably not. You buy products that address your needs or solve your problems. Otherwise, you don't want them.

Ideas are the same. People, including children, are receptive to ideas that benefit them. They are not open to ideas that are not beneficial or are forced on them. Rabbi Eliyahu Dessler put it succinctly:

> Every person is interested in his own needs more than yours; therefore, show him how your needs agree with his. Do not try to influence the other person just to *do* the new thing, but to *want* to do it. Then he will be happy doing it ... Do not talk too much about yourself; talk with the other person about himself, and he will have an interest in listening (Rabbi Eliyahu Dessler, *Michtav M'Eliyahu,* vol. 4, p. 244).

Let us take a look at how Reuven, the son of Yaakov, used this principle to persuade his brothers to change their plan to kill Yosef:

> Reuven's intent was to save Yosef. If he had simply said, "Let us not kill him," the implication would be that he was hesitating due to his mercy for Yosef. Therefore, he said, "Let us not kill *a soul.*" This implied that he only cared about them, not about Yosef. It is the same when he said, "Let us not spill blood," and he did not say, "*his* blood." He implied, "I also hate Yosef, just as you do, and I do not care about his life at all. I only care about you, that you should not be murderers" (Rabbeinu Bachya, *Bereishis* 37:21,22).

Everyone tunes in to station WII FM — "What's In It For Me?" Successful salespeople know this. They know that everyone is looking out for his or her own best interest. When presenting a new product, they ask themselves, "What's in it for the customer?" Successful parents can ask the same question, "What's in it for my child?" They can then show the child how the product addresses his or her needs.[1] This notion is reminiscent of the Rambam's teaching, quoted at the beginning of Chapter Three, about the wisdom in motivating people with rewards that are beneficial to them.

What if a salesperson does not know what the customer's needs are? He finds out. The first thing he does is listen carefully to the other person.

Listen carefully. Discovering someone else's needs is not difficult. It requires effective listening. We did not say *listening* — we said *effective listening.*

Did you ever talk with someone and get the feeling that he was not listening carefully? Instead, he was thinking about his upcoming response or something totally unrelated. Many people do this. An effective listener, however, listens carefully to the other person. He makes an effort — and it does take effort — to open his mind to the other person's ideas. He detaches himself from all other unrelated thoughts at that moment and connects with the other person.

> "A wise person ... does not interrupt the words of his friend, and he is not quick to respond." The wise person allows the other person to speak until he finishes all his words; then he gives an answer (Rabbeinu Yonah, *Avos* 5:7).
>
> "The one who answers a word before he understands, it is foolishness to him and an embarrassment." It is necessary to listen to the points of the questioner and all his doubts, and afterward to come to a clear decision. He earns the questioner's respect by doing this (Malbim, *Mishlei* 18:13).

---

1. See *Chovas HaShmirah,* last footnote in the preface: It is easier for a person to perform *mitzvos* when he knows that his life depends on it. In other words, people are motivated when they see value in an activity.

Good salespeople listen to their prospective customers and seek to understand their needs. Then they talk to the customers *with those needs in mind* and show how their product can help. The customers see what's in it for them and feel that their needs have been recognized. This increases their chances of buying. Parents and teachers can follow the same plan.

Diagnose before prescribing. Imagine going to a doctor, complaining of stomach pains. The doctor invites you into his office and you describe your pains. He immediately writes out a prescription and moves on to the next patient.

The doctor has not taken a history of the problem or performed an examination. He does not know much about the pains, yet he prescribes a treatment. He may be making a big mistake. How much confidence would you have in this doctor?

Successful doctors first diagnose by gathering all the pertinent information. Then they prescribe. Successful salespeople also diagnose first, and only after they understand the customer's problem do they prescribe a solution. Successful parents do the same; they first assess the needs and problems of their child, and then find a solution that addresses the child directly.

Let us illustrate with a dialogue between a young boy named Yaakov and his father. Yaakov's father tries persuading Yaakov to be nice to another boy.

Father: Please be nice to Chezky.

Yaakov: I don't want to be nice to Chezky.

Father: You have to be nice to everyone.

Yaakov: But I don't like Chezky.

Father: It's an *aveirah* to be that way.

Yaakov: Why? He deserves it. He does bad things.

Father: Two wrongs don't make a right.

Yaakov: Yes, but ...

Father: Yaakov, you know how to act properly. I want you to be nice to Chezky even if it means going out of your way.

Yaakov's father prescribes ("Be nice to Chezky") and even passes judgment ("It's an *aveirah*") without first understanding *why* Yaakov has not been nice. He never diagnoses the problem — that is, the reason for Yaakov's attitude — and his solution does not really solve the problem. Instead, he forces a behavior which Yaakov probably resents.

If Yaakov's father would listen to his son, he would discover the *reason* for the problem. He may then devise a solution that would answer the "What's-in-it-for-Yaakov" question. His son would see the benefit and might commit himself to the plan.

Yaakov's father would first ask questions to elicit the necessary information. The dialogue might go like this:

Father: Please be nice to Chezky.

Yaakov: I don't want to be nice to Chezky.

Father: Really? Tell me about it.

Yaakov: Chezky isn't nice to me.

Father: That must make you feel bad. What does he do?

Yaakov: Yesterday, he pushed me when we were playing in the yard.

Father: You must have really resented that. Why do you suppose he did that?

Yaakov: I don't know.

Father: Did something happen right before he pushed you?

Yaakov: Well, I did grab the ball away from him.

Father: Is there a connection between that and his pushing?

Yaakov: Maybe he got angry at me.

Father: Maybe. What if you hadn't taken the ball. Would he have pushed you?

Yaakov: Probably not.

Father: So it looks like there is a connection. (pause) Yaakov, do you want to be friends with Chezky?

Yaakov: Yes.

Father: So what plan can we make to keep you friends?

Yaakov: I don't know.

Father: What if you are nice to Chezky — would that help?

Yaakov: You mean I'll be nice to him, then he'll be nice to me? That sounds like a good plan.

In this dialogue, Yaakov's father gathers the pertinent information to make a diagnosis. He learns that Yaakov wants to be friends with Chezky, but instead is driving him away. He then finds a solution — that Yaakov try being nice to Chezky. What's in it for Yaakov? A renewed friendship with Chezky. And Yaakov wants that.

Yaakov doesn't need convincing because he sees the benefit in his father's plan. His father also gets what he wants. And because Yaakov is interested in the solution, his father is confident that he will actually make the effort.

Yaakov might have a different problem. He might be jealous of Chezky and is covering up by saying that Chezky is not nice; he might have a false perception of Chezky altogether; or Chezky might really be a bully. Each scenario requires a different solution. And the only way to formulate one is to get the pertinent information and make a diagnosis.

First, listen. Discover the child's needs. Then find a solution that addresses those needs. Ask, "What's in it for the child?" When the child sees that you are connecting to him, he will become receptive to your idea.

Sell them what they want. Salespeople do not sell what *they* think the customer needs, but what the *customer* thinks he needs. We will illustrate this with an example of what *not* to do.

> Rabbi Levy wants his students to review some important school work instead of going out to recess. He produces a crossword puzzle to provide the review. He believes the puzzle will be so much fun that it could even replace the fun of recess. Here, Rabbi Levy tries persuading his students to accept his plan:

Rabbi Levy: Why do you want recess?

Students: It's fun to play outside.

Rabbi Levy: Look what I have for you. A crossword puzzle. It's also fun.

Students: But we want recess fun.

Rabbi Levy: Fun is fun. It shouldn't make a difference to you. Besides, this is educational fun, so it's better.

Rabbi Levy actually thinks he is doing the right thing. He asks, "What's in it for them?" He knows they want fun, and since his crossword puzzle is also fun, he believes it is a valid substitute for recess.

Rabbi Levy does not realize that along with their *needs,* he should also address their *wants.* If the children don't want it, they won't appreciate the benefit. They will resent the plan and will probably not perform well.

This pattern applies in a home setting, too. Suppose a child says she wants to take up a hobby, and her mother thinks that baking is a good idea. Before persuading the child to learn baking, the mother should first find out if the child is interested in it altogether. Just because a parent thinks baking is important does not mean that the child wants to learn how to bake. She may prefer sewing, and will resent being pushed into something she doesn't want to do. As a result, she will not perform as well as she might.

When persuading children, don't sell them what *you* think they want; sell them what *they* think they want. Align yourself with your children and find solutions which address both their *needs* and *wants.*

All this does not mean that parents should enlist their children's approval for every goal. We have mentioned several times that parents should expect their children to be obedient. Parents frequently set goals, and rightfully so, that children are not happy with. They assign chores that children do not want to perform; they make rules that children say are fit for a prisoner; they make household schedules that children consider too restrictive. Yet the children must comply, no matter how much they dislike it.

Ideally, children *should* be obedient. However, many children do not respond this way. They are motivated only when they see a personal benefit. For this reason, it is more productive to align yourself with the child.

Align yourself with the child.

> When we want to influence another person, we should direct his will to meet our demands and goals. We will be more successful not when we try to get a response to our demands through inflexibility and commands, but when we give the child appropriate freedom within the framework of his natural tendencies toward the good and proper, and we mix firmness with love and warmth (Rabbi S. R. Hirsch, *Yesodos HaChinuch,* Netzach Publishers, p. 66).

Aligning yourself with your children is not a sign of weakness; on the contrary, it is a sign of strength. It shows that you have considered the most effective way of reaching each individual child. This requires self-discipline and strength of character.

When you align yourself with your children, you draw their support. If they agree to the goal, they will be committed to it and will achieve the kind of success you want them to have. They will also be left with good feelings toward you. This enhances your potential to influence them in the future.[1]

There is a benefit in this approach even if they only *partially* agree to the goal. The more they understand, the more they will accept. And the more they accept, the more effort they will put into reaching the goal.

There is a benefit in this approach even if they *totally* disagree with the goal: the value you have given them by creating good feelings and making the effort to relate to their needs will go a long way. When performance time comes, they may appreciate your sincerity and be more cooperative.[2]

---

1. See a full discussion on this topic in Rabbi S. R. Hirsch, *Yesodos HaChinuch,* pp. 65-69.
2. See Rabbi S. R. Hirsch, *Judaism Eternal,* vol. 1, p. 230: Parents should not appear autocratic; they should give reasons for the things they want their children to do. The concept of understanding the reason for one's actions is also seen in the *mitzvah* of belief in Hashem — "And you shall know today and you shall take to your heart that Hashem is G-d" (*Devarim* 4:39).

Tap into the child's values. There is a way of making a goal so important to children that they *want* to "buy" it. Tap their own values. Show how your goal addresses their priorities.

Values are ideals which are important to a person. Values say what a person stands for and give direction to his or her life. If you want to know what is close to a person's heart, look at his or her set of values.

You can connect with other people and stand on equal ground with them by relating to their values. When you make this connection, you are "speaking their language." People naturally want to talk in terms of their own priorities and will therefore be more open to your ideas.[1]

This is the approach Reuven used to persuade his brothers to spare Yosef. He talked about the sin of murder, a concept which was part of their value system. He did not talk about the compassion they should have for Yosef because this was not part of their framework.[2]

Parents can use persuasion by tapping into their children's values, too. Let us illustrate:

> Shimi, twelve years old, has many opinions and loves to express them. He is assertive and tries to influence others to follow him. He reads all that he can about politics and leadership. He plans to become a community leader one day.
>
> At this time, his parents are not thinking of his plans for the future. They just want him to get along better with his siblings and some of the other children on the block. They have tried motivating him to reach this goal. They have preached, punished, reprimanded and rewarded. Now they are trying something new. They are persuading him by tapping into his own values.
>
> They explain to him that learning to get along better with others will give him the practice needed for leadership. They help him understand that if he masters human-

1. Rabbi Eliyahu Dessler, *Michtav M'Eliyahu*, vol. 4, p. 244.
2. Rabbeinu Bachya, *Bereishis* 37:21,22.

relations skills today, he will become a better leader tomorrow.

Shimi is now interested in learning human-relations skills and is motivated to practice them with his siblings and neighbors.

Shimi's parents asked the question, "What is in it for him?" They thought about his values and found the answer — the concept of leadership. This appealed to Shimi and made him less resistant. He and his parents are now on common ground. They are speaking his language and he is open to their ideas.

Does this sound manipulative? It would be if the parents alone stood to gain something by it. But Shimi has something to gain, too. He *wants* to reach the goal and is looking forward to the benefit.

In Shimi's case, the value his parents tapped was related to the goal itself, which was to improve his social skills. His *value* was leadership and the chance to practice it. Shimi was motivated to reach his parents' goal because he wanted to improve his own human-relations skills. All three were on common ground.

Unlike Shimi's case, there are times when the goal itself has no value to the child — but the *by-product* of the goal is still meaningful. Let us illustrate:

Josh's parents wanted him to play a musical instrument. They talked about the beauty of music, the enjoyment he would have, the pride they would have in him and the fact that he could earn extra money playing at *simchas.* But Josh could not be persuaded.

They decided to tap into his values. They asked themselves, "What is important to Josh?" They realized that Josh valued his individuality and loved to stand out in a crowd. Now they had a new approach.

"None of the other children in your group play a musical instrument," they told him. "Do you realize that if you would play a musical instrument, you would be the only one? You would be able to stand out as having a talent that nobody else has. You would be unique."

This appealed to Josh, and he agreed to begin music lessons.

Josh agreed because he saw what was in it for him — a sense of individuality. This feeling was only the by-product of playing an instrument, not the actual goal of playing itself. Nevertheless, it motivated him.

Here are some more examples of tapping into values that relate to the by-products. In some cases, the by-product is a natural consequence of reaching the goal; in others, it is provided by the parents.

Value: A sense of importance
Say: If you gather the *siddurim* after *shacharis,* the *shul* will be neat and prepared for *minchah.* People will be able to *daven* better in a neat *shul,* and Hashem will also be happy. What you do *really* counts.

Value: Recognition
Say: If you learn well, you will become a *talmid chochom* and people will look up to you.

Value: Being independent, autonomous
Say: If you do your chores all by yourself, you will prove that you are capable of being independent. I will then be able to give you more independence in other activities.

Value: Comfort, pleasure
Say: If you don't go to bed on time tonight, you will have to go to bed early tomorrow.

The last example is called negative reinforcement. The child is motivated to perform properly out of a desire to *avoid* a negative consequence. Unfortunately, this approach is used too often. We say "unfortunately" because it is negative and its long-term effect is limited.[1] The use of too many negative reinforcements may also hinder the parent/child relationship.

When a child has a mistaken assumption. When a child is operating under a false assumption, you can point out the mistake and make the correction. Sometimes, however, the child will disagree. He has his opinion, which is part of his value system, and

---

1. Rabbi Shlomo Wolbe, *Alai Shur*, p. 261: "Praise and prizes are more effective than threats and punishments."

he is not prepared to modify it. He needs time to become comfortable with the new idea. How can you persuade this child *now?*

Speak with the child as though his assumption were correct. Show him that, even according to his assumption, the new idea has merit. Speak his language. We mentioned earlier that this is how Reuven persuaded his brothers to spare Yosef. Your child will also appreciate the approach and may become receptive.[1]

Rename the task. The name attached to a task may lead one to think that the task is difficult. Thinking about the difficulty that lies ahead, the child may not be motivated to tackle it. After all, who wants to do something that smacks of hardship? However, the same task can generate greater interest if it has a pleasant connotation.

Take, for example, math problems that children do for homework. Solving problems is a chore which nobody likes. Who wants to spend several hours a week involved in an unpleasant activity? Homework is usually unappealing, but referring to it in terms of *problems* reduces the appeal even more.

Instead, try calling the homework "math *challenges.*" Challenges are exciting. They are certainly more interesting than *problems.* It is the same work, but giving it an appealing name generates more interest. Many students, for instance, complete school worksheets more happily when they are called "fun sheets."

Perhaps children don't like performing household chores. Can you blame them? A chore is drudgery and is not very appealing. Try calling the tasks instead "helpful deeds," "household *mitzvos,*" "acts of *chesed* " or "household contributions."

Think of other unpopular tasks and consider renaming them. This may rekindle your children's interest.

Be sincere and pleasant. There is a well-known saying: "Words that leave the heart enter the heart."[2] This means that when you present a new goal or idea, you should feel love and compassion for the other person. Make it clear that your only interest is his welfare and that you have nothing to gain personally. Be sincere. Your words will then be accepted.

---

1. See Vilna Gaon, *Mishlei* 26:5.
2. Rabbi Moshe ibn Ezra, *Shiras Yisrael,* p. 156.

Your tone of voice and choice of words should be friendly, warm and sweet; they will be more easily accepted. King Shlomo said it well:

> Pleasant words are like a honeycomb, sweet to the soul and healing to the bones (*Mishlei* 16:24).
>
> Points presented in a very pleasant way are sweet as honeycombs to the listener, and they help the soul and body. This is the way to draw the people's hearts to one's opinion, whether it is related to an ethical matter or a physical necessity (*Metzudas David, Mishlei* ad loc.).[1]

Make the goal attainable. Children are not motivated to work toward a goal that they perceive as unattainable. Even if they appreciate the goal's benefit and begin with commitment, they will quickly lose interest. What else can you expect? For this reason, it is important to consider the feasibility of the goal before setting it.[2]

Sometimes, the goal really is unattainable. Other times, it is attainable, but the children feel unable to reach it. They lack confidence or have what is called "a mental block." To them, the goal is unreachable.

In these cases, the parent should lead the children toward the final goal in stages. Motivate them to reach the goal at a lower level or to reach just one portion of it. After they achieve this, motivate them to come closer to the final goal. As it comes within reach, they will see that they can achieve it.

The Action Plan

The most important part of a sales presentation is the follow-up, or action plan. After the salesperson creates a sense of urgency and the customer agrees to the necessity of the product, the salesperson must follow up with a request for action. The two of them discuss the number of items to be purchased, the color,

---

1. See also Talmud *Shabbos* 34a: "... say it pleasantly so that it should be accepted." See also Rabbi Shlomo Wolbe, *Alai Shur*, p. 261: "Words which are not said quietly and patiently are not accepted." See also Vilna Gaon, *Even Shlaimah* 6:5.

2. See Rabbi Shlomo Wolbe, *Alai Shur*, p. 263: "Any demand that is above the age level of the child is likely to have a negative impact on his soft heart."

delivery date, schedule of payments and any other detail of the transaction.

Similarly, after parents show the child how a goal benefits him and he agrees to it, they should follow up with a request for action. If possible, they should formulate the action plan together with the child. This enhances the child's commitment to the goal.

Let's illustrate this point with Yaakov, the boy who agreed to be nice to Chezky. He and his father agreed on the goal of being nice, but exactly what does "nice" mean? They should discuss it and agree on terms. They may agree that being nice means speaking respectfully to Chezky, offering assistance when requested, and refraining from hitting him, calling him names and grabbing a ball away from him.

Next, they should agree on the skills needed to be "nice." Yaakov may have to learn how to be more respectful or self-disciplined. He may have to create a new state of mind that will help him see Chezky in a favorable light. He may need assistance, either from his parents or from a professional counselor. This will enable him to reach the goal.

Putting it all together. Let's see how Naomi's mother, whom we met at the beginning of the chapter, can use these principles to motivate her daughter to study *dikduk* (Hebrew grammar). The first step is to create good feelings and to gather the pertinent information for a diagnosis. Let's watch how she does it.

Mother: Naomi, honey, I noticed you didn't study for the *dikduk* test.

Naomi: I don't want to study.

Mother: I'm interested. Tell me about it, please.

Naomi: I don't like *dikduk.*

Mother: It's not fun studying things you don't like, I know.

Naomi: That's right.

Mother: Is that the only problem?

Naomi: I also don't see any reason to learn it.

Mother: So you don't like the subject and you see no reason to study. I can understand your problem.

The mother creates good feelings by giving Naomi value. She is calm, non-judgmental and genuinely concerned. She also seeks to understand Naomi's problem so she can make a diagnosis and formulate a solution that addresses her daughter's needs.

Naomi's mother never agrees with her, yet she is sympathetic. She uses the "mirroring" method of sympathizing, in which she reflects Naomi's feelings back to her and shows understanding. Naomi appreciates her mother's understanding and becomes more receptive.

Even if they have a poor relationship, the mother's decision to treat Naomi with respect and to show sincere interest will enhance her daughter's receptivity in this particular instance. It may even be the beginning of a new, improved relationship.

The next step in the persuasion process is to complete the diagnosis and offer a solution that Naomi can appreciate:

Mother: Why don't you like the subject?

Naomi: Because it's too hard.

Mother: In what way is it too hard?

Naomi: I can't remember the rules.

Mother: Do you think that if you reviewed them a few times every night, you would remember them better? If you'd like, I am available to study with you. I can even suggest ways of remembering the rules.

Naomi: But I thought you don't have time.

Mother: For you, I have time. I would be honored to study with you.

Naomi's mother discovers the reason that she does not study — she does not remember the rules, and as a result, has difficulty with the subject. Her mother could say, "So study harder," but Naomi would reject that. Instead, she *aligns* herself with Naomi and formulates a solution that her daughter can appreciate.

The solution, however, is not complete. While having assistance will lighten the load, Naomi still does not have an interest in the subject. Her mother now has to arouse her interest:

Naomi: Even if I study, who needs *dikduk* anyway? It's not so important to know.

Mother: You mean you think there is no value in knowing *dikduk?*

Naomi: That's right.

Mother: Can I show you something about *dikduk?*

Naomi: Okay. What do you want to show me?

Naomi is frustrated and does not want a sermon on the importance of *dikduk.* Nor does she want her mother to force her own views on her. For these reasons, her mother requests permission to show Naomi why *dikduk* is important. If Naomi gives permission, she will be more receptive than if she were force-fed the information.

Now let's see how Naomi's mother sparks her interest:

Mother: Look at this word. (She opens a *Chumash* and shows how knowledge of simple *dikduk* helps translate words and understand the text. She gives several examples and presents a convincing argument.)

Naomi: That is interesting. And you're only using the simple rules.

Mother: That's right. Just knowing the simple rules can be very helpful. (pause) Naomi, you want to do well in your studies, don't you?

Naomi: Yes, I do try.

Mother: Knowing *dikduk* will really help you in all your school work. And I can help make it easier to learn.

Naomi's mother shows her what is in it for her. She points to the benefit of excelling in her studies and taps into Naomi's value of doing well in school. She hopes that the appeal to her value system and the appreciation for its importance will motivate her daughter to study. If Naomi's mother had ordered, "Study harder and improve your grades," Naomi would probably have resented it and would not perform well. Why should she? She sees no benefit.

Now that the benefit is recognized, the two of them need an action plan:

Mother: Do you think you want to begin reviewing with me?

Naomi: Yes.

Mother: How many times should we do it?

Naomi: Is ten minutes a day good enough?

Mother: If we review every night for ten minutes, you will learn it. And I'm sure you will get at least ten points higher on your next test. Can we agree to that, too?

Naomi: Yes.

Together, they formulate a plan of action. Naomi is now committed to studying every night and to improving her grades.

Motivation is an ongoing effort. Both Yaakov and Naomi have work to do. Yaakov must learn to get along with Chezky, and Naomi must discipline herself to study a difficult subject. As they encounter difficulties, they will have to make adjustments to old routines and attitudes. Being persistent and making adjustments is not easy. For this reason, their parents will have to continue motivating them. Motivation is not a one-time effort; it is an ongoing process.

Focus on the benefits, not the difficulties. Parents should not focus on difficulties by saying things like, "We know this is unpleasant, but you have to do it anyway. Life is not easy, you know." This does not make the goal easier to reach.

Instead, they should focus on the benefits. They should inspire their children by saying things like, "Look at the benefit you will gain," "You will have so much fun with your new friend," "You will be so much more successful in school," "Somebody with your capabilities can surely meet any challenge that arises." Focusing on the rewards of success is more inspirational than focusing on its difficulties.

Overcoming Resistance

Persuasion implants new ideas in the minds of others. If they are open and willing to entertain those new ideas, they may accept them. But if they are closed and resistant, they will not accept them.

The problem is that most people are resistant to new ideas, at least to some degree. As a result, persuasion is a difficult job.

> All the ways of man are pure and straight in his eyes, and even if he does a wrong thing, he shows how he is going in the proper way (Vilna Gaon, *Mishlei* 16:12).

Furthermore, when a person is emotionally invested in an opinion, it is especially difficult for him or her to change.[1]

Because people are resistant to new ideas, we presented the professional sales approach as a way of enhancing receptivity. There are some people, however, who do not respond to the sales approach. Even after seeing the benefits and feeling good about the persuader, they remain unreceptive. They are comfortable and secure with their familiar ideas and unwilling to entertain new ones. They appear stubborn and set in their ways. They resist.

In these cases, the persuader should ask, "What is stopping them? The benefit is there, so why are they not buying? What problems or difficulties are holding them back?"

If the product that is being sold is a goal, the first thing to do is to show that there is nothing to be afraid of and that the goal can be reached. Give them ideas for overcoming the obstacles, and if needed, give them assistance to get them started.

If, however, the lack of receptivity is due to an inner resistance that is unrelated to fears or doubts, the persuader will have to use a different approach. First, we will briefly describe the five types of resistance that people display. The ability to recognize various resistance styles enables us to deal with people more effectively.

Type One: In the first type of resistance, a person is reluctant to adjust familiar ideas because he is already comfortable with them.

---

1. Maharal, *Derech Chaim, Avos* 4:19.

> Mrs. Rosen tries to motivate her children to cooperate by criticizing and screaming at them. Friends have told her about the disadvantages of this approach and have recommended that she use praise and rewards. She has even spoken with a professional who concurred. But she is sure that her method is correct and continues to use it.

Mrs. Rosen is secure with her approach because it is the only method she is familiar with. Opening up to new methods requires effort, experimentation and risk-taking. That is too much work. Therefore, she is unreceptive to new methods.

Here is an example of a child who is comfortable with an old idea:

> Mirel holds a pencil awkwardly. Her parents and teachers have tried to show her the proper way of grasping a pencil but, because she is comfortable with her method, she refuses to accept the suggestion.

Mirel is comfortable with her own method. To change it, she would have to experiment and try something new. That is too much work.

Type Two: In the second type of resistance, the person has put a great deal of effort into his first position and does not want to adjust it.

> Mr. Levine has been thinking about his vacation for several weeks. He has finally decided to go on a sightseeing trip. His brother suggested he change his plans and go to the family reunion scheduled for that time, which would give him a chance to meet distant family members. Besides, he could take the sightseeing trip at another time. Although it makes more sense to go to the family reunion and postpone the trip, Mr. Levine keeps his original plan.

Mr. Levine spent two weeks thinking about his vacation. He put time and effort into the decision and doesn't want to put any more time and effort into changing it. So he stubbornly resists.

Here is an example of a child who has put effort into an idea and does not want to change it:

> Ari planned to make a birthday party for his brother. He called his friends and told them what to bring, and he made all the other arrangements. He planned the party for 5:30 in the evening, but he did not know that his parents were planning to go out that evening.
>
> When Ari told his parents about the party, they told him that the time was a problem. They wanted to be home to supervise the party, so they asked Ari to change the time. Ari became very angry about this.

Ari had put time and effort into his plans and didn't want to put any more time and effort into changing them. So he stubbornly resisted.

Type Three: In the third type of resistance, the person has no apparent reason to resist. Rather, she is unwilling to redirect attention to a new idea.

> Hindi mops the floor and leaves it full of puddles. Her mother suggests that she squeeze the mop one more time before each use, but she refuses. Her mother asks why she disagrees, and Hindi simply answers, "No reason."

Hindi could do as her mother suggests; it is not that difficult. But she is comfortable with her way and reluctant to change. Unlike Mr. Levine and Mrs. Rosen, Hindi has no rationale. She is just unwilling to redirect her attention to a new idea.

Type Four: In the fourth type of resistance, the person is unwilling to redirect attention to a new idea because she is preoccupied with other concerns. For example, a child may just have been rejected by a friend or denied a part in the school play. She may be suffering from a poor self-image or may just have noticed a new pimple on her forehead. Turning her attention to another thought takes too much effort, so she appears stubborn and resistant.

In the first two types of resistance, Mr. Levine, Mrs. Rosen, Mirel and Ari have reasons for not wanting to change their attitudes. They consider the alternatives and decide that their plan is best. Before changing their minds, they would have to do more than redirect their attention to a new idea. They would first have to uproot a conflicting set of ideas.

The third and fourth types of resistance are different. These people have no particular reason for feeling as they do. They do not have a conflicting set of ideas that must be uprooted. Their only task is to redirect their attention to new ideas.

Type Five: In the fifth type of resistance, people push away new ideas as a way of satisfying emotional needs. For example, children with a need to express control or be independent may resist new ideas — even if those ideas are reasonable and appropriate — as a way of saying, "I am in charge and nobody can tell me what to do." Self-centered children may resist an idea that requires them to consider the welfare of others. Children who insist on extraordinarily high standards of cleanliness and perfection resist any standard lower than their own; they have a fetish, a psychological fixation, that must be satisfied.

Before changing their minds, these children have to do more than redirect their attention or uproot a conflicting set of ideas. Because their resistance is a fundamental part of their psyches, they must first find a way of satisfying their emotional needs.

These five types of resistance are due to ulterior motives of which the children themselves are probably unaware. The job of parents is to break down their resistance and to enhance receptivity. How can they do it?

Ask questions and create dialogue. Questioning invites people to find answers and to respond. It spurs them to think. Wise men throughout the centuries have used the questioning technique to clarify their points and to persuade others.

When you are questioned, you are pushed to make the uncomfortable effort to think about something you would otherwise not think about. But once your attention is redirected from what *you* want to think about to what the *other person* wants you to think about, you become open to those ideas. In the process, you may even discover flaws in your own position.

Before buying a new suit or dress, you first try it on to see how it fits. You don't just hold it up and observe it from a distance; rather, you remove your current set of clothes and try on the new ones. Before "buying" a new idea, you do the same. You see how it fits mentally by forgoing a familiar idea — even discarding it — and trying on a new one.

A question spurs you to do this. As you search for an answer, you may think of things that never entered your mind before. You view these ideas from different angles and see how they fit your mental "body." You also examine your familiar position. If you discover a flaw in it, you discard it and replace it with something new.

When dealing with unreceptive children, don't try to persuade them with points that are clear, convincing and logical to *you*. You are both wearing different suits of ideas and are comfortable with your respective outlooks. They may not buy your idea. Rather, help them *discard* their familiar idea and *try on* a new one. If they find it comfortable, they will probably accept it. How can you do this?

Ask questions. Let the children do the thinking, talking and discovering. Help them find flaws in their old ideas and think about new ones. Let us illustrate.

> Judy, twelve years old, does not complete her homework. Her father thinks the problem is that she leaves it until the end of the night and forgets to complete it. He wants her to begin homework shortly after arriving home from school.
>
> He could simply ask Judy to adjust her schedule, but judging from past discussions on the topic she would not be receptive. So he uses the questioning technique to enhance receptivity.
>
> He first has to break the ice and begin the discussion. He senses that a direct question would put Judy on the defensive, causing her to be uncooperative, so he makes a statement that implies a request for a response. This has the same effect as a question, but without the defensive side effect.
>
> **Father:** Your teacher mentioned that you have not been completing all your homework assignments.
>
> **Judy:** I do it most of the time.
>
> **Father:** Does "most of the time" meet class standards?

(This question pushes Judy to talk about her position and search for a flaw.)

Judy: I guess not.

(Here she finds a flaw. Hopefully, she will now be more receptive to new ideas.)

Father: So why do you think it happens?

(He now tries to find out if there is a problem he should be aware of.)

Judy: I try but I just don't seem to get it done.

Father: When do you do your homework? What is your schedule after school?

(He suspects that she does not manage her time well, a typical cause of the problem, and is now pushing her to consider her time management.)

Judy: After getting home I have a snack, go outside to play, come back in for dinner, talk on the phone with my friends, do some things in the house and then, if Mom doesn't ask me to do chores, I do my homework.

Father: Do you think your schedule may be contributing to the problem?

Judy: Maybe I wait too long before starting my homework and then I forget about it.

Father: Is there any way of adjusting your schedule to alleviate the problem?

(Father is leading Judy toward adjusting her schedule. Hopefully, she will try on some new ideas and find a solution.)

Judy: I guess if I start homework right after my snack, I won't forget to do it.

(Here she tries on a new idea and finds that it fits the values that compose her "mental body.")

Father: So let's review. What will be your schedule after school?

(This is the call to action, the final step in a goal-setting discussion.)

Judy: After arriving home, I'll have a snack, do my homework, go outside to play, eat dinner, talk to my friends and do the chores.

In the past, Judy did not want to adjust her schedule. But now her father has persuaded her to consider it. First, he asked questions that pushed her to examine her position. She found a flaw and became receptive to a new position. Then he invited her to try on new ideas.

He had a goal for Judy: to complete her assignments. He suspected the cause of her problem: poor time management. He formulated questions that would test his suspicion. Then he led Judy to his goal by using short, non-threatening questions.

At one point, Judy's father asked for her opinion. This is another important benefit of the questioning technique; it provides an opportunity to get all the necessary information before coming to a conclusion.

There are several other benefits as well. One is the ownership that Judy feels in the new plan. She feels closely committed to it because she has had a role in devising the plan. Another benefit is Judy's boosted self-esteem. Her father shows her respect and is truly interested in her answers. This also strengthens their relationship.

Sometimes the questioning technique will not work. You may have to try something else. We will now present several alternative approaches.

Postpone the discussion. If you sense that a child is completely closed to your idea, wait for a time when he or she will be more receptive. As moods change, so does receptivity.

Although this seems like an easy way out, it isn't. If children are closed, your persistence may cause them to dig their heels in deeper and intensify their opposition. This further reduces your chances of persuading them, now and in the future.

Sometimes parents can enhance receptivity without postponing the discussion. This will be discussed next.

If children need recognition, give them recognition. A

child may resist as a result of his need to be recognized and understood. Once recognized, the child will become receptive to a new idea.

> During recess, Motti refused to share a school-owned ball with his classmates. His teachers explained that the ball was to be shared by everybody, but he continued to keep it for himself. This was a daily routine, and Motti's teachers could not get through to him.
>
> Motti's parents knew him a little better. They knew that he needed to be recognized by others as being independent. Keeping the ball away from others was his way of satisfying that need.
>
> So they suggested a different approach. During the school day, his teachers would take him aside and talk with him about his capabilities, independence and leadership qualities. They would catch him doing things right and coach him when he did things wrong. They would *willingly* give him the recognition that he had been *forcing* them to give through his negative behavior.
>
> His teachers complied with the plan and his parents provided additional support at home. Once Motti's need for recognition was satisfied at various points during the day, he became less obnoxious and more receptive to his teachers during recess. He no longer kept the ball and was more willing to share.

Motti was taking the ball because he wanted the recognition that came along with it, not because he wanted the ball. The new approach provided that recognition, so Motti no longer felt the need to keep the ball. And even when he did keep it, he was more receptive to negotiation because his dominant need was being satisfied elsewhere.

Sympathize with the child. A child's need for recognition may not be as extreme as Motti's. He or she may simply want to be understood and sympathized with. This is human nature — even for adults. People generally want to be understood and supported by their superiors. Sympathy has a medicinal effect, which in turn makes people more receptive to the suggestions and direction of others.

In Motti's case, he may have been keeping the ball because he wants to be understood as a person who is in need of independence. He may want his teachers and parents to sympathize and say things like, "You want to feel in charge. Sure you do. It is nice to feel in charge and independent." They do not condone his action, and he does not necessarily *want* them to. He just wants them to sympathize with his sense of independence.

Children like this find it difficult to be receptive until their emotional needs are satisfied. When you satisfy those needs, you also generate trust and respect, important factors in the exchange of new ideas.

Sometimes, people are in a state of natural receptivity. Catching children in this state avoids the challenge of resistance. This will be discussed next.

Use the inertia of an agreeable mood. If you jump from a moving vehicle, you continue moving at the same speed until friction and gravity stop you. This is the law of inertia. It states that an object continues in its state of motion until an outside force acts upon it.

Our response system is the same; when we are in a negative mood, we tend to perceive things negatively. When we are in a positive mood, we tend to perceive things positively. Similarly, when we are in an agreeable mood we behave in a spirit of approval and compromise. But when we are in a disagreeable mood we act in a contrary and difficult manner. In other words, our mood influences our receptivity.

Building on this notion, the time to present new ideas is when children are in an agreeable frame of mind. Pay attention to their moods and use the inertia of their moods to enhance receptivity and cooperation.

What if the children are in a disagreeable mood? Is there anything you can do to change it? Yes, there is. You can create an agreeable mood by asking several questions that you know will receive a "Yes" response. Responding "Yes" repeatedly creates a receptive "Yes" mood. Once the inertia is directed toward agreeability, present your new idea. See Chapter Nine for an example of this strategy.

Dealing with irrelevant responses. Did you ever speak to someone about an important matter and find his response irrelevant to your point? You wondered, "Why is he saying that? Did he hear what I said?"

He may not understand your point. He may disagree with it, or perhaps the point may be unimportant to him. But most likely, he is using the conversation to satisfy his need to discharge his own feelings about the irrelevant issue. People are like that — they often become preoccupied with other concerns and have a need to talk about them. And it makes no difference to them if their remarks are unrelated to the issue at hand.[1]

As long as the other person is preoccupied with his feelings and is looking for ways to discharge them, he will not give you much attention. One effective way of getting his attention is to let him express himself first and to show that you understand his issues. Having satisfied his need to share, he will begin to direct his attention toward you.

When children make irrelevant responses, let them express themselves freely. This breaks their preoccupation with those points. But do more than that; give them value and make them feel important by listening carefully and showing understanding. Sympathize with them. Their issues are important to them, and when you give them value, you create good feelings and enhance receptivity.

Encourage With Role Models

Children frequently need encouragement. They do not resist the goal or disagree with its importance — they simply feel incapable of reaching it.

Some parents try to encourage their children by reminding them of their strengths and capabilities. They say things like, "You can do it." Sometimes it works; sometimes it doesn't.

Parents can also encourage a child to reach difficult goals by alluding to others who have reached similar goals under identical or worse conditions. These role models prove that the goal can be reached. The child is left thinking, "If they can do it, so can I."

1. See Talmud *Yoma* 75a on *Mishlei* 12:25: A person wants to talk to others about his concerns.

Let's take a look at professional sports for an illustration. The world record for running a mile was set at four minutes in 1945. It was not until 1954, nine years later, that Roger Banister broke that record. Since then, many other athletes have broken the four-minute record.

For nine years nobody was able to break the record. Why? Psychologists believe that the goal was not the problem; rather, it was the athletes themselves. They thought it impossible to run a mile in less than four minutes and imposed limitations upon themselves. But Mr. Banister did not impose limitations on himself. He believed it was possible and reached his goal. Other athletes viewed him as their role model. They said, "If Banister can do it, so can I."

Perhaps you want to teach your children to swim or play ball, but they think they are incapable. Perhaps you want your son to become a *talmid chochom,* but he thinks it is too difficult. Allude to others who have made the effort and have succeeded. Leave your children with the feeling, "If they can do it, so can we."

Dealing with failure. Children often become discouraged when they fail. As they see it, failure is a proof of their inadequacy. This only intensifies their negative self-image.

You can help your children redirect their energies toward succeeding. Allude to others who failed, but who learned from their mistakes and went on to succeed. Read them biographies of people who have succeeded after failing. Maybe you can find a few people in your neighborhood with success stories of their own. Visit them or invite them in to share their outlooks and experiences with the children. Let the children visit their work places to get a first-hand look at their approach to life.

Prove to children, through role models, that failure does not preclude success; rather, failure is part of a natural progression toward success. Let your children get the feeling, "If they can succeed after failing, so can I."

To whom should you allude? A role model can encourage children to persevere only if the children believe that they can duplicate the role model's performance. For this reason, allude to people whose stature is within reach. The children will then be able to identify with those people and will be motivated to emulate their performances.

When encouraging a child to emulate a role model, do not allude to a genius or someone with extraordinary capabilities, even a great Torah personality. Instead of becoming encouraged, the child may become discouraged and say, "There is no way I can do what he did — I'm just not good enough" or "Of course he can do it. He's a genius. But I'm not a genius, so I can't do it."[1]

Be careful as well not to allude to someone who reached the goal at a younger age than your child is now. Instead of becoming encouraged, the child may suffer a blow to his ego and say, "I'm already older than that person, and I still can't do what he did. I must be retarded." This can result in a defeatist attitude.

Validate With Role Models

Did you ever try to persuade children to do something that they believed was unimportant? They didn't resist; they simply did not agree that the goal was valuable. As a result, they were not very committed to it.

The way to overcome this challenge is by showing your children that the goal has value. You can do this with role models. Here is an illustration:

> Shaindi was learning about *chesed* (kindness). Her mother told her about the various levels of *chesed,* from convenient favors to acts of self-sacrifice. Shaindi found it difficult to believe that anybody would, or should, take a personal loss to help someone else. She thought, "It's just Mommy talking. She's not the last word."
>
> Before Shaindi would understand the importance of *chesed* or make a commitment to practice it, even at a low level, she needed proof that her mother was correct.
>
> Shaindi's mother validated her point by recounting a famous story of the Chofetz Chaim: There were two grocery stores in the Chofetz Chaim's town. He owned one. People patronized his store and neglected the other one. The Chofetz Chaim closed his store for several hours each day so that people would patronize the other store. When

1. Heard from Rabbi Michel Twerski.

> this did not help, he closed his store completely. This is an example of kindness at a high level.[1]
>
> Shaindi was amazed. She had to hear it a second time to believe it was true. She then understood the importance of *chesed,* and while she was not prepared to take any big losses, she was prepared to do *chesed* on her own level.

Shaindi's mother was trying to impress upon her the importance of an ideal, but Shaindi could not comprehend or relate to it. She found the concept difficult to believe, so her mother used a role model to authenticate her point. Her message was: "If the Chofetz Chaim was willing to take a personal loss to help someone else, the ideal must be true — and important."

You can give weight to difficult concepts by alluding to esteemed role models. You are not necessarily implying that the child should emulate the exact behavior of the role models, which is exceptional and difficult to imitate. Rather, you are using the role models to *validate* a difficult concept.

When teaching your children new ideals or reinforcing old ones, provide them with books about great people who exhibit those principles. Introduce them to prestigious Torah personalities. Let them meet and observe the people who represent those ideals.

To whom should you allude? When validating a difficult concept, allude to role models of high stature — even if their achievements are beyond the reach of your child. The greater the personality, the more authentic the ideal. After all, if it weren't authentic they wouldn't practice it.

Mention to the children that you are alluding to the role model only to validate your point and that you do not expect them to duplicate the role model's achievements; they are exceptional people capable of exceptional performances. Sometime in the future they can duplicate those performances, but not now. Otherwise, the children may become discouraged because they know they cannot replicate the role model.

---

1. Story is found in *Michtav M'Eliyahu*, vol. 1, p. 135.

Inspire With Storytelling

Have you ever listened to a speaker and found your mind wandering? Suddenly, the speaker began telling a story and you found your attention recaptured.

Everybody loves a good story. A story stirs the imagination. Its vivid illustrations serve as mental pegs that assist in the comprehension of abstract ideas. A story appeals to the emotions and encourages receptivity.

A story can be inspirational. Take, for example, a story about the Torah sage, the Netziv. As a young boy he neglected his studies, until he overheard his father making plans for him to become a wagon driver. He realized that he was not living up to his potential and decided to become serious. He made a turn-around and began applying himself, and he became a Torah giant.

Children who have wasted years of their lives chasing trivialities while neglecting the important matters often feel that it is too late to begin a program of change. Hearing this story may inspire them to begin, even at a later age.

You may have your own personal experience to share or you may have read a story about someone else's experience. You can also ask people with inspirational stories to give your children a personal account of their experiences.

Tips for good storytelling. Use rich adverbs and adjectives to paint lively, colorful images. Use body language and voice intonations to convey your thoughts in a dramatic way.

Grab the listener in the beginning and separate him from his preoccupations with family, finances, social or academic concerns. Start with a shocking question ("What would happen if ...?"), a challenge ("I challenge you to raise your grades by five points!"), a shocking statistic ("Did you know that you can actually raise your IQ by improving your thinking skills?"), a relevant news item ("You have been taking care of your baby brother. Researchers just discovered that siblings who care for brothers and sisters ...") or a personal revelation ("After living in this town for five years, I have discovered that ...").

Use Metaphors and Stories to Clarify an Idea

Chassidic Rabbis, the Dubno Maggid, the Chofetz Chaim and many others used metaphors and stories to explain their wise insights. They found that a metaphor or a story, called a *mashal,* could illuminate new or abstract concepts.

Here is an illustration of clarifying an abstract concept with a metaphor:

> Nachman had just started to learn *Gemara.* The language was unfamiliar and the concepts abstract. He feared that he would not do well.
>
> Nachman's father told him that finding the task difficult is a common reaction, not only for children beginning *Gemara* but for anybody embarking on any new undertaking. He told Nachman that *Chazal* said, "All beginnings are difficult."[1] Nachman listened but he could not relate to the concept.
>
> His father thought of a metaphor which clarified the point. He told Nachman that an airplane needs a tremendous amount of power to begin its flight. Once it becomes airborne, it travels hundreds of miles per hour on *less* power. The airplane has a difficult beginning, but once airborne, it has an easier time. People are similar. Beginning to learn *Gemara* is difficult but as the weeks and months go by it becomes easier.
>
> Nachman was familiar with airplanes and was able to relate to the metaphor. He now understood that difficulty is natural to all beginners, and he felt more comfortable with his own situation.

Jewish tradition is replete with stories about kings, masters and servants. Since people identify easily with these relationships, the storyteller uses them to clarify new or difficult concepts concerning the relationship that we are supposed to have with Hashem. People first see how the concept applies to the familiar king/servant or

---

1. Rashi, *Yisro* 19:5.

master/servant relationship; then they can apply it to their relationship with Hashem. The concept becomes clear and, hopefully, it leads to greater commitment.

Here is another important tip for using metaphors and stories:

> We must be careful to tell a *mashal* in its proper form as if the occurrence really happened, because a child's nature is such that, although he knows it is only a *mashal*, when he hears it he sees the whole occurrence in his imagination as if it really happened, and he becomes inspired and motivated by it ... (*Chovas HaTalmidim*, end of ch. 1).

Love Being a Parent

Harry Winston, a renowned diamond merchant, once put a very valuable diamond up for sale and advertised all over the world. A man entered his boutique and Mr. Winston assigned his best representative to the sale. After a short time the customer decided to leave. When Mr. Winston saw this he approached the customer, took hold of the diamond and began to talk at length about its exceptional beauty. He continued talking about how everyone looking at it will appreciate it, too. The customer soon decided to purchase the diamond. He then asked Mr. Winston a provocative question: "Why do you think I agreed to purchase the diamond from you now, while I was ready to walk away from the salesman a few moments ago?" Mr. Winston answered, "Because the salesperson just *knows* diamonds, but I *love* them."

Influence means helping people change the way they think and motivating them to take appropriate action. Harry Winston was influential because he *loved* the object of his profession — diamonds. Parents can also be influential if they love the object of their profession — their children and the goals they try to persuade them to reach.

Your attitude determines your altitude. A positive attitude will not only sustain you through the most challenging times, it will also enable you to be a successful parent.

Chapter Five

Teach Responsibility and Independence

We have all come in contact with people who do not fulfill their responsibilities. We ask them to do something and they agree, but when the time comes to perform they do not carry through. We may depend on them again, but apprehensively.

What if they would disappoint us a second time? Would we rely on them again? Probably not. When a job has to get done, we delegate it to people we can trust, or we do it ourselves.

Did you ever wonder how successful these irresponsible people are in their family relationships, business endeavors and personal growth? They may not be able to hold on to a job; business managers want dependable people working for them. Family members learn that they are "all talk, no substance" and lose respect for them. Irresponsibility also impairs a person's self-esteem, development of *middos,* social and family relationships, attitude toward *mitzvos* and relationship with G-d.

You are probably acquainted with people who have a strong sense of responsibility. They may have become Torah scholars or independent business people. They may have become successful parents or teachers. They may have succeeded in breaking a bad *middah* or in developing a good one. No matter what the success is, they all have something in common — they decided to reach a goal, made the commitment, and accepted the responsibilities that went along with it. After a great deal of work, they reached the goal. These people became successful because they were responsible first.

Responsibility Motivates

> ... Go to an ant, observe its ways, and become wise. Without a chief, overseer or ruler, it prepares its bread in the summer and gathers its food in the harvest (*Mishlei* 6:6-8).
>
> This ant has three chambers. It does not use the upper one because of moisture. It does not use the lower one because of mud. But it uses the middle one. It only lives six months ... and its total life intake is one and a half kernels of wheat. Yet in the summer, it goes and gathers all it finds ... Why does it do this? Because it says, "Maybe Hashem will give me long life and I will be prepared to eat" (*Midrash Rabbah, Shoftim* 5:2).

The ant has a responsibility — to prepare for the future — and is committed to fulfill it. The ant is motivated to reach its goal in an extraordinary fashion. Why is it so motivated? Because of its clarity of mission and its attitude toward responsibility.

The lesson for us is that when we recognize our responsibilities and have a clear understanding of our mission, a strong inner drive emerges and we become motivated to reach our goals.[1]

Life is full of challenges, and a motivated person overcomes them. He finds ways of reaching goals, ways that an unmotivated person would not find.

> The lazy person says, "An old lion is in the way, and a young lion is between the streets" (*Mishlei* 26:13).

---

1. Rabbi Chaim Mordechai Katz, *Be'er Mechokek*, pp. 21-22.

The lazy person is unmotivated. He does not even try to avoid the lion — or any other obstacle. But the motivated person avoids the lion, or obstacle, by digging a tunnel or climbing the rooftops. No matter what the problem is, he searches for solutions. He is creative and finds ways of overcoming difficulties. He focuses on his mission and has a strong inner drive to succeed.[1]

You want your children to seek greatness and pursue excellence in all their activities. You want them to be true to their word and to fulfill all their obligations. The first step in helping them to succeed is to inculcate a sense of responsibility. How can you accomplish this?

Assign Responsibilities

Infants have no responsibilities. But as they mature, they learn to do more by themselves. This does not mean that they *want* to do more by themselves. Why should they want to wash themselves in the morning if Mommy will do it for them? Why should they want to lift the fork to their mouths? It is more fun to play "airplane" with Abba. And why should they want to dress themselves? It is easier to let big sister do it. They enjoy attention and pampering, and often resist a parent's attempt to cut the apron strings.

If parents allow this to continue, the children will not learn to be responsible or independent. But parents who require their children to perform with responsibility teach them valuable life skills. Here is the key to learning responsibility:

> ... As we teach a child to walk, the father does not explain the specifics of walking, nor does he talk about its importance. Rather, he teaches the child to walk by walking. This is the way he should teach all good traits and *mitzvos* — by doing them, and only through doing them (Rabbi S. R. Hirsch, *Yesodos HaChinuch,* p. 55).

Once children are capable of doing a task by themselves, let them do it. Make it a requirement. Require them to wash themselves, brush their teeth and feed themselves. Assign household

---

1. Ibid., p. 21.

chores, too. Require them to straighten their rooms, put away their toys, take care of their clothes and clear the dinner table. This is the way to teach responsibility.

If they do not want to fulfill these requirements, you have a problem. On one hand, you should avoid coercion because it impairs relationships and generates rebellion. On the other hand, the children *must* fulfill their requirements. What can you do? You can use the motivation techniques discussed in this book. Once children are motivated, they will perform.

Assign appropriate tasks. When assigning responsibilities to children, consider their age, capability and temperament. Be sensitive to each child's nature and try to make the chores enjoyable. Otherwise, they may become overwhelmed and resist. They may also be left with emotional scars.

> Any demand that is above the age level of the child is likely to have a damaging impact on his soft heart, an effect that will have a negative influence on all his future affairs. The effect may be in the form of phobias, nervousness or failing to become independent at the age that independence is expected. This applies to such simple things as cleanliness, sitting properly at the table, etc., which parents often require their children to perform several years before the appropriate time (Rabbi Shlomo Wolbe, *Alai Shur*, p. 263).

Consider the nature of each individual child. Every child has his or her own individual nature and abilities. A task that is interesting to one may not be interesting to another. Just because one child can perform a particular task does not mean that the others can.[1]

Don't assign too many tasks at one time. The children may resist. After they are comfortable with one task, add another. Adding new tasks slowly can eliminate a lot of aggravation.

Tightening up is preferable to loosening up. This means that if you make appropriate demands and the children are receptive, you

---

1. Rabbi S. R. Hirsch, *Yesodos HaChinuch*, pp. 55-56. Also see Rabbi Yeruchom Levovitz, *Daas Torah, Shemos*, 19:3; Vilna Gaon on *Mishlei* 16:4 and 22:6; and *Midrash Rabbah, Bamidbar* 21:15.

can add new tasks later, and they will probably continue to be receptive. But if you make inappropriate demands and the children resent it, they retain those feelings even after you remove some of the tasks at a later time. Lingering resentment may choke off the possibility of the child fulfilling future assignments.

Allow independence. There is more than one way to complete any task. Whether the task is balancing a checkbook, straightening up a house or getting dressed in the morning, everybody has his or her own way of doing it. There is no right way or wrong way; it is a matter of preference.

Keep this in mind when your children are completing their tasks. Assuming they are not causing any damage, give them independence to do things their way, even if it is different from yours. It should make no difference how the job gets done — and besides, who says your way is best? Maybe *their* way is.

Also, don't breathe down their necks. If they have a responsibility, assume they will do it. Don't keep reminding them or giving advice. Give them some freedom. If you act like a slave driver, you may cause them to rebel one day. The results could be disastrous.[1]

Offer help when needed. Sometimes children are capable of a task but need some help. Let them do as much as they can and help them with whatever they cannot do. In many cases it is just a matter of rearranging the child's environment.

> Rivkah, six years old, could not hang her dresses in the closet because the hanger bar was too high. Sometimes her mother would pick her up so that she could hang up her dresses. Other times, Rivkah would put her dress on the hanger, and her mother would hang it up.
>
> Then Rivkah's mother thought of a new plan. She put a stool in the closet for Rivkah to stand on. Now Rivkah could do the entire job herself.

Let your children know that you will do everything in your power to bring out the best in them, but make it clear that they still have to fulfill their requirements.

---

1. Rabbi Shimon Schwab, *Selected Speeches*, CIS Publishers, pp. 102-103.

Create schedules. Responsible people recognize that it is not enough to perform well; they must do so at the proper time. The time to eat dinner is at dinnertime, not thirty minutes after dinner is served. The time to clear the dinner table is immediately following dinner, not one hour later. The time to wake up in the morning is one hour before school starts, not twenty minutes before.

Children are not household guests, each with a private schedule. They are active members of the family. Make them feel that way. Create schedules which must be followed, including times for waking up, returning from school, eating dinner and going to bed.

Assign chores that have value.

> Dovid was a disorganized child. His mother never asked him to watch his baby sister because he would get involved with something else and forget about her. She never sent him to the store because he would forget to buy one or two items. She could not trust him to do anything important.
>
> Dovid's mother wanted to get him used to responsibility, so she found something for him to do: sweeping the dining room floor *before* dinner. If he would do it incorrectly or forget to do it altogether, there would be no big loss.
>
> Dovid did his chore willingly until he realized that he was not collecting much dirt. After several days, he finally protested; "Why should I sweep the floor? It's not important. If it isn't done, it makes no difference."

Can you blame Dovid for feeling this way? He had been asked to do a task with no apparent value. He felt used and put down. Had his mother pointed out the value in the activity — assuming there was one — he would have been more willing to do it.[1] But she should not have asked him to do a useless task.

Require excellent performance. Any task can be completed to varying standards. You can perform excellently, you can just get by or you can choose one of the many levels in between.

---

1. See *Chovas HaShmirah*, last footnote in the preface: It is easier for a person to perform *mitzvos* when he knows that his life depends on it. In other words, people are motivated when they see value in an activity.

Children who are assigned responsibilities will fulfill them to any standard they want — unless they are *required* to meet a specific standard. This is where parents come in. They can guide their children by requiring high performance standards.

Parents can inculcate the value of excellence in their children by requiring — and enforcing — a high standard of quality in everything they do. If the children are capable of excellence and enforcing it does not interfere with their self-esteem or the parent-child relationship, parents should not accept anything less than excellence. They should require the children to repeat the task until it is performed properly.

Did your children ever bring home a school assignment that seemed meaningless? It was obvious that the assignment was nothing more than busy work. Nevertheless, the children completed it because they knew that all school work must be done, but they felt forced and made no effort to do it well. You would have liked them to do a better job, but you could not find the words to motivate them.

These are the unenjoyable responsibilities of life and there is no way of avoiding them. Since they must be done, parents have an opportunity to instill in their children an important *middah* — excellence. Teach them that any task a person does should be done well.

Why is this an important principle to learn? Because a half-hearted approach to one task may create a *middah* of carelessness which will carry over to all of life's activities. If a task must be done — although it has no apparent value — do it right. This in itself is a value.[1]

Requiring and enforcing high standards engenders a winning attitude and an appreciation for excellence. Imbued with this attitude, children will do the best they can in all their activities. They will want to do their very best because the quality itself is important to them. They are on their way to success in life.

Hold them accountable, but be flexible. If children complain about a task or find excuses not to do it and you give in, they may learn that complaining or making excuses gets them off the hook.

---

1. Rabbi Yaakov Kamenetsky, cited in *Reb Yaakov*, Mesorah Publications, 1993, pp. 325-326.

And if they do not perform and you do not hold them accountable, they may learn to disregard other expectations. We don't want this. But if you *never* forgive and never give in, they may perceive you as a cruel taskmaster and may begin to rebel against your future wishes. The question is, when should you insist and when should you be flexible?

You can find the answer by analyzing the nature of the child, the difficulty of the task, the reason the child does not want to complete the task and the impact of the consequence on the child. Based on these considerations, you can decide to uphold your rule or to make allowances. Obviously, each situation is different. Let's look at one example.

> Asher made plans to sleep at a friend's house. When it was time to go, his parents noticed that he had not completed his chores. They asked for an explanation, and he admitted that he had been busy playing with his toys and talking on the telephone.
>
> Asher's parents had to make a decision: should they keep him at home or allow him to go? Keeping him at home might be harsh and overbearing, but allowing him to go might teach him that he did not have to follow rules.
>
> The parents knew that Asher was looking forward to staying with his friend. If they were to take that privilege away, Asher would be very hurt. They decided that the consequence was disproportionate to the offense of carelessness. But they could not just let Asher go without informing him of their dissatisfaction.
>
> They told Asher, "Since staying at your friend's house is a special event, we are making a special exception in the rule. We decided to bend the rule in this case and allow you to go. We are not letting you get away with anything. You are still responsible for your chores."

If Asher's parents had kept him at home, he would have been very unhappy. He might even have turned rebellious in the future. But by making an allowance and creating good will, Asher may reciprocate with better behavior in the future. Flexibility, in this case, may be a motivator.

However, where the consequence is not so serious, parents should consider letting the child experience it. If they were to remove the consequence, they would send the message that complaints or excuses will get the child off the hook. This is not a time to build good will and enrich relationships.

Children are always looking for their parents' weak spots. The more parents give in and show their vulnerability, the more their children will oppose or disregard their demands. On the other hand, the more parents insist that assigned responsibilities be fulfilled, the more children respect their demands. With time, they learn to comply dutifully with their parents' expectations.

Be fair, friendly and sincere. Children appreciate and trust parents who are also their friends because they know that their parents only have their welfare in mind. They will be more responsive to parents who are fair and friendly than to those who are oppressive and autocratic.

Don't do the children's work for them. Parents who do their children's work may be handicapping them for life. Here are two examples:

> Yitzy Friedman, eleven years old, does not like doing homework. When homework time comes, he dawdles. His mother coaxes him to do it, but Yitzy thinks of excuses: the work is too difficult, his hand hurts, etc. Mrs. Friedman becomes frustrated and screams at Yitzy, who begins to cry. Finally, Mrs. Friedman gives him the answers; it is easier than fighting or seeing him fail.
>
> Sarah, Yitzy's sister, is supposed to sweep the floors on Friday afternoons. She dislikes this chore and finds excuses not to do it: friends to play with, school work to do, a twisted ankle, etc. Mrs. Friedman coaxes and cajoles. Sometimes Sarah resentfully complies. Other times, Mrs. Friedman does it herself; it is easier than haggling with her daughter.

Mrs. Friedman is sending her children a message: if they do not fulfill an obligation, she will do it for them. They just have to make a nominal effort, if any, but once the job becomes inconvenient, they can always count on her to come to the rescue. Dawdling and complaining, they surmise, have a benefit.

As Yitzy progresses through school, he will continue to depend on his mother. But what will happen when he leaves school and does not have his mother to depend on? As a child, he is developing a trait that may persist throughout life. He may not be able to cope with the challenges of adulthood.

Sarah, too, is developing a dependency on her mother. As an adult, she may not be able to cope with unpleasant responsibilities.

But if their mother would hold them accountable for their work, they would be used to fulfilling responsibilities and they would be better prepared for adulthood. Picture this scene as part of the Friedman story:

> Yitzy refuses to do his homework. Mrs. Friedman provides encouragement and urges him to do it. As he continues dawdling, she says, "It is your assignment and I will not do it for you. You will not be able to play with your friends until it is done."
>
> When Sarah refuses to perform her chore, Mrs. Friedman says, "This is your responsibility and I will not do it for you. You will not go outside until you finish it."

Mrs. Friedman provides encouragement but refuses to do their jobs for them. She wants them to learn that if they don't fulfill their obligations, nobody will do it for them. Mrs. Friedman does not like seeing her children unhappy, but she realizes that this is the only way to break them of their old dependencies and to instill in them a healthy sense of duty.

Chazal tell us, "If I am not for myself, who will be for me?"[1] This means that people should assume the responsibility of doing a job independently. Mrs. Friedman can foster this ideal by *demanding* that her children complete their assignments.

---

1. *Avos* 1:14.

Life Demands Work

When children are required to fulfill responsibilities, they learn that life demands work. They learn that work is the medium through which they can succeed and feel good about themselves.

> Love work (*Avos* 1:10).
>
> A person may think that when he sits, inactive from work, he is experiencing tranquility; on the contrary, he attains tranquility with toil ... as it is written in *Mishlei* 20:4, "Because of the winter a lazy person does not plow; he will seek in the harvest time and there is nothing" (Rabbeinu Yonah, *Avos* 1:10).[1]
>
> Wealth that comes from inactivity will dwindle and go away. The one who progressively gathers with his hand will increase and succeed (*Mishlei* 13:11).[2]

There is no better way to instill the value of work than by requiring children to do all their tasks independently and to a high standard.

Teach Alacrity

Procrastinators have a motto: "Why do it today if it can be done tomorrow?" Parents typically respond, "Do it anyway."

Procrastinators believe they are right. They think they should not have to do a task today if they can do it just as well tomorrow. They don't even need an excuse — the possibility of doing it tomorrow justifies the plan. Saying "Do it" does not address their attitude, nor does it teach them anything.

---

1. See Rabbeinu Yonah there: If a person does not work in the winter plowing season because he is uncomfortably cold — a seemingly valid reason not to work — he will have nothing to harvest.

2. As translated by Vilna Gaon. *Chazal* have more to say about the importance of work. Here are six examples: "Torah which does not have work with it will be abandoned in the end and causes sin" (*Avos* 2:2). "The one who works his field will be satiated with bread, and the one who pursues vain things will be satiated with poverty" (*Mishlei* 28:19, translated by Ralbag). "Say a little and do a lot" (*Avos* 1:15). "Action is the priority, not study" (*Avos* 1:17). See *Avos* 3:10 concerning inactivity and time-wasting activities. See also *Avos d'Rav Nosson*, ch. 11, concerning the importance of work.

Here are two ways of dealing with procrastination:[1]

1) When children want to postpone the task so that they can do some other time-wasting activity now, say, "If doing it tomorrow means that you will waste time now, you must do it now. The Torah forbids a person to waste even a moment's time."

2) Whether or not they want to do another time-wasting activity, say, "You may not be able to do it tomorrow. Another urgent matter may arise, requiring your attention."

When children express the procrastinator's motto, be prepared with the proper responses. It is an opportunity to create a healthy attitude and to motivate the children to perform.

Help Children Learn to Manage Time

Children have many competing interests. When they come home from school there is homework to do, dinner to eat, friends to play with and household chores to perform. If they play first, there may not be sufficient time for the other important activities. But if they address the other activities first, they may not have time to play. How can children organize themselves so that they will reach *all* their goals? They can learn to manage time effectively.

Time management is a three-part strategy. First, prioritize activities. Next, estimate the time required to complete each activity. Then, use this information to formulate a schedule.

A chart can be a helpful time-management tool. At the top of the next page is a sample time-management chart. Parents should produce the skeleton and then fill in the three columns together with the child. After the chart is filled in, hang it in a conspicuous spot as a reminder to the child.

The schedule may not always go as planned; any activity may take more or less time than originally anticipated, or other unexpected events may interfere with the plan.. Nevertheless, the chart provides a basic structure which children can follow to reach goals. Once they commit themselves to the plan, they can refer to the chart periodically to make sure they are on schedule. Scheduling

---

1. Rabbeinu Yonah, *Avos* 1:14.

WEEK OF PARASHAS *Va'eira*		ARRIVE HOME AT *4:30*
ACTIVITIES	TIME NEEDED	SCHEDULE
PLAY WITH COMPUTER	***20 Minutes***	***5:00-5:20***
PLAY WITH FRIENDS	***40 Minutes***	***5:20-6:00***
EAT DINNER	***45 Minutes***	***6:00-6:45***
WASH DISHES	***15 Minutes***	***6:45-7:00***
DO HOMEWORK	***1 Hour***	***7:00-8:00***

releases parents from the traditional police duties of coaxing and threatening.

Following a schedule has another advantage. It puts organization into children's lives. They will be less likely to make mistakes or to become confused when carrying out responsibilities.[1] Organization will also help them think more clearly and attain peace of mind.[2]

Enforcing Responsibilities

Earlier, we told the story of Yitzy and Sarah Friedman. Yitzy refused to do his homework, and Sarah refused to perform her assigned chore. Mrs. Friedman informed them of the forthcoming penalty — losing the privilege of playing with their friends. She hoped this would motivate them.

What should she do if they are not motivated to cooperate and still refuse to do their work?

Mrs. Friedman knows that the only way her children will learn responsibility is if she carries out the threat. She would probably say, "You are not doing as you are supposed to do. I warned you about the punishment. Now you are not allowed to play with your friends. This will teach you for the next time."

How would they respond? With tears and arguments, they may say, "That's not fair," and think of reasons not to be punished.

---

1. See *Sefer HaChinuch, mitzvah* 72.
2. Rabbi Chaim Mordechai Katz, *Be'er Mechokek*, p. 153.

Nevertheless, Mrs. Friedman is secure in her approach and insists that they suffer the consequences. Yitzy and Sarah must learn to fulfill their obligations, and she feels this is the way to teach them. Another result of the punishment is friction and mutually hurt feelings.

Does this sound familiar? Mrs. Friedman is using the traditional approach of enforcing responsibility. But there is another way.

Before presenting it, keep in mind that we are not finding fault with the traditional approach. Experts find it effective and recommend using it. We are presenting another approach, one that motivates children to comply with rules and at the same time builds their sense of responsibility — with minimal friction. Parents who frequently engage in power struggles with their children may find it especially useful.

Give choices. After the children refuse to comply, the parent informs them of the negative consequences for non-compliance and the positive consequences for compliance. The parent then gives the children the choice to comply or defy. After enduring the negative consequence several times, or maybe even once, the children will realize that their original action is the cause of their discomfort. Hopefully, they will begin to choose their options more prudently.

In the case of Yitzy and Sarah, their mother would say:

To Yitzy: "If you do not do your homework, your teacher will assign his usual penalty assignment. If you do your homework, there will be no penalty. It is your choice."

Or:

"You have until seven o'clock to do your homework. After seven, you will not be allowed to complete it. What you do is your choice."

To Sarah: "You can either sweep the floor and help prepare the house for Shabbos or you can stay home during the *Oneg Shabbos* tomorrow. It's your choice."

Mrs. Friedman then steps back and allows Yitzy and Sarah to pick the action and consequence of their choice. If Yitzy decides to neglect his assignment, he will take his penalty the next day. If Sarah neglects her chore, she will take her penalty the next day.

In Sarah's case, Mrs. Friedman will have to sweep the floors herself. But when Sarah suffers the uncomfortable consequence of staying home from the *Oneg Shabbos*, she will begin to do her chore. Even if Sarah does not learn her lesson this time, after suffering the consequence several more times she will learn that neglecting a responsibility is no longer profitable.

Choice-giving can be used anytime except in cases where an *aveirah* would be committed or in dangerous situations. For example, if a child is about to eat non-kosher food or runs out into the street, it is inappropriate, for obvious reasons, to let him make his own decision. A clear directive — even through physical means — would suffice.

Giving choices is a very effective method of enforcing responsibilities. We will now discuss its benefits and the reason it is so effective.

The law of cause and effect. This law states that every action has a corresponding reaction. Applying the law to everyday life, we can say that to the degree that people adhere to rules, they will move toward success or failure. Adhering to rules has a positive consequence called "benefit" or "reward." Disregarding rules has a negative consequence called "loss" or "penalty."

For example, doing homework results in praise, higher grades and continuation of privileges. Not doing homework, on the other hand, results in penalty assignments or loss of privileges. Peforming household chores results in continuation of privileges. Not performing chores results in loss of privileges.

When children understand this law, they will realize that they are in control of their lives. When they receive a negative consequence as a result of an improper action, they can see the relationship between their action and the consequence. They cannot detach the action from the outcome and say, "Hashem wants it that way. I have nothing to do with it." On the contrary — they can see that they caused it. Negative behaviors bring about negative results.

When you hold a stick at one end and raise it from the ground, what happens to the other end? It rises, too. It is one stick, and you cannot expect the other half to stay still. Knowing that a stick has two ends, your decision to raise one end is also a decision to raise the other.

Every action has a logical reaction. It is one of life's natural laws. Choose an action and you concurrently choose the outcome, the other end of the stick. The consequence of the action is just as much a part of your decision as the action itself. Your choice of action is also a choice of reaction.

Suppose a parent tells a child, "If you touch the hot stove, you will get burned." The child goes ahead and touches the hot stove and gets burned. Can he have a grievance against the parent? Of course not. The penalty of getting burned was a direct result of touching the stove, and it is the child's decision to touch it. He knew he would get burned, yet he chose it anyway.

Children can choose to comply with or disregard rules and expectations. This is response-ability: the ability to choose a response. But if they want the outcome to be rewarding, they must comply and perform well. Otherwise, the outcome will not be satisfying. If they do not like it, they will have nobody to blame but themselves.

Giving choices to children and letting them suffer or enjoy the consequences of their decisions puts control in their hands. It teaches them to think about the logical consequences of their actions *beforehand.* Once they make the connection, they will become responsible decision makers.

Project the outcome. Before acting, children should learn to project the consequences of any proposed plan of action.

> "Which is the good way to which a person should cling? ... [He] should see the outcome" (*Avos* 2:9). He looks carefully at everything and sees all the outcomes before they happen. When the thing is rewarding in the beginning but leads to a loss in the end, he avoids it. By doing this he will never sin, because he considers the reward of a sin in relation to its loss. Therefore, a person should cling to this way, to think in the beginning what will be in the end, and to plan all affairs with this idea (Rabbeinu Yonah, ad loc.).
>
> At the beginning of your actions look at the end and consider the loss of a *mitzvah* against the benefit it

brings, and the benefit of a sin against the loss it brings, because the wise person has his eyes in his head (*Orchos Chaim LeHarash* 46).

By focusing on the short-term effects of a decision and ignoring the long-term effects, many people end up with poor health, financial upset and disappointing personal relationships. A responsible decision-maker, however, looks both to the short- and long-term effects. He realizes that both short- and long-term effects are the other end of the stick. If a particular action will be detrimental in the future, although it is beneficial in the present, he avoids it.

Children need to learn the skill of seeing both ends of the stick — that is, projecting results. Before doing anything, they should ask, "What will happen if I do this?" Focusing on the future is a good habit that will last throughout their lives.[1]

To help children project outcomes parents should clarify the rewards and penalties from the start. The children will then know what they are working for and can make decisions based on it.

An illustration of choice-giving. When I teach elementary-age children, I give a beginning-of-the-year speech on the first day of school. I discuss rules and consequences and use the following allegory to motivate students to follow rules:

"Picture yourself driving down a country road on a beautiful summer day. As the road reaches a cliff, it turns to the right. You have a choice — you can turn to the right and follow the road, or you can continue going straight off the cliff. If you turn, you will enjoy the rest of the day. If you go straight, you will fall over the cliff and be injured. Don't say, 'The steering wheel steered me right off the cliff' or 'The gas pedal powered the car off the cliff.' You control the car, so you can only blame it on yourself.

"Following rules in this class is the same. You can choose to follow the rules and continue having a wonderful year, or you can break the rules and have an unhappy year. Just don't blame it on

---

1. *Chazal* have more to say about projecting outcomes. Here are three examples: "When a person considers the end, whatever he does will be profitable. But when one does not project the end, all his work will be lost" (*Mishlei* 21:5, according to Vilna Gaon); "The thoughts of a person who plans are worthwhile" (Rabbeinu Yonah, *Mishlei* 21:5); "Consider the benefit gained from a sin against the loss it brings" (*Avos* 2:1).

me. It is *your* decision. I hope you decide to make your trip pleasurable."

This speech conveys the cause-and-effect message and transfers responsibility to the students. Its effects last for the remainder of the year.

One of the rules in my class concerns recess. When the bell rings to signal the end of recess, students must line up immediately. If they do so, they have outdoor recess the following day, but if they continue playing, they lose the privilege. Complying with the rule results in a benefit; not complying results in a loss.

When we go outside for the first time and the bell rings at the end of recess, students are not sure if I will really enforce the consequence. So, as children do, they test me by continuing their ball game. After they finally line up, I announce that they will lose recess the next day. Then I give another unsolicited speech: "You were informed of the rule and the consequence. You had the choice to line up immediately or to continue playing. You chose to play, which means that you have also chosen to lose recess tomorrow."

I make it clear that losing recess is not a punishment; rather, it is a natural consequence of something the children have *chosen* to do — and for which they are responsible. I am emotionally detached and have no vested interest, and I do not argue the point with them. After one or two episodes, they make the cause-and-effect connection and begin to follow the rule on their own.

If I would react emotionally to their disobedience, some children would consider it a victory. They derive benefit from angering teachers and parents, because it gives them a feeling of control. And they are willing to pay the price — even if it means losing recess — for the opportunity to control their authority figure. But when I remain calm, they have nothing to gain by breaking the rule other than a few more moments of play.

Let us stop to analyze the advantages of this approach:

1) Children recognize that the decision to continue playing is also a decision to lose recess the following day. It is the other side of the stick. They learn to take responsibility for their actions because they see the connection between the action and the outcome.

2) I do not assume the role of judge or "bad guy," deciding guilt

and declaring penalties. I am a facilitator, enforcing the choice that the *children* make.

3) Children learn to avoid the *behavior*, not *me*. They do not see me as the cause of their penalty, and our relationship does not suffer.

4) I am relieved of the tensions and pressures that are commonly associated with emotional attachment.

5) Some children are argumentative, rebellious or controlling. They are constantly struggling for power. But when they are given choices, they have no need to struggle. They can choose as they wish, without anyone telling them what to do. If they choose to defy the rule, no one is punishing them; they are receiving the natural consequence of their action.

How would the traditional teacher handle the recess problem? He may say with emotion, "I said that you would lose recess for playing after the bell. You must learn that you cannot do what you want. I hope this punishment teaches you the importance of following rules."

This traditional teacher takes an authoritarian role and declares the students' guilt, a position which openly invites children to engage in a power struggle with him. He is obviously frustrated. He is allowing undesired pressure to enter his day, which then vents itself in an emotional display. This in turn may affect all subsequent interactions with his students.

Furthermore, with the traditional approach, the students may not connect their behavior with the penalty. Instead, they may blame it on the "mean" teacher — the "bad guy" who delivered the punishment. They may not take full responsibility for their actions.

Call it consequence, not punishment. Punishment connotes retribution, and sometimes retaliation. It is attributed to a person in a position of power who judges and decrees. Consequence, on the other hand, is an outcome, a result of another action. It is attributed to a person who is in control of the action. In our case, that person is the child.

When giving choices, parents and teachers do not *give* consequences — children *take* them. Parents and teachers assign responsibilities and enforce consequences; they do not judge or control children. The children can be their own judges. They know when they have broken a rule, and they know that their behavior brings about the consequence. They can understand that suffering a negative consequence is not punishment, but rather the natural result of poor performance.[1]

Enforce consequences immediately. We want children to recognize the cause-and-effect relationship between their actions and the consequences. That connection is most apparent when the consequence immediately follows the performance. Enforcing a consequence at the right time has the greatest impact.

Create realistic consequences. Sometimes parents become so upset and/or forceful that they say things like, "If you do such-and-such, you will lose your bicycle privileges for a year."

Both the parent and child know that this consequence will not be enforced. If so, what good is the threat? The child only learns that the parent makes empty threats, and he may begin to disregard other rules that have more realistic consequences.

For this reason, plan the consequence for each violation carefully. And make the consequence realistic — not too severe and not too weak. The child will see that you really plan to enforce it and he will make the effort to avoid it.

Why does choice-giving work? First, let us address a related question: How does choice-giving give children control in the first place? You offer only two options, one of which carries a penalty. This is not much of a choice! Can we fool children into thinking that they have a choice when in fact their control is so minimal?

To children, the world is chaotic. There are many decisions to make and many directions in which to go, and they are not secure choosing these paths all on their own. They want structure. They want adults to give them direction by setting guidelines for them and creating a framework of rules in which they can live comfortably. Although their actions may indicate that they want full independence and control, deep down inside they do not want it. They do not want to be told what to do, but at the same time they want rules that will bring security to their lives.

---

1. Similarly, it has been suggested that the Jews wandered in the desert for forty years to strengthen their faith in Hashem. This decree was the natural consequence of their sin of weakened faith.

Giving choices satisfies this need. With this approach, children are not given carte blanche to determine their direction. That would be too chaotic for them. Rather, they are provided with a framework in which to operate. And within that framework they have choices, enough to feel some control. That is the key — *some control.* They receive a measure of independence and at the same time a structure that gives direction.

The following diagram illustrates this idea. The arrows point outward to a world of chaos. The box represents the framework — the security shed — which parents build for their children to separate them from this confusing world. The children have some choices within the framework, enough to feel in control. The choices are represented by the C's.

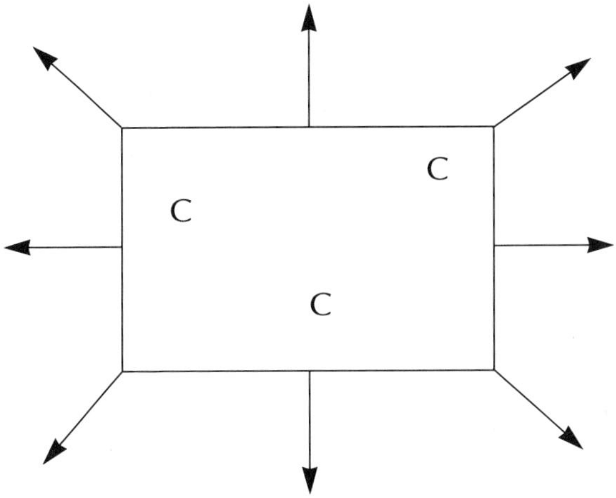

The traditional approach, on the other hand, seizes all control from children. Parents tell them, "You must do this" or "You must do that." Then they judge the children, and if they find them guilty, they punish them. This approach is confining and promotes rebellion.

Furthermore, when children are told what to do without being given a choice, they feel forced to go in one predetermined direction. This means that all other options are forbidden. Since forbidden options have a curious appeal, children may feel drawn to experiment with them.[1] To the authority figure, this will appear to be rebellion.

1. See *Mishlei* 9:17: "Stolen water is sweet."

But when a particular undesired behavior is part of a child's package of options, it does not have the same allure. Children are less likely to choose that option when they have the freedom to accept or reject it.

Motivate by giving choices. I once advised the parents of an uncooperative five-year-old boy to motivate their child by giving him choices. Here is their story:

> Tzvi was often uncooperative — even rebellious. When it came time to get dressed in the morning, he flatly refused, but when he was asked to get undressed at night, he would quickly change into a fresh shirt and pants. Another problem was that instead of talking, Tzvi screeched. The more his parents insisted that he stop, the more he screeched. It was obvious that he was bidding for power.
>
> There was one particular routine that his mother could not tolerate. When he was told to get ready for bed, he would go to his room and remove all the blankets and sheets from his bed. He would then screech, "I can't sleep in this bed." His mother would become infuriated and scream, "What's the matter with you? Of course you can't sleep like this! Don't you ever do that again!" After losing her temper, she would proceed to make up the bed.
>
> This routine repeated itself every night. Tzvi was truly winning the power struggle.
>
> One night, Tzvi's mother decided to deal with the problem differently. Before he undid his bed, she calmly told him, "If you undo your bed, you will have to sleep in it that way. I will not make up the bed for you. Whatever you decide is okay with me."
>
> When bedtime came, Tzvi announced once again that he had removed the sheets and blankets. His mother said calmly, "I'm sorry, but you will have to sleep in the bed that way tonight. You decided to undo the bed, and it doesn't bother me."
>
> Tzvi could not believe his ears. Dumbfounded, he screeched, "You mean you're not going to make my bed?"

"That's right," his mother responded. "Now go to your room. It's past your bedtime." Tzvi gave her another confounded look, then ran to the maid and instructed her to make up the bed.

The maid did make up the bed, but Tzvi never undid it again.

Let's analyze this story. Tzvi's mother wanted him to go to bed on time and to leave the sheets and blankets in place — simple enough. But Tzvi wanted power. How did he get it? By undoing the bed, thereby angering his mother and causing her to remake it.

Without realizing it, Tzvi's mother was giving him power every night. And by giving him power, she was rewarding his behavior. The rule of reward says that the behavior that is rewarded will be repeated. Tzvi repeated his routine because he was rewarded every time.

Mother and son were locked in a power struggle. As hard as the mother worked to win the battles, Tzvi triumphed every time — that is, until his mother removed the reward. She stopped becoming angry and instead created a penalty for his behavior: he would have to sleep in an uncomfortable bed. The only power she gave him now was the power to make his own choice.

Why is it that a routine that had lasted for months stopped so suddenly? Because Tzvi had nothing more to gain. He no longer had any reason to struggle for power, because he had it. He had the choice of leaving the bed the way it was or undoing it. And now that his mother was remaining calm, he no longer derived any benefit from her emotionality. If Tzvi had derived benefit from telling the maid to make his bed, his mother would have intervened and instructed her not to do it; but this did not come into play, as Tzvi found it too much trouble to go after the maid. The alternative was to sleep in a messy bed. Since that was not pleasant, Tzvi quickly gave up his routine altogether.

Tzvi's parents applied this approach to other behaviors as well. The result was that their son became a more cooperative individual.

Is this the Jewish way? People often question if choice-giving is the Jewish way. They say, "Children should not get choices. We should expect them to follow rules and reach goals obediently.

Looking at the Torah as a model, we are expected to follow *mitzvos* obediently, and we should train children to do the same with our demands."

Ideally, we *should* expect children to be obedient. However, we are now concerned with children who are typically labeled "disobedient." They have different reasons: some are seeking control, some have conflicting interests, and some simply don't like the task that is set before them.

Using forceful measures with disobedient children may impair relations and intensify rebelliousness. Instead, the children need a form of enforcement that befits their particular set of circumstances. King Shlomo said, "Train a child according to his way."[1] In other words, teach a child according to his individuality. *This* is the Jewish way.

The notion of choices is not new to Judaism. Hashem suggests that we *choose* to observe the *mitzvos;* He does not force it upon us.[2] We also find the concept of free choice in many rabbinical works.[3]

Providing positive consequences for good performance and negative consequences for poor performance is also a Torah concept.[4] In Torah terms it is called *s'char v'onesh.*

Giving choices teaches independence. When parents order a child to do something and the child complies, he or she has not gone through any sort of thinking process. But when parents give a choice, even if it is only between two options, the child must think independently about the most beneficial option. Choice-giving, then, is more than a tool that enforces responsibility; it is a tool that encourages independence.

When a child constantly misbehaves at the dinner table, you can motivate him to behave properly and independently by combining choices with rewards. Place five coins at the child's plate. Tell him that he may keep them all if he behaves properly during

---

1. *Mishlei* 22:6. See Vilna Gaon and Rabbeinu Yonah.

2. *Devarim* 30:19.

3. For example, Rabbi Eliyahu Lopian, *Lev Eliyahu,* vol. 1, p. 253; Rabbeinu Yonah, *Avos* 4:2.

4. See the Thirteen Principles of the Rambam.

the meal. But if he misbehaves, he will lose one coin for each infraction. As he sits at the table, those coins act as a constant reminder of what he is supposed to do. He will think two or three times before misbehaving because he will not want to lose any coins. He has the choice. And he learns to behave properly — and independently.

Don't protect your children from the penalty. Why is it important to make the cause-and-effect connection? So that children will become rational thinkers and consider the consequences of their actions before acting, a trait which will remain with them throughout life.

How can parents teach children to make the connection between their actions and the outcome? By letting them experience the penalty for poor performance rather than protecting them from it. Let's illustrate how covering up a penalty can be detrimental.

> Avi's school was running a candy sale. There were prizes offered to all children who sold over $50 worth of candy. Avi wanted the prize and planned to sell, but he always found other things to do. By the time the deadline came, he had not sold any candy.
>
> He approached his father and asked for help, telling him how much the prize meant to him. His father did not want him to feel bad, so he bought $50 worth of candy from Avi on the spot.

What lesson did Avi learn? He learned that a penalty does not necessarily follow a poor performance. He learned that just as his father saved him from losing the prize in this incident, he will probably save him from other penalties, too. And if he doesn't, someone else will.

What will Avi do when nobody is available to "save" him? He may not perform properly because he has not yet learned to project results. And when he receives the penalty, he may not understand that he himself caused it. His father, in effect, is fostering an attitude of dependency which will persist throughout Avi's life. Here is another illustration:

Avi frequently forgets his lunch at home. His father does not want him to borrow food or return home for his lunch. He also does not want him to have to eat the school-prepared peanut butter sandwich, so he delivers Avi's lunch to school.

If Avi's father continues doing this, his son will never learn to take his own lunch. Why should he? He can get it hand-delivered. If Avi's father would stand back once or twice and allow him to feel the discomfort of returning home for lunch, borrowing food from friends or eating the school sandwich, Avi might learn to take his lunch. Instead, he is learning that irresponsibility carries no penalty.

No parent wants a child to experience an uncomfortable consequence. But when a child feels the penalty and recognizes that he caused it, he will try to avoid it the next time. This attitude will grow with him, transferring to other areas of life as well. The child is on his way to becoming an independent and responsible individual.

Hillel, fifteen years old, enjoyed sleeping late in the morning. His parents didn't want to fight with him, so they let him sleep after the wake-up call. When he finally woke up, he would ask for a ride to school. His parents didn't want him to be late, so they gave him a ride.

One day, Hillel's father realized that he was protecting him from the consequences of tardiness. He also realized that he was rewarding Hillel for his negligence by driving him to school every morning.

He devised a new plan of action. He told Hillel's teacher to penalize him for coming late by assigning extra work or keeping him after school. He told Hillel about the penalty, informing him that he would no longer provide a ride when Hillel woke up late. He said, "You can wake up on time, arrive at school on time, and avoid the penalty. Or you can wake up late, arrive at school late, and take the penalty."

Hillel did not immediately change his ways. But after several days of suffering the penalty, he began waking up earlier.

Hillel's father did not protect him from the penalty. He even went one step further; he encouraged the teacher to penalize his son for his negligent behavior. Hillel corrected himself without a confrontation or a power struggle.

So when a child is not diligent in his school work, don't blame the teacher. Putting blame on the teacher actually harms the child. The child learns to blame the teacher too, and never accepts responsibility for his own negligence. As he matures, he will continue to find fault with others and to blame them for his mistakes.

There is a story of a young man who was a compulsive gambler. He issued bad checks and had been charged for fraudulent use of credit cards. Rejecting a therapist's advice, his father did not let him face the charges. He also covered the son's bad checks. Several years later, the son was still a compulsive gambler, but the situation was worse. He and his family were penniless and homeless. The father's "kindness" had not helped the son; rather, it enabled the son to continue his destructive habit and eventually dealt the innocent wife and children a cruel blow.[1]

Had the father accepted the advice of his therapist, he would have let the son experience the bitter consequences of his crimes. This may have deterred him from pursuing his destructive habit.

Let children feel the penalty of their inappropriate actions. This is not punishment; rather, it is the natural consequence of negligent behavior. Don't accept weak excuses such as "I forgot" or "I lost it." These excuses indicate carelessness, and carelessness too has consequences. Allowing children to feel the discomfort will motivate them to be more careful next time.

Don't remind constantly. Children do not need to be reminded of their responsibilities and of the penalty for not performing. Say it once or twice and leave the rest up to them. It is their responsibility, and they need to remember to do it on their own.

Be consistent. Every time parents enforce a consequence, positive or negative, they provide an opportunity for their children to see themselves as being in control of their own outcomes. This is the way children learn to take responsibility for their actions.

---

1. Told by Rabbi Abraham Twerski, M.D., *Jewish Action*, Summer 1993, pp. 57-59.

For this reason, it is important to enforce consequences for *every* action, not just now and then.

Parents who do not enforce consequences are doing their children a disservice. These parents send the message that they are not completely serious about the performance. What happens then? Their children will continue to break rules or to perform poorly. Additionally, they will not understand the consequences of their behavior and will not learn that their actions bring about unpleasant results. This unhealthy attitude transfers to other areas of life, too.

We mentioned earlier that within the parameters of consistency, there is place for flexibility. If you think that the child will react to a consequence in a disproportionately negative way, you should consider being flexible. Tell the child that he really deserves the consequence but that you decided to forgo it in this case. Let him know that his action is unacceptable and that the consequences will still stand in the future.

Rules show you care. If parents would not make rules and enforce them, their children might think that they do not care about them. But when there are rules to follow and consequences to pay, they know their parents care about them. Here is a story which illustrates this point. The story was told by a friend who experienced it as a child.

> Nosson was a mischievous child. His father set rules for him and consistently enforced them, and Nosson did not like it. He often told his father, "You don't care about me. If you would care, you would let me do the things I want." One day, his father said, "So you think I don't care about you. I will show you what not caring really means."
>
> That day, Nosson's father did not enforce a single rule. He allowed Nosson to do whatever he wanted and said nothing. Nosson took advantage — he went where he wasn't supposed to go, he did not keep schedules, and he even broke a dish or two. His father said nothing about it.
>
> By the end of the day Nosson had a terrible, empty feeling. He felt that his father did not care about him. He

> learned to appreciate the rules that his father made for him, and the enforcements, as a reminder that his father really cared about him.

This story illustrates how children appreciate rules, structure and consistency. They want their parents to care about them. And enforcing rules is the way to show it.

Provide rewards when they are earned. Some parents, in an effort to be kind, shower their children with all sorts of goodies. They do not give these goodies as a result of any particular behavior; they just want their children to be happy.

What do these children learn about the law of cause-and-effect? They learn that rewards are available for doing nothing. In life, rewards are usually the outcome of effortful activity, but these children may not learn it. This does not mean that you should never give gifts to your children; it means that you should not give an excessive number of gifts.

Even worse, some parents provide rewards after a poor or mediocre performance, which gives their children the message that weak performance is acceptable. The children will not then see any reason to improve. They will simply fulfill the principle that the behavior that is rewarded will be repeated.

Provide rewards for your children only when they truly deserve them. Just as a penalty should follow a poor performance, a reward should follow a good performance. And when they do get a reward — or for that matter, any kind of benefit — make the connection and remind them that it is a direct result of their good performance. This reinforces the cause-and-effect connection.

Urge Children to Find Solutions to Their Own Problems

> Yussy and his sister Leah are playing while their mother is baking in the kitchen. Suddenly, Leah comes in screaming, "Mommy, Mommy, Yussy took the game away from me."
>
> Mother stops her work to investigate the claim. She

asks Yussy, "What is going on? Is it true that you took the game away from Leah?"

"Leah was playing for a long time and it is my turn now," he responds.

Mother must solve the dispute. She asks whose game it is, how long it takes to play and other pertinent information needed to make a judgment. After hearing both sides, she decides that Leah should play with the game for ten minutes, and then Yussy should have it. Yussy is not happy with this decision and runs out screaming. Mother reconsiders and asks Leah if she would mind letting Yussy play with the game first.

"No, that's not fair. I was playing with it," Leah howls.

"What's the matter with you children? Why can't you play nicely? I wish I wouldn't have to settle all your disagreements," Mother yells in despair. She is frustrated and gives the final verdict: "Since you cannot agree, nobody plays with it." Now, nobody is happy.

Is there a better way of resolving this problem? Does Mother have to play the role of judge and jury, hearing both sides and coming to a verdict?

There is another way: she can let the *children* find the solution. When Leah presents the problem, Mother can say, "I see you are unhappy about this. What do you think can be done to solve the problem?" Leah may very well come up with a viable solution.

If she does not have a solution, Mother may say, "You feel that Yussy took the game away unfairly. That is not a nice feeling. I am wondering if you might let Yussy play with it first, while you do something else? Afterwards, you can get it back."

Here, Mother first sympathizes with Leah and then gives a suggestion. She sympathizes because she knows that children often just want to be understood. When Mother sympathizes with Leah and shows that she understands the problem, Leah may become more receptive to a suggestion. She may decide to be flexible rather than fight.

If Leah insists on playing with the game first, Mother may meet with both children and say, "You are disagreeing about who will play with the game first. I am not going to tell you what to do. You must find the solution yourselves." Without asking for both sides of the story, she can lead them through a problem-solving process. The dialogue may go like this:

Mother: I see two children who want to play with the same game. Is that correct?

Children: Yes.

Here, Mother confirms that there is a problem. Sometimes at this point, one child may decide to give in to the other; he or she may say, "Oh, I don't care. Let him/her have it." This solves the problem with minimal hurt feelings.

If not, Mother begins the problem-solving process by urging the children to find a solution:

Mother: There is only one game like this in the house. Both of you want it first, but only one can have it. Think of a plan that will make you both happy.

Yussy: It's not fair. I want it. It's my turn.

Mother: You feel that it's not fair. It does not feel good to be treated unfairly. Now, I have a question which I would like both of you to think about. How can both of you play with the game and be happy about it?

Here, Mother listens and sympathizes with Yussy but refuses to be drawn into the argument. She then brings the discussion back to the point. Finally, Leah responds.

Leah: (pensively) I guess if I play with it and Yussy plays with it we will both be happy.

Mother: (to both) Okay. Now, who will play with it first? Only one of you can play with it first. I am not going to decide. You will make that decision.

Yussy: Leah already played with it. She could have it for just a *little* while longer and then I will have it for a *long* time.

Mother: Yussy is willing to let Leah play with it first. Since Leah has already been playing with it for a while, Yussy thinks she should have it for a short time and then he should be able to use it. Leah, what do you think?

Leah: Okay, I will play for a little while, and then Yussy can have it.

Here, Mother paraphrases Yussy's suggestion in a way that emphasizes its fairness. She remains detached by not judging its validity or persuading Leah to accept it. Leah finally agrees.

Not all solution sessions go this quickly or have a happy ending. Sometimes the parent has to stimulate the dialogue by asking more leading questions. Sometimes the children cannot agree on a plan. If Yussy and Leah had not agreed, for example, their mother could have taken the game and said, "I want both of you to be able to play with the game and be happy about it. When you come up with a solution, tell me and I will return the game to you."

During a problem-solving session, the parent listens, sympathizes and offers help. She is a facilitator, assisting her children in the process of finding solutions, rather than a judge and jury. Because of this, the children cannot say, "Mother is not fair." It is *their* decision, not hers.

Another advantage of this approach is that it eliminates power struggles between parents and children. The parents remain detached from the process, and the children have the control to decide on a plan of their own.

This technique may be used in other situations, too. Here is an example:

> Sruli, four years old, was having a good time in the playground. He was going from the swings to the climber and back to the swings. Then he decided to go on the slide. As he approached the slide, he saw that he was not able to reach the ladder. He broke out in tears and came running to his mother.
>
> "Mommy, Mommy, I want to go on the slide," he cried.
>
> His mother walked him over to the slide and began a problem-solving session:

Mother: (calmly) I see the ladder is too high for you. What do you think can be done?

Sruli: (still crying) I don't know. I want to go on the slide.

Mother: (gently) I know that. It doesn't feel good to want something and not get it. Now, what do you think will make it possible for you to go on the slide?

Sruli: (after thinking) You could lift me up to the ladder and then I could slide down.

Mother: Good idea. You found a solution.

Some parents would expect the dialogue to continue like this:

Mother: Now, let's see if you can ask me nicely to lift you.

Sruli: Please lift me up to the ladder.

This last part may or may not be a problem, depending on the child. If the parent thinks that the child will happily make the formal request, she should ask him to do it; it teaches the child that he must ask politely for what he wants. But if the child becomes irritated by the notion of a formal request, the parent should refrain.

Suppose your spouse knows what you want and forces you to articulate a request. How would you feel? You would probably be irritated. The child may feel the same way.

Our goal is to encourage Sruli to find a solution independently. He did it, and his mother recognized him for it. She should think twice before asking him in addition to articulate his request.

Make a list of solutions. Another problem-solving technique is to make of list of solutions. The parent and child first share their feelings; then they work together to find a solution that is agreeable to both. Let's illustrate:

> Goldi, six years old, often wakes up in the middle of the night. She frequently comes into her parents' bedroom, wakes them and finds a place next to her mother for the remainder of the night.
>
> Goldi's parents have asked her to stay in her room, but she does not cooperate. As the weeks pass, they

become increasingly irritated by the disturbances. They do not want Goldi to feel unwanted, but at the same time, they want her to stay in her own room.

Goldi's mother comes up with a new idea. She approaches Goldi with a blank paper and crayon, and begins a problem-solving session. This was their dialogue:

Mother: Can we talk about our middle-of-the-night problem?

Goldi: Yes.

Mother: We have a problem that we are both unhappy about. Would you like to tell me how you feel about the situation?

Goldi: I wake up in the middle of the night and I feel that I just have to go into your room.

Mother: I'd like to tell you how I feel. I am unhappy about it because it disturbs my sleep. Let's see if we can think of a solution that will make both of us happy.

Mother shows Goldi respect for her position. She is concerned for her daughter's feelings and asks her about them. She then shares her own feelings. This sets the stage for a problem-solving session.

Let's continue the dialogue:

Mother: (taking paper and crayon) Let's write down some solutions. First, we'll give our solution, then I'll write it down, and lastly, we'll decide which ones are good for me and which are good for you.

Goldi: You are going to make a list?

Mother: Yes. Would you like to offer the first solution?

Goldi: I can come into your bed when I need to. (Mother writes down each suggestion as it comes up.)

Mother: Any other ideas?

Goldi: I can just wake you up to talk to you.

Mother: You could read a book when you feel the urge to come into my room. (She continues writing.)

Goldi: I could color in a special coloring book. (pause) Mommy, can you get me a special middle-of-the-night coloring book? (Mother writes.)

Mother: If I am awake and I see your light on, I could come to your room to see how you are doing.

Goldi: I can write you a letter and draw pictures of how I feel.

Mother: Can you think of any more ideas?

Goldi: No.

Mother: Okay. Now let's look at our list and decide which are good for me and which are good for you. (She looks at the list.) Coming to my room is not going to make me very happy, so we have to cross that one out.

Goldi: But if you see my light on, can't you come to see if I am okay?

Mother: Yes, I can do that.

Goldi: And if I had special coloring books and reading books for the times I want to come into your room, I would feel better.

Mother: We can get you some special books. And if you need more crayons, we can get that for you, too.

Goldi: That sounds good.

Goldi and her mother solved a problem that a week's coaxing and pleading did not solve. Goldi was cooperative because she knew that her feelings were respected; why else would her mother take the time and effort to record her ideas? She also knew that her mother had her welfare in mind and wanted to do what was best for both of them.

Problem-solving teaches independence. Parents have a natural tendency to want to solve their children's problems for them. When a problem is presented, they give orders or offer suggestions in the hope that their children will comply. The disadvantage is that the children are not learning to be independent; rather, they are learning to depend on their parents for solutions. What happens when they have to make decisions for themselves? They will not have the skills or confidence to do it.

But if parents let children work out solutions to their own problems, they are helping them develop a skill which will enable them to live more successful lives. Once children become accustomed to problem-solving, they are able to work out all kinds of problems, even the differences they have with their brothers and sisters.

In summary. A parent who urges children to find their own solutions sends this message: "You are responsible for your life, and you must seek solutions to your own problems." In this way children learn to be independent and to take responsibility for their own decisions.

If children have a disagreement with a teacher or an argument with a friend or sibling, if they have trouble with an unclear homework assignment or cannot find a lost article, encourage them to find a solution. With a little effort, they will solve the problem efficiently and independently.

When a child asks permission to do something, say, "It's okay with me. I'm happy you made your own decision." This is the same as saying "yes," but it encourages independence and transfers responsibility for the decision to the child.

Problem-solving may require parents to go against their nature. It requires time, effort and thoughtful planning. But the benefits are worth it, for their children will master a strategy that can be applied to all areas of life. They will learn that solutions can be found if one takes the trouble to look for them. They become independent and do not rely on others to solve their personal or interpersonal problems. And since the solution belongs to the children, they are committed to it.

Be a Role Model

We have been discussing ways of teaching children responsibility. One effective method — possibly the most effective — is to be a good role model. Responsible parents teach responsibility by example.

Some parents behave irresponsibly and still demand that their children act responsibly. They say, "Do as I say, not as I do," and actually expect their children to listen to them. It doesn't work. Children follow their parents' actions, even if their words give another message. Parents can influence children to do as they say only if they "walk their talk."[1]

Create an Atmosphere Conducive to Success

We are all familiar with the powerful influence our environment has upon us. For this reason, parents want their children to be in an environment that contains only positive influences. They pay close attention to the friends their children choose because a "bad" friend can undermine the attitudes that they are trying to promote in the home.

The environment that parents create in their home has a strong influence on a child. How can parents create a positive home atmosphere? By doing all the right things. This means that they display happiness and enthusiasm and behave as paradigms of excellence. They recognize their children's excellent performances, and they offer praise, rewards and certificates of merit for jobs well done. They talk about how proud they are of their children and they make parties in honor of excellent performances. In time, the children will become imbued with an attitude of excellence and will express it in all their activities.

Encourage children to succeed by reminding them of their capabilities. Discover their personal interests and goals, and create opportunities for each one to succeed. Don't call children to task for every failure, but allow them to experience failure and all the lessons that come along with it.

Preparing Children for a Successful Future

Prepare children for school. School-age children spend more time engaged in school-related activities than in any other activity. They walk or ride to school, sit in school, play in school, eat in

---

1. Chazon Ish, *Emunah U'Bitachon, 4:16.*

school, learn in school, purchase clothing and other things for school, etc. They also study, take tests, follow school schedules, do homework, etc. They are expected to perform according to standards set by school authorities. Indeed, children are professional students.

Being successful in school is important. It is more than important; it is critical. As children succeed in school, they develop positive perceptions about their capabilities and learn to respect themselves. On the other hand, if they do not succeed, they develop negative perceptions about themselves and have less self-esteem. As we mentioned in the first chapter, the attitudes they develop today determine the success they will have tomorrow. In other words, successful experiences nurture success-oriented attitudes, which in turn produce more successful experiences.

You can prepare your children for success in school by helping them break old dependencies and develop a strong sense of duty. Assign responsibilities, hold them accountable, urge them to solve their own problems, let them manage their time and train them to project outcomes.

Prepare children for adulthood. Every human being makes the transition from infant to youngster to adult. An infant has no obligations and is totally dependent on parents. As the infant matures, parents and teachers begin to make demands, and life becomes more complex. When the youngster becomes an adult, a myriad of new responsibilities is added to the list. And more frequently than not, nobody is available to help.[1]

Some adults, after being thrown into a position of responsibility, lament the fact that their parents did not prepare them.

> Chana is twenty-six years old. With three children under the age of five, her daily routine is very demanding. She never has a day off, and when she is sick, there is no time to stay in bed to recuperate properly. Chana feels she has too many responsibilities and that she cannot cope.

---

1. See Rabbeinu Yonah, *Avos* 2:5: Where there are no people to help a person do *mitzvos* and to chastise him, he must act properly on his own accord. Obviously, people need training for this kind of independent living.

Chana dreams about the days when she had few responsibilities. When she had a problem with school work, Mother supplied the answer. When she fought with her brother, Mother consoled her with a goody. Mother never accepted a teacher's claim that Chana was defiant or spoke with *chutzpah* — "Not my Chanala," was her reply. Mother assigned few household chores because she believed that childhood was meant for fun, not work. Indeed, life was easy.

Intellectually, Chana knows she must be devoted to her three children, but emotionally, she is not satisfied with her life of unceasing responsibility. She longs for the day when she can retire from it all.

As a child, Chana was protected from responsibility, but as an adult, she has no way of escaping it. At twenty-six years old, Chana is paying the price for a mistake her mother made a long time ago. Her mother should have prepared her for the responsibilities of adulthood.[1]

I have an acquaintance who had her first child after ten years of marriage. She assigned him household chores, taught him to be independent, and never allowed *chutzpah.* Friends said, "Why don't you enjoy your son? After ten years of waiting, he is so special. Why not treat him specially?" She responded, "Just because I had to wait ten years doesn't mean that I should make him a brat and ruin his life." This parent did not want her child to pay Chana's price.

True, it is during adulthood that people have most of their responsibilities, but they cannot wait until then to develop a *sense* of responsibility.

You can cultivate a young plant to become a properly aligned tree, but it is very difficult to straighten a plant after it has grown with a bend. A person is the same. While he is still young, it is easy to go on the good path and depart from the bad, but if he grows old with his evil ways, it is difficult in his eyes to change (Rabbeinu Yonah, *Avos* 1:14).

---

1. Rabbi S. R. Hirsch, *Yesodos HaChinuch,* pp. 49-56.

> When a person habituates his limbs to be inactive from work, his hands are held back (when he decides to start) because habit controls them (Rabbeinu Yonah, *Avos* 1:10).

Habits, routines, and attitudes become well-established and are difficult to change during adulthood. Therefore, the time to prepare people for adulthood is when they are young. Parents who teach their children at a young age to accept responsibility imbue them with a value that sustains them throughout life.[1]

---

1. See Malbim, *Mishlei* 20:4: Although a person's psyche is full of distractions when he is young and settled when he is old, the time to plant the seeds of wisdom is during youth. See also Rabbeinu Yonah, *Mishlei* 22:6.

Chapter Six

Expect the Best and Treat the Child as a Winner

Can you recall a time you were motivated to reach a goal because someone expected you to reach it? That person may have been a parent, teacher, friend or relative. He or she expected the best of you and had confidence in your ability. You may even have thought that it could not be done, but you made the effort and met the expectation.

How did this person motivate you? What was the secret? The answer is that he or she believed in you, expected the best and treated you as a winner.

This is called a self-fulfilling prophecy. A prophecy is self-fulfilling when the expectation of an event induces behavior that increases the likelihood of the event. It is also called the Pygmalion effect. It is more than an abstract idea or concept; it is a reality, a fact of life.

A self-fulfilling prophecy can work vis-a-vis a person's expectation of himself and his subsequent behavior, or his expectation of someone else and that person's subsequent behavior. We will be discussing the latter — how a parent's expectation of a child's success induces behavior that increases the likelihood of that success.

The Self-fulfilling Prophecy

Rabbi Shamshon Raphael Hirsch wrote about the self-fulfilling prophecy. He wrote that parents should expect the best of their children and treat them as winners.[1]

To explain the idea, he told a story of a rabbi who accepted a position in a new community. Some people, with good intentions, wanted to help him by making a list of all the community members along with a short description of each member's character. But the rabbi rejected the offer. Here, in his words, is the reason:

> In most instances, this knowledge holds the rabbi back from performing with proper guidance and influence. It is better to assume that each person has good character and to firmly resolve that they all want to be straight and ethical, with love for other people and prepared for sacrifice, compromise and *mitzvah* performance.
>
> When the rabbi publicizes his opinion to the community, every person will try to prove that the opinion is correct. As the relationship between rabbi and community grows, people practice these traits and an impact is made on them. The person who lacks a particular trait will become the kind of person the rabbi wants him to be.

This rabbi used the self-fulfilling prophecy to shape and improve people. He expected the best from all community members and treated them as if they already were what he wanted them to be. They in turn met his expectation by behaving that way. He prophesied good behavior, and because he treated the people with that expectation, the prophecy was fulfilled.

Another recognized educator once said that this technique can

---

1. Rabbi S.R. Hirsch, *Yesodos HaChinuch*, p. 63.

be used to change the habits of a miserly person. Praise a miserly person for being a gracious contributor and treat him as though he already were this way, and his buried trait of philanthropy will be uncovered. The newly found trait soon wins over his miserliness, and he becomes a bona-fide philanthropist.[1]

In the same way, you can bring out the best in your children. Search for their good traits and articulate your expectations. Share your belief and confidence in your children by saying things like, "You are such a capable person. There is no doubt that if you apply yourself, you can reach your goal."[2]

Experiments have demonstrated the self-fulfilling prophecy. Researchers have performed many experiments to demonstrate the effect of expectations and the self-fulfilling prophecy. These experiments involved ordinary people in social settings, athletes in sports settings, patients in medical settings, workers in occupational settings, children in school settings and animals in laboratory settings.

One researcher studied members of a bowling team.[3] The researcher observed that on any given evening, members "knew" how each player would bowl. When a particular player was expected to bowl well, he did. When he was expected to bowl poorly, he did. The expectations of team members seemed to determine the performance of the players.

The researcher explained that team members subtly communicated their expectations to each player, which in turn influenced performance. Players who were expected to perform well received encouragement. This increased their motivation to perform well and decreased the interfering effects of anxiety. But players who were expected to perform poorly received negative messages. This increased their anxiety and hindered their performance.

In a social setting, a shy and socially inept woman became relaxed and self-confident when she was among people who deliberately treated her as a social favorite.[4]

---

1. Rabbi Klonimus Kalmish Shapira, *Chovas HaTalmidim*, ch. 1.
2. Ibid.
3. William Whythe, 1943, cited in *Pygmalion in the Classroom*, Robert Rosenthal and Lenore Jacobson, Holt, Rinehart and Winston Inc., 1968, p. 4.
4. E. R. Guthrie, 1938, cited in ibid., p. 5.

Another researcher made an interesting observation in an occupational setting.[1] In the early 1900's, the United States Census Bureau installed a new machine called the Hollerith tabulating machine. Mr. Hollerith, its inventor, trained the first group of clerks. He told his trainees that the machine was very difficult to operate and that he did not expect them to punch more than 550 cards per day.

Once the clerks became acclimated to the new machine, they found that they were able to comfortably process 550 cards per day, just as Mr. Hollerith expected. When they tried to exceed this number, they became tense and exhausted.

However, clerks who were trained afterward were able to process three times as many cards. The only difference between the two sets of clerks was that the second group was not informed that the machine would be hard to operate.

Yet another researcher showed how expectations play a role in a medical setting.[2] He was working in a psychiatric hospital and told the nurses and attendants that he had administered a new test to ten patients. The test, developed at Harvard, predicted that six particular patients — and he named them — would begin to have a surprising improvement in their condition. Nothing was said about the other four. The nurses and attendants now had different expectations for the two sets of patients. What they and the patients did not know was that all ten patients were randomly selected to be part of their respective group.

At the time of discharge, the six patients who were expected to improve actually *did* improve more than the other four.

Another interesting study was conducted in an animal setting.[3] Students in an experimental psychology class were divided into twelve groups, and each group was given five laboratory rats. Six groups were told that they had specially bred "bright" rats, and six were told that they had specially bred "dull" rats. In truth, all the rats were ordinary laboratory animals.

The students were to train their rats to run to the dark side of

---

1. J. Jastrow, 1900, cited in ibid., pp. 5-6.

2. Taylor, 1966, cited in ibid., p. 19.

3. Robert Rosenthal and K. L. Fode, 1963, cited in ibid., pp. 37-38.

a maze by rewarding them with a bit of food every time they reached their destination. After five days, the experimenters gave their reports. The groups that believed their rats were "brighter" reported more successful runs and viewed their rats as more pleasant and likeable than those that believed their rats were "dull." They also handled their animals more often and more gently than the other groups did.

The most successful groups expected the best of their animals and treated them that way. The animals *believed* to be better performers *became* better performers.

Two researchers reviewed these findings and posed the question: If animals perform better as a result of their trainers' positive attitudes toward them, would school children perform better if their teachers think they are bright?

The researchers set out to answer the question. They administered tests predicting future academic progress to children of a San Francisco elementary school. Teachers were given to believe that those with high scores would show a spurt of academic progress during the school year. They did not know that the test scores were randomly assigned and did not correlate at all with the students' true potential.

The researchers tested the students again at the end of the year. They found that those who were expected to have a spurt in their performance actually did improve. Their teachers also rated them as intellectually curious, happier and less in need of social approval.[1]

The only difference between the two sets of students was the expectations the teachers had of them. The teachers nurtured and motivated the high expectation students more than they did the others, treating them as winners. The children began to believe it; and in choosing to live by their strengths, they attained success — the same success that the other students could have had if they had been treated the same way.

You can deduce teacher and parent expectations. If you carefully observe the interactions that teachers and parents have with children, you can often deduce the kind of expectations the adults have. Their gestures, body language, facial expressions and

---

1. Robert Rosenthal and Lenore Jacobson, 1966, cited in ibid., pp. 174-178.

tone of voice are more positive and encouraging with children for whom they have high expectations. They watch these children more closely and give them more compliments. They give them more time to respond to questions. They are also polite, saying "please" and "thank you," to these children more often than to those for whom they have low expectations.

Children respond to the expectations adults have of them. When teachers and parents have high expectations of children, their attitudes and behavior toward the children are advantageous. The converse is also true. Children sense it and respond in kind.

> During the three Shabbos meals, Mr. Schwartz discusses the weekly *parashah* with his twin sons, Tzvi and Moshe. They are both of average intellect, but Tzvi is vivacious, full of self-confidence, and ready to show how much he knows, while Moshe is reserved and slow to share his thoughts. Tzvi actively participates in the discussions while Moshe hesitates.
>
> Mr. Schwartz has learned to expect more from Tzvi than from Moshe. When he asks a question, he looks at Tzvi with an anticipatory gaze. If Tzvi does not respond, he looks at Moshe, but without the same anticipation. He also gives Moshe less time to respond than Tzvi.
>
> If neither knows the answer, he encourages them both by saying, "Come on. You can do it," but he looks at Tzvi with a smile and may even give him an encouraging touch on the hand.
>
> Mr. Schwartz loves both his sons and wants to see them both succeed. But as they mature, Tzvi continues to take the lead while Moshe continues to lag behind.

Moshe needs prodding and more time to respond. That's how some people are; there is nothing wrong with it. If Mr. Schwartz would provide for his need, Moshe would probably progress at the same rate as Tzvi. Instead, Mr. Schwartz has instinctively assumed that Tzvi is both knowledgeable and interested in his Torah discussions, while Moshe isn't. He has grown to expect more from Tzvi, and without realizing it, treats his sons differently. The differences are subtle, but Tzvi and Moshe are aware of it, and they respond in kind.

At first, Moshe probably said to himself, "Father knows Tzvi has the answer, so he looks at him and gives him time to think. But he feels I don't know the answer, so he doesn't do the same for me." With this attitude, Moshe doesn't even *try* to participate at the next table discussion. Why should he? In his mind, he has already decided he is inadequate. And even when he does try, his self-confidence is so low that he gives up quickly. His negative attitude carries over in school, where he also gives up quickly and experiences many failures. He performs exactly as his father expects, proving to both of them that he is inept. As the vicious cycle continues, Moshe deteriorates — and the original cause of his failure may never even be discovered.

Tzvi, on the other hand, believes he is capable of good performance. Why not? His father treats him as a winner. He believes in him and encourages him to participate. Tzvi's self-confidence grows as a result, and he makes the effort to perform well. The better he performs, the more strongly he proves to himself and to his father that he is a budding Torah scholar. As the cycle continues, Tzvi blossoms.

Mr. Schwartz has brought out the best in Tzvi by teaching him indirectly that he is a winner. But he has inhibited Moshe's growth by teaching him indirectly that he is inadequate. Had he looked for Moshe's strengths and given him the necessary time and attention, he could have brought out the best in him, too.

Sometimes, a parent may even bring out the *worst* in a child. Take, for example, a mother who believes her child will behave poorly in public. She subtly conveys her expectation by adopting the role of policeman, guarding the child against imminent wrongdoing. She requires him to stay home or forbids him to participate in certain activities. The child senses his mother's expectation and responds defensively. An adversarial relationship develops. Just to prove his worthiness and independence, he will exhibit the very behavior that his mother wants him to avoid.

I am acquainted with a parent who helped her daughter fail a mathematics course. Here is the story:

Malka did not understand mathematics and was failing every test. The teacher tried to tutor her, but Malka did not even make an effort to understand. She had a defeatist attitude and often said, "I'm bad in math. I'll never understand it."

The teacher decided to discuss the problem with Malka's mother. As they talked, she discovered that the mother also had a negative attitude about herself, only stronger. She said, "I was never good in math, and neither were my sisters and brothers. None of my other children were. My family is just not good in math." Her mind was made up, and her attitude was so negative that she didn't even agree to a plan of action.

The teacher now understood why Malka was failing. Her mother expected failure and indirectly taught her to expect failure, too. She conveyed the message in many subtle and not-so-subtle ways. Malka "knew" she would do poorly — it was in her genes. So she gave up without even trying.

On the flip side of the coin, there is a story of a teacher who turned the school's "bad" boy into a fine student. When she met her class on the first day of school, she told this boy, "I understand that you have many leadership qualities. This class is going to be the best in the school and I expect you to help get us there." That day, whenever he performed well, she praised him and reminded him of his reputation and of her expectations. She did this consistently day after day, until he actually became the leader that she expected him to become.

The teacher bestowed upon this boy a virtue — she gave him a fine reputation — which he did not yet have. He did not want to disappoint her, so he felt obliged to live up to it.

There are many stories of parents and teachers who have bestowed labels upon their children, both good and bad, which the children then upheld. One child, for example, always threaded her grandmother's needles. The grandmother was always so impressed and would say, "You have *goldeneh hendt* (golden hands)." The girl believed she had skillful hands, and later on she became a dentist. Then there is a story of a little boy who always told his father about the dreams he had. His father would say, "Son, you dream on high, but your feet are always on the ground" — meaning that he aimed high but he was also realistic. The son took this attitude with him into adulthood and attributed many good decisions to it.[1]

There are other stories of children who lived up to negative labels until their parents adjusted the labels. One little girl, for example, was constantly being told that she was "bossy." She became more and more bossy until her parents adjusted their view of her and began treating her as if she were agreeable. There was also a stubborn little boy who was constantly told, "You are a stubborn mule." He continued behaving stubbornly until his parents adjusted their view of him and began treating him as if he were flexible.

You get what you expect. The opinion parents have of a child influences the kind of interaction they have with the child. For this reason, parents should never make up their minds that a child is "bad" or a "failure." If a child is faltering, they should look for her strengths and *believe,* with sincerity, that she is basically good and has the potential to improve. Then they should convey their belief to the child; otherwise, she may never improve.[2]

The saying goes: "Treat a person as he is, and he will remain as he is; treat a person as if he were what he *could* be and *should* be, and he will become what he could be and should be." This does not mean that a parent or teacher can actually control the level of success another person has. There are many other factors, internal and external, working for and against that success. Rather, the saying expresses the idea that parents and other authority figures play a primary role and have a strong influence on the lives of others. Through their expectations, they influence — not control — another's behavior, both positive and negative.

The Sh'lah saw this concept in the words of *Mishlei*:

> "Do not rebuke a scorner lest he hate you; rebuke a wise person and he will love you" (*Mishlei* 9:8). When you

---

1. These stories are told by Adele Faber and Elaine Mazlish in *How To Talk So Kids Will Listen & Listen So Kids Will Talk,* Avon Books, 1982.

2. Rabbi S.R. Hirsch, *Yesodos HaChinuch,* p. 64.

> rebuke another person, do not degrade or insult him by saying, "You are a scorner," because he will hate you and will not listen to you. But "rebuke a wise person" and say to him, "You are so wise. Why are you doing this?" and he will love you and listen to you (Sh'lah, cited in *Chovas HaTalmidim,* ch. 1).

Treat your children as if they already are what you expect them to be and help them become what they are capable of becoming. Develop high expectations and treat them accordingly, and they will perform according to your expectations. Expectations of success breed success.

Talking to Children in the Positive

If a child steals, don't say, "You are a thief" or "You are not worthy of anything good." The child may continue to steal and become exactly what you don't want him to be. Say instead, "You just stole something" or "You just behaved poorly." Then say, "You are better than that and you know better." This generates a positive attitude. The child will probably stop the undesired behavior and will become the refined person you want him to be.[1]

When a child receives a failing grade in school, don't say, "You are not living up to your potential." Say instead, "You have great potential, and I know you can do well. These grades do not reflect your true ability."

Rabbi Abraham Twerski wrote that as a youngster his wise father would rebuke him with the words, *"Es past nisht."* It means, "This is not for you. You are better than that. You are expected to live up to the high standards which you already have." He emphasized how the behavior was incompatible with a child of such high caliber.[2]

When you dwell on the negative, the effects are negative; when you dwell on the positive, the effects are positive. You can bring out the best in a child by being positive and encouraging. You can even

---

1. Ibid.; also Rabbi Klonimus Kalmish Shapira, *Chovas HaTalmidim,* ch. 1.
2. *Generation to Generation,* CIS Publishers, vol. 1, p. 15.

tell a scorner that he is wise — and it is not a lie because he probably does have many wise qualities. He will then respond in kind.

When a child hears encouraging words about himself, he develops a healthy self-image. His confidence grows, and he becomes instilled with an "I-can" attitude. His expectation of success energizes him to continue trying and develops into a self-fulfilling prophecy.

Find ways of expressing your expectations positively. If a child holds a pencil incorrectly, say, "Hold the pencil like this ... It's not hard. You can do it. Then you will have a beautiful handwriting." The message communicates confidence and high expectation. It inspires an "I-can" attitude.

Recognize good performance. Catch your children doing good things and praise them for it. Say, "I noticed you doing ... I am proud of you and I am proud that you are part of my family." If they come home from school with excellent grades, publicize the achievement in the home by talking about it at the dinner table and displaying the paper on the wall.

What an impact praise makes! It shows appreciation for the children, and at the same time emphasizes and reiterates the high expectations you have for them. This motivates the children to continue performing well.

If you want, you can add weight to the compliment by providing a tangible reward. It can be food, an extra privilege, a certificate, a star on the chart, or any other item that has meaning to the children.

A Positive Relationship Motivates Children to Fulfill Your Expectations

A veteran high school teacher once told me his secret to success. He works to develop a positive relationship with his students. Once they learn to love and respect him, they want to please him. They do not want to let him down, so they produce good grades for his sake, to satisfy his expectations. They want him to be proud of them.

This approach is not new. Thousands of years ago, Aharon HaKohen, the brother of Moshe Rabbeinu, used the same technique to motivate people to fulfill his expectations.

> When Aharon walked on the street and met an evildoer, he would say "Hello." The next day, when that man

> considered committing a sin, he would say to himself, "Woe is me. How will I look at Aharon? He greeted me, and I will be ashamed." That person would reconsider and would not commit the sin (*Avos d'Rav Nosson* 12:3).

What was the key to Aharon's influence? A simple "Hello" could not possibly have had such a powerful effect. Rather, his influence resulted from the overall relationship he had with people. People loved and respected him, and they wanted to please him. They knew what he expected, and he did not even have to express it. They met his expectations because they did not want to let him down.

Look for Hidden Ability

How do parents form the expectations they have of a child? Many parents simply observe the child's performances and instinctively derive conclusions about his or her ability, just as Mr. Schwartz did in an earlier scenario. If they conclude that the child's ability is strong, they form high expectations; if they conclude the opposite, their expectations are reduced.

These parents, in effect, have unconsciously appointed themselves judges of their child's ability. If a child performs well and appears interested, as in the case of Tzvi Schwartz, the verdict is "strong ability." The child is then awarded high parental expectations. However, if a child appears dull, performs poorly or displays little interest, as in the case of Moshe Schwartz, the verdict is "weak ability" and he or she is sentenced to low parental expectations.

The problem is that the child may have hidden talents and abilities which are only waiting to be uncovered. If the parents would detect them, they would certainly try to bring them out. Instead, they rely on their own instincts and form negative conclusions, allowing the hidden talents to go untapped. They suppress growth and condemn the child to a life of mediocrity.

Children often have more drive and potential than parents attribute to them. History shows us many such cases. Rabbi Akiva, for example, was an ignoramus up until the age of forty. He and others believed that he had no talent for Torah learning. When he married, the bride's wealthy father disowned her because he felt that Akiva was an unworthy individual. We are all familiar with the greatness that Rabbi Akiva achieved.

Rabbi Eliezer ben Hurkenus is another example. He was also considered inept. At the age of twenty-eight, before he began studying Torah, he did not even know how to read *K'rias Shema.* When he decided to leave home to study Torah, his father wanted to disinherit him. But to his family's surprise, he became a towering Torah scholar.[1]

King Dovid, about whom we say, "Dovid, king of Yisrael, lives forever," was considered the least worthy of his seven brothers. When Shmuel the prophet asked Yishai, Dovid's father, to present all his sons so he could designate the one Hashem had chosen for the kingship, Yishai did not even bring Dovid from the fields. When Shmuel finally met Dovid, he too felt that this son was not fitting and even asked Hashem to confirm that Dovid was in fact the chosen one.[2] Dovid went on to become one of our greatest leaders.

These "world-class" success stories were all based on hidden talents which emerged over time. Any child may be a late bloomer, with hidden talents waiting to emerge. Wise parents are always on the lookout for these latent talents. As one expert said, "There is something greater than ability; it is the ability to *see* ability."

For this reason, we are instructed to have many students, even if they are all on different levels, because we don't know how many or which ones will succeed.[3] Even a seemingly unworthy student may surprise us and take a place above all the others. Rabbi Yochanan ben Zachai illustrated this point:

> Hillel gathered all his students and said to them, "Are all of you here?" They said, "Yes." Then one student said, "All are here except the smallest of them all." Hillel said to them, "Let the small one come. A generation of people will follow him." And they brought Rabbi Yochanan ben Zachai to him. [The lesson is] we should not push away the small ones from before the big ones because lambs eventually become grown sheep (Rabbeinu Yonah, *Avos* 1:1).

---

1. *Pirkei Rabbi Eliezer*, chs. 1-2.
2. *1 Shmuel* ch. 16, and *Yalkut Shimoni* there.
3. Rabbeinu Yonah, *Avos* 1:1.

Every human being has great potential and a wealth of hidden ability, and all are capable of more than they are presently accomplishing. We are all obligated to say, "When will my actions equal those of my forefathers?"[1] Rabbi Eliyahu Dessler deduced that since we are *obligated* to aspire to higher levels, it must be that higher levels are within everyone's reach.[2]

Secular thinkers agree. William James, the father of American psychology, said that people utilize only a fraction of their true abilities. Another expert put it this way: "What lies behind us and what lies ahead of us are tiny matters when compared to what lies *within* us." Yet another student of behavior put it this way: "Everyone is a potential winner. Some people are disguised as losers. Don't let their appearances fool you."[3] One self-confident youngster offered his own version of the idea: "G-d don't make no junk!"

All children are created in the "image of G-d" and are endowed with "pure souls created by G-d."[4] They possess hidden strengths, and you never know how much they will accomplish.

A teacher who withholds a Torah law from a student because he thinks the student will not understand it is called a thief. The student is *entitled* to that information and the teacher is required to share it with him, no matter how intelligent the student appears.[5] The same can be said concerning any growth opportunity consistent with Torah ideals — a child is entitled to it and a parent must provide it, even if the parent thinks the child is inept.

The Baal Shem Tov compared the Jewish nation to stars. Stars appear to us as tiny specks, but in reality they are gigantic. The Baal Shem Tov said that the Jewish nation is the same; although it has an insignificant appearance in the world, the world exists because of it. In reality, every Jewish person possesses greatness.[6]

---

1. *Tanna d'Bei Eliyahu Rabbah* 25.
2. *Michtav M'Eliyahu*, vol. 3, pp. 21-23.
3. *The One Minute Manager*, Blanchard and Johnson, copyright 1982 by Blanchard Family Partnership and Candle Communication Corp., by permission of William Morrow and Co., Inc.
4. Said in the morning prayers.
5. Talmud *Sanhedrin* 91a, according to Maharsha.
6. Cited in *Mayanah Shel Torah, Bereishis* 15:5.

Form Realistic Expectations

With all this talk about high expectations, how high should you go? Does it mean that the higher you set your expectation, the greater the effect? Let's look at a story that answers this question.

> Devorah was not doing well in school. She did not study for tests or complete homework assignments. She disturbed the class with loud outbursts and was often reprimanded by her teacher.
>
> Devorah's parents wanted her to improve. They decided to motivate her by expecting the best and treating her as a winner. When she came home with a failing grade, they told her how smart she was and that she could get 100% if she would only try. When she brought home notes about misconduct, they told her that she was capable of being the best-behaved child in the class. They talked with her as if she were already the success they expected her to be.
>
> At first, Devorah liked hearing the positive talk, and she even tried to fulfill her parents' expectations. But she never met their high standards. As time went on, she became less motivated and finally asked her parents to stop talking about her "great potential."
>
> Devorah's parents were confused. They had tried to treat her as a winner and did not understand why she rejected their efforts.

The problem was that Devorah's parents expected too much. She didn't have the drive or the background to score 100% on tests. For now, 80% was more reasonable. And she was too fidgety to be the best-behaved student in the class.

Devorah tried at first to meet her parents' expectations, but she couldn't. And with each shortcoming, she became more convinced of her inadequacy. She no longer wanted to hear about goals she could not reach or abilities she did not have. It depressed and irritated her.

Let's go back to the original question — how high should you go? There is no rule and no easy answer. On one hand, you should believe that the child has greater potential than he or she displays.

On the other hand, you cannot expect more than the child can achieve. It isn't easy to determine.

But one more thing is certain — if the child is capable of reaching certain goals, expect him or her to reach them. If the child is not capable, do not expect it.[1] Why? Because expecting a child to reach an unattainable goal will result in failure, and failure only adds fuel to a negative self-esteem, jeopardizing future achievements.

So how can you determine realistic goals? Get to know your child as well as you can. Carefully observe his or her performances. Create a total perception of the child, using as many available resources as you can. Speak with teachers, relatives and friends who come in contact with the child and who see him or her under a different set of circumstances. Once you have the "big picture," you are in a position to form reasonable expectations.

Consider individual needs. People have many kinds of needs. They have low-level needs such as food, shelter and clothing. They have higher-level needs such as security and safety, and above these the need for such things as love, respect and a sense of belonging. The highest level is the need to excel and fulfill one's potential. Psychologists call this "self-actualization."

A person who has not fulfilled lower-level needs does not focus on higher-level needs. For example, a person who does not have food or shelter does not feel a strong need for safety. For this reason, he may do something considered unsafe in order to get food and shelter. Once satisfied, he will no longer engage in those unsafe acts because he now wants to satisfy his need for safety and security. Once he feels safe and secure, he strives for love and respect. Only after he satisfies all his lower-level needs does he begin to be concerned with self-actualization.

Parents and teachers expect children to make school a major part of their lives by paying attention in class, studying at home and doing well on tests. What they are unwittingly assuming is that their children have satisfied all their basic needs and are ready to take the steps toward self-actualization. For this reason, parents and teachers become frustrated when children do not live up to their high expectations.

---

1. Heard from Rabbi Shimon Schwab.

The problem is that the children may have lower-level concerns on their minds. They may be more concerned with avoiding the class bully than with doing well on a test. They may be more concerned about their low self-esteem and the constant criticism they receive at home than about paying attention in class.

They are not meeting the expectations set by the authorities because they are not on that level. They have more important matters on their minds. Parents and teachers would do better to address those matters first, or at least alongside their other expectations.

Set different standards for each child. Because children's needs are a function of their personalities and their lifestyles, parents have to look at each individual and understand what his or her particular set of needs is before forming expectations. Otherwise, the standards may be unrealistic. No two children in any family are alike. Each is an individual. Each has his or her own needs, abilities, strengths and weaknesses. One may blossom as a result of a particular treatment, while another sinks.

Therefore, you cannot have identical expectations for each child. "Draw a picture" of each child and provide the individual treatment that he or she deserves.[1]

Forming Expectations for the "Difficult" Child

When we observe a "difficult" child, we are not looking at a whole person. We do not always recognize his or her personal problems, pressures, moods and predispositions. Professional counselors who meet with these children can tell you that they are ordinary people with a particular problem that compels them to misbehave.

If you have a "difficult" child in your family, make an effort — and it does take effort — to discover what is causing the child's behavior.

Try to understand the child. Analyze the relationship you have with the child. Question your treatment to see if it is causing the

---

1. See *Midrash Rabbah, Bamidbar* 21:15: A leader must deal with each person according to his individual traits. See also Rabbi Yeruchom Levovitz, *Daas Torah, Shemos* 19:13; Vilna Gaon on *Mishlei* 16:4 and 22:6; and Rabbi S. R. Hirsch, *Yesodos HaChinuch*, pp. 55-56.

behavior. Very often, parents treat a child in a way that creates the very attitudes and behaviors they are trying to eliminate. This was discussed in the first chapter.

Ask the child, "Do you realize you are acting this way? Can you tell me why?" If the child senses that you are sincere, he may open up. The odds are that he also wants to behave appropriately but has a problem that is causing him to misfire. Talk about the problem. Negotiate solutions.

Speak with professionals or other people who understand the way children think. Open your mind to new ideas and new ways of dealing with children. Getting a fresh perspective may enable you to deal more effectively with the child.

Your attitude is the key. Most importantly, develop a proper attitude toward the "difficult" child. Your attitude and the expectations you have of the child are your keys to success. Rabbi Shamshon Raphael Hirsch gives an apt description of the proper attitude:

> Parents and teachers should forget the past mistakes of their children. We do not act for the past but for the future. We set our hopes and aspirations on the foundation of the future, not on the foundation of the past ... Hashem is always prepared to erase the sins of our past and to give us the opportunity to lead our future lives in a more careful way ... We should be careful not to express any bitterness toward our children and students even when their behavior warrants it; and not only this, but we should hold in our hearts a love and compassion for them ... There should be a new hope that today, after a period of mistakes, they will improve their ways (Rabbi S. R. Hirsch, *Yesodos HaChinuch*, Netzach Publishers, p. 68).

There is a great deal of responsibility placed on the parents of a "difficult" child. These parents cannot isolate and focus on the child's poor behavior only. They must also examine their own attitudes and behaviors to see if they are thinking and acting appropriately.

Rabbi Hirsch addresses several areas of examination, and we will now elaborate on his insights. But before going further, please go back and review his words carefully.

Disregard past misconduct. The past is gone forever. It may have been very different from the present and future, but what happened then does not necessarily predict what will happen later. For this reason, people should look to the future when setting any kind of goal.

A child's behavior is no different. If a child behaved inappropriately last week, it doesn't mean that he will repeat that behavior this week or the following week. The past does not necessarily predict the future. If it did, the words "improvement" and *"teshuvah"* would not be part of our language. Just as Hashem looks beyond our old misconduct and forms new expectations of good behavior, parents should do the same with their children.

Look for the child's good points; no doubt there are many. Make a list of them. Then, in your mind and on paper, separate the good behaviors from the poor ones. You will soon realize that the child has numerous qualities worthy of praise and appreciation.

Train yourself to focus on the positive. Point your antennae toward the things the child does right. Appreciate his attributes. Be a "goodfinder," not a faultfinder. This doesn't mean that you should take a Pollyanna approach and treat the child as if everything he does is perfect. But it does mean that you should *adjust* your view of the child and form new, positive expectations for him.

There are many stories of children who performed so poorly in school that their teachers gave up on them. When the principals saw what was happening, they informed the teachers that these children had high IQ's and strong potential. The teachers, not knowing that the information was not necessarily true, changed their attitudes toward the children. They disregarded past performances and adjusted their expectations for the future. They began treating these low achievers as winners. In time, the children began to improve.[1]

Have love and compassion. Withhold bitterness. Parents typically become disappointed and upset when a child performs poorly or behaves improperly. This is normal, but it is important not to hold bitter feelings toward the child. Even if the child's misbehavior is severe, they must treat him lovingly. Just as Hashem

1. *Pygmalion in the Classroom*, p. 56.

encourages improvement with love and compassion, parents should do the same.

View each day as an opportunity for improvement. Each day is new, holding new potential and new opportunities for improvement. Expect the best and treat the child as if today is his first day of improvement. If there is no improvement today, expect it tomorrow. Do this every day. If the child senses that you have given him a chance — and he may need many weeks or months to get this feeling — he may begin to change.

Remind the child how great he can be. Sometimes, "difficult" children are unaware of their true abilities. Is it any wonder? For years, their parents and teachers have been recognizing them for their inadequacies.

You can change that around. Believe in them and inform them of the possibilities that exist. Let them know that they have the potential to reach great heights. Let them know that you expect it.[1]

Don't give up on the child. If you give up hope and decide that the child is a failure, not only will the child lose your valuable encouragement, he will also give up on himself. He will begin to think that he is a lost cause and that improvement is impossible.

> When we give up on our children and do not persist in helping them improve, they also give up on themselves. They close the gates of *teshuvah* on themselves, as they think that all the powers in the world are unable to lift them from their low level. Therefore, we should express our hopes to them, and with our support they will be lifted and empowered to overcome their weaknesses ... With every interaction we have with them, they must sense that we are inviting them [to take the opportunity of making this day the first day of improvement] (Rabbi S. R. Hirsch, *Yesodos HaChinuch,* Netzach Publishers, p. 69).

Control your personality. All this may sound difficult. It is. It's not easy to disregard past mistakes and misbehaviors, withhold

1. Rabbi Eliyahu Dessler, *Michtav M'Eliyahu,* vol. 3, pp. 21-23, and *D'rashos HaRan,* beginning of ninth *d'rashah.*

bitterness, praise good performances, believe in your child's worthiness and set high expectations — especially if at first glance the child's behavior seems to call for the opposite response. It is even more difficult if you have your own personal problems, such as ill health, marital difficulties, emotional instability or other pressing issues. You already feel frustrated, and your natural tendency is to condemn and to lapse into anger and bitterness — all the things you are supposed to avoid.

However, you don't have to live according to your personality. You don't have to let your natural tendencies control you. Being positive is certainly a challenge when you are feeling down or have a difficult child to deal with. But you can make the effort to be mentally strong and to control your responses. It is worth the investment, because the success you have with your children and the success they have in their lives depend on it.

How to Treat a Child as a Winner

We have been saying that if you treat a child as a winner, he will become one. Now the question is: *How* do you treat a child as a winner? We have already discussed some basic "winning treatment" guidelines, but there are more.

All the guidelines share a common ingredient — a message that says: "You are special. You can do it. I have confidence in you. I expect big things from you. I won't give up on you."

The message is sent through words, actions and general attitude. The latter two are important, because if your words are going to make an impression on the child, your gestures and attitudes — the unspoken words — must convey the same message. They are all building blocks for a productive relationship where children respond in kind and show how special they really are.

How can you *properly* send the message that you have high expectations for your children?

Give genuine respect.

> Mr. Goldstein is a Torah scholar and spends the whole day and a good part of the night in a *kollel.* He is a hard worker and sets high goals for himself. He also sets high goals for his children. He often tells them that they are

special, and he talks about the expectations he has for them.

But Mr. Goldstein doesn't spend much time at home. When he *is* home and his children want to be with him, he says, "I don't have time now" or "You didn't do your homework yet" or "Go study for your test. That's more important."

Mr. Goldstein rarely praises his children's good performances. But when they do poorly in school, he is quick to point out their mistakes. When they misbehave at home, even slightly, he responds with a sharp reprimand or punishment.

As his children grow older, Mr. Goldstein begins to notice that they are not responding to his expectations. He is especially disturbed by the ever-decreasing influence he has on them.

Mr. Goldstein's children are probably saying to themselves, "He doesn't respect us. He doesn't like us. He doesn't think that we are worthy people. That's why he always criticizes us and doesn't spend time with us." Why should they think differently? All of their father's actions lead to that conclusion.

Since the children sense that he does not respect them, they in turn do not have positive feelings for him. And in that case, why *should* they care about the expectations he has for them? Why should they want to prove to him how special they are?

The children's assumptions might be incorrect. Mr. Goldstein may indeed respect his children. The problem is that he only knows how to behave negatively toward them. Maybe his parents acted that way toward him. Maybe he feels that it is the proper way of raising children. Whatever the reason, his children don't know it and don't really care. They only care about what they see and experience.

If Mr. Goldstein would *show* more respect for his children, their relationship would improve and they would want to meet his expectations. Showing more respect means spending more time with the children at home, talking about their good qualities, asking for their thoughts and opinions, taking an interest in their lives and giving them 100% of his attention, whether they ask for it or not. Showing respect means talking with children the way one talks with any important person.

Use positive body language. There is a saying, "I can't hear *what* you're saying because *how* you're saying it is so loud." A smile, frown, look, touch, jump, handshake, nod of the head or a sincere "please" and "thank you" — or lack of any one — tells a child what you really think of his actions and how much you really respect him, no matter what you say.

Body language confirms the sincerity of your words. Suppose you told a child how special he is, but when he talks to you, you frown or show little interest. What will he think? He will probably think that you are really dissatisfied with him. But if your face lights up with genuine interest, he will see that you are sincerely satisfied with him. Non-verbal signals always convey their own strong message.

Be sincere. Picture a father encouraging his daughter to achieve a goal. He says, "You are capable of big things. Just try and you will do it." After a short pause he adds, "And I don't mean what I just said."

How would his daughter feel? She would be insulted by the bogus encouragement.

No parent would ever do this. But some parents do similar things. They compliment their children or offer encouragement, but they aren't really sincere about it. True, they do not say so explicitly, but the message will probably get across in some other way. The tone of voice, apparent lack of interest or preferential treatment of another child will make the lack of sincerity obvious. And once the child senses that half-heartedness, the effect is no different than if it had been explicitly said.

Sincerity is the most important element in treating someone as a winner. You know it from your own experiences; you appreciate honest praise and encouragement, but you detest phoniness. Children are no less astute. They can detect insincerity and will respond in kind. They also see through phoniness and manipulation.

Some parents do not talk positively because they do not see positive qualities in their children. They cannot honestly say, "You are capable of big things." Because they want to be sincere but cannot, they are not positive at all.

These parents can try the following exercise: Consider the child's potential and take an inventory of his or her strengths. Write the ideas down on paper. As the list grows, it will become obvious that the child really is capable of big things. Now try talking to him or her about it — sincerely.

Praise good performance with enthusiasm. Suppose a child performs well and you say nothing. What message have you conveyed? Is the child a winner? If he is, how much of a winner is he? It is not clear.

Suppose you say, "Good" or "Okay" to the performance. What is the message now? The child knows that the performance is acceptable, but he doesn't know if it meets your high standards? Is the child a winner? Once again, it is not clear. You haven't supplied enough information.

Compare these weak responses with an enthusiastic one: "That's great! You did it! I'm so proud of you!" Now we can answer those questions. Yes, he is a winner. Yes, he met your high standards. The child will then be motivated to repeat the performance. And when you specifically describe the good parts of the performance, the message sounds more sincere and has even greater impact.

Offer encouragement. When a child is faltering and you encourage him or her to perform well, the message you are sending is, "I really care about your performance. I have confidence in you and believe that you can do well." Such a message can have a powerful effect on a child who is struggling.

Never give up on a child; believe that each one has hidden potential. If a child is shy, draw him out. If his self-esteem is low, build it up. If a child shows weak progress, help strengthen it. And when a child needs help, give him 100% of your attention.

Even if a child is not competent in certain areas, but he thinks he is, support him. Don't tell him what you really think; it would crush him. Build his self-confidence by supporting his fantasies of competence. He may begin to improve.

Enforce your expectations. Parents may expect the best, but if they don't hold the child accountable, what message will he get?

Tuvia was a cooperative ten-year-old boy. He got along nicely with his brother Eli and always shared his toys with him.

One day he suddenly became uncooperative. His parents wanted to see Tuvia play nicely with his brother and talked to him about their expectations.

The next day, Eli came crying to his father because Tuvia wasn't sharing. His father wanted him to stop crying, so he gave Eli another toy to play with. He then gave Tuvia a gentle reminder of his expectation.

The next day Eli came again with the same problem. His father quickly gave him a candy to get him to stop crying, and again he reminded Tuvia of his expectation.

This went on for weeks, but Tuvia did not improve. A friend advised the father to avoid the easy solution by confronting Tuvia and inducing him to share his toys — in other words, *enforcing* the expectation. He did this, and eventually the fighting stopped.

At first Tuvia was getting a mixed message. On one hand, he heard his father say he had to share. On the other hand, the order was not enforced. Tuvia deduced that if his father did not push him to share, it was not so important. He did not relate to the spoken message — "Share." Rather, he related to the unspoken message — "It is not so important to share."

But at the end, Tuvia's father began to enforce his words. Both the spoken and unspoken messages became identical. Tuvia knew that sharing was important and so he improved.

Parents can expect the best, but if they do not enforce the expectation in action, it loses its effect. The enforcement tells the child how important the standard is, and that there is a difference between upholding it and ignoring it.

Attribute success to skill, not luck. When a child succeeds at a task — whether it is solving a problem, passing a test, winning a ball game or creating a Purim masquerade outfit — don't say, "You did that nicely. You are so lucky." Attributing success to luck is another way of saying, "You don't have the skills. You aren't really capable of succeeding unless an outside force intercedes for you." The low expectation is obvious.

Instead say, "You did that so well. I always knew you had the skills to do such a good job." This says that you expect good things from the child because he has the *ability* to succeed.

Don't play favorites. Several pages ago, we saw how Mr. Schwartz favored Tzvi over Moshe. He assessed his sons' abilities and concluded that Tzvi was more interested in Torah scholarship than Moshe, so he gave him more attention and encouragement without even realizing it. Not only did Moshe feel jealous, he began to experience failures in other areas, too. As a result, he deteriorated.

Parents often favor one child over another. Sometimes they realize it, but most times they don't. When parents play favorites, they send the message: "I don't expect this one to do as well as that one. That one is better than this one." The less-favored child senses that his position is lower and feels that his parents are discriminating against him. In addition to suffering jealousy, he will not reach his potential.

Frequently, one child *is* actually more capable than another. If parents were to treat them equally, they would be addressing the needs of neither. The stronger one would not develop quickly enough, and the weaker one would feel unreasonably challenged.

Nevertheless, parents can treat both children fairly and without preference. The answer is to give equal attention and encouragement, treating each child as a winner *in his or her own right.* Although the level of challenge may be different for each, both will sense that they are expected to do their best, and both will try to meet their parents' expectations.

Chapter Seven

Motivate With Constructive Criticism

The word "criticism" typically has a negative connotation. It conjures up thoughts of hurt feelings, scolding and nit-picking. A person who criticizes is regarded as a faultfinder, someone who is looking for deficiencies to point out. Criticism is so frequently used in unpopular ways, is it any wonder that it has such an unpopular reputation?

Yet the Torah requires us to offer *tochachah* — rebuke, a strong form of criticism — to other people.[1] Does this mean that we are supposed to find fault, nit-pick, scold and hurt people's feelings? Surely not. That would violate another prohibition.[2]

Rather, the Torah's concept of criticism is constructive and beneficial. It is supposed to create peace and stronger relations, not resentment.[3] It is supposed to be positive and motivational, not negative and demoralizing. It flows from love, not tension. Criticism does not have to be critical.

---

1. *Vayikra* 19:17.
2. *Vayikra* 25:17.
3. *Sefer HaChinuch, mitzvah* 239 and *Sifri, Devorim* 1:1.

In its pure form, criticism is benign. It is simply the act of pointing out another person's faults. What is wrong with that? Every Torah-observant Jew is supposed to seek improvement, which must sometimes come through the observations of others.

These observations, however, can be either constructive or destructive. Constructive criticism has the recipient's welfare in mind and is corrective in both the short- and long-term. It leaves the recipient with his self-esteem intact, and it also leaves him feeling good about the criticizer.[1] Destructive criticism, on the other hand, causes the recipient to lose respect for himself. It is usually not corrective and may not even have the recipient's welfare in mind. As a motivational technique, we are only concerned with the constructive approach.

Criticism can be given on various levels. On a low level, it is a casual reminder or a gentle nudge. On a high level, it is a tough reprimand. There are many levels in between. The principles in this chapter apply to all levels.

The Necessity of Criticism

Parents must offer constructive criticism to their children. King Shlomo, the wisest of men, said that constructive criticism is the cornerstone of successful child-rearing. Used properly, it prepares a child for a successful life.

> A wise son is the product of a father's instruction, and a scorner is the product of not hearing rebuke[2] (*Mishlei* 13:1).
>
> The one who withholds his rod hates his son, and the one who loves him instructs him early[3] (*Mishlei* 13:24).

King Dovid was censured for not reprimanding his son Avshalom. Because he received no rebuke, Avshalom went on to live a life of depravity. He became one of Dovid's greatest antagonists and even wanted to kill him.[4]

---

1. Ibid.
2. Translation follows Vilna Gaon.
3. Translation follows Ralbag.
4. *Midrash Rabbah, Shemos* 1:1.

What if a child is obstinate? Should parents give up hope? No, never. They should ignore the child's unyielding manner and continue to offer constructive criticism:

> Instruct your son because there is hope, and do not pay attention to his cries[1] (*Mishlei* 19:18).

Constructive criticism is so important that it is better to show hate — which is undoubtedly not ideal — than not to criticize at all:

> A person who rebukes his friend by speaking harshly to him, informing him of the truth and displaying hate in his words — this person is better than the one with hidden love, who loves his friend deep in his heart but does not rebuke him for the things he sees in him (Rabbeinu Bachya, beginning of *Nitzavim,* explaining *Mishlei* 27:5).

Children should accept constructive criticism. Hearing one's shortcomings and learning how to improve is the stepping stone to wisdom and success in life.[2] One should be very happy to hear as much constructive criticism as possible.[3]

> Listen to advice and accept instruction, so that you will be wise in your later years[4] (*Mishlei* 19:20).
>
> A fool despises the instruction of his father, and the one who retains rebuke will become wise[5] (*Mishlei* 15:5).
>
> The one who loves instruction loves knowledge, and the one who hates rebuke is a bore *(Mishlei* 12:1).
>
> For a *mitzvah* is a candle and Torah is light, and the way of life is [to take] instructional rebuke (*Mishlei* 6:23).

Rabbi Aharon Kotler went one step further. He said that accepting rebuke is more than a wise thing; it is an integral part of the *mitzvah* of *tochachah.* Just as people are obligated by the Torah to

---

1. Translation follows Rabbeinu Yonah.
2. Ralbag, *Mishlei* 15:5 and *Metzudas Dovid, Mishlei* 12:1.
3. *Orchos Chaim LeHarash* 45: "Be happy when you hear rebuke, as one who finds great plunder."
4. Rabbeinu Yonah commented that this statement is directed to children.
5. Translation follows *Metzudas Dovid.*

offer rebuke to those who need it, the ones who hear it are obligated to accept it.[1]

Constructive criticism is the greatest blessing. When our forefather Yaakov blessed his sons, he also pointed out their shortcomings. He reprimanded them and urged them to correct their ways. What kind of blessing is this?

Rabbi Chaim Mordechai Katz explained that the greatest blessing one can receive is the opportunity to improve faults. By informing his children of their faults, Yaakov gave them that blessing.[2]

Although criticism is so beneficial, people have an aversion to it. They do not like to be criticized even by individuals who are sincere and have their welfare in mind. If you were to ask a person if he wants constructive criticism, he would either refuse or say with a sigh, "Okay, if you have to. But let's get it over with quickly." It is the rare person who says, "Please tell me. I want to hear about my faults."

For this reason, King Shlomo probably made a considerable effort in *Mishlei* to describe the benefits of criticism. He was aware that people dislike it and wanted to convince them otherwise.

Since receiving constructive criticism is so beneficial, why do people shun it? Why don't they continually seek criticism and improvement? The answer to this question is vital. It is the key to using criticism as an effective motivational technique.

Why People Do Not Like to Be Criticized

Criticism, even in its most positive form, sends an unspoken message; "You are not good enough. You need improvement." This is stinging. It is an attack on the very essence of the person who receives it. Nobody likes hearing this kind of message, neither children nor adults.

The strongest force in a person's psyche is the drive to feel important and to be recognized as important.[3] People want to be recognized for their successes and attributes, not for their failures

---

1. *Mishnas Rabbi Aharon*, vol. 1, p. 242:4.

2. *Be'er Mechokek*, pp. 83-86.

3. *Mesilas Yesharim*, ch. 19. Also, see the beginning of the second chapter for a discussion of this point.

and misgivings. They have pride, and it hurts them to have a fault pointed out. They feel violated and become defensive.

Additionally, people do not see their own faults.[1] They believe that what they do is right, and when they make a mistake, their pride drives them to justify their actions. When someone calls attention to the mistake, their first instinct is to defend themselves.[2]

With this insight into human nature, it is not difficult to understand why people find any kind of criticism distasteful. But there is more.

Most people are set in their ways. They are naturally inclined to hold on to their ideas and opinions. When you introduce new ideas to them, you are working against that force, especially if your suggestions are contrary to their current positions. It is very hard for them to see, let alone appreciate, your point of view.

> All the ways of man are straight in his eyes (*Mishlei* 21:2).
>
> It is natural for a person to see all of his traits as pure, whether they are good or bad; therefore, correcting traits is very difficult (Rabbeinu Yonah, *Mishlei* 16:2).

Because people are so set in their ways, King Shlomo made an unpopular suggestion. He advised that we minimize our verbal exchanges with other people. The reason is that if the other person offends us during a conversation, we are forbidden to pretend that we are not hurt and act as if nothing happened. Torah principles require that we say something. But herein lies the problem — if we tell the other that his remarks were offensive, he will accuse us of being misguided and irrational. He will reject our reproof because he is set in his ways, convinced that his actions are meritorious. He may even begin to dislike us. To avoid this "no-win" situation, the best policy is to minimize verbal exchanges with others.[3]

Another reason people resist criticism is that they experience

---

1. Talmud *Kesubos* 105b.
2. Rabbi Eliyahu Dessler, *Michtav M'Eliyahu*, vol. 4, p. 244.
3. Vilna Gaon, *Mishlei* 10:18-19.

emotional pain when they become aware of an error.[1] To avoid this pain, they become defensive and resistant.

Chazal tell us yet another reason people reject criticism. Everybody has faults — and they are not hard to find. Thus, whenever a person gives criticism, there is a credibility gap. The recipient's reaction is; "What right do you have to point out *my* faults. *You* have a *greater* fault." The recipient will probably then disregard everything the criticizer says — even if the points are valid.[2]

A person with an undeveloped or negative self-image may find criticism even more difficult to accept. Because he already feels rejected and inferior, criticism, even valid and constructive, only serves to intensify those feelings. To protect himself from the pain, he defends himself by saying, "I didn't do anything wrong."

People who have a need for control or independence also reject criticism of any kind. Similarly, children who engage in power struggles with their parents will consistently reject the parents' criticism. In their minds, accepting criticism represents submission and compliance — and that is against their nature. Their reaction is, "You can't tell me what to do."[3]

Recognizing people's natural aversion to criticism, the first rule Dale Carnegie put forth in his classic work on making friends and influencing people is: "Do not criticize." This may be a good suggestion for the person who wants to have a superficial relationship, but a deep relationship includes some constructive criticism, too. And, as we previously mentioned, a parent/child relationship *requires* it. For this reason, we have to find a way to enhance our children's receptivity to constructive correction.

Developing a Strategy to Enhance Receptivity

Just as you prepare a meal when you have people who will eat it — otherwise, the food will go to waste — you should only offer criticism to a child who is receptive and ready, to some degree, to

---

1. Rabbi Chaim Shmulevitz, cited by Rabbi Z. Pliskin, *Growth Through Torah*, Benei Yaakov Publications, 1988, pp. 67-68.

2. Talmud *Arachin* 16b.

3. See Maharal, *Avos* 4:9: People hold on to their opinions when they are emotionally invested in them.

accept it. Otherwise, your remarks will go to waste. In fact, if you think your criticism will go to waste, it is a *mitzvah* to say nothing.[1]

To be effective, then, parents should first break down, or at least reduce, the natural resistance their children have to criticism. How can parents do this? How can parents make criticism more palatable and kindle in their children a desire to improve? How can parents minimize resistance and maximize cooperation?

The best strategy takes into account the child's "resistance buttons." The challenge is to discover what those buttons are and to learn how to push them. We just talked about some natural resistance buttons. Now we will discuss the important topic of pushing them.

The first step in our strategy is to use constructive criticism for the purpose it was devised — to correct mistakes.

Constructive Criticism Is Corrective

You want to bring out the best in your children. Therefore, when you see them making a mistake, you try to motivate them to improve. One way of motivating is simply to point out the problem and tell them how to correct it. This is the essence of constructive criticism.

Constructive criticism, used properly, is a corrective measure. It is not a protest against an unacceptable action, nor is it a way of venting personal displeasure over a child's undesirable behavior. It clarifies.[2] And it has a purpose — to bring about change. Constructive criticism is a *means* to an end, not an end in itself.

> This is the concept of rebuke: to motivate a person to fulfill his responsibilities to follow the *mitzvos* of Hashem ... The *mitzvah* of rebuke has one condition — that the rebuker senses that his words are accepted, and that his words should help the recipient do *teshuvah* for his

---

1. Talmud *Yevamos* 65b: "Just as it is a *mitzvah* to say something that will be heard, it is a *mitzvah* not to say something that will not be heard." See also Rabbi Chaim Mordechai Katz, cited later on this page; *Shulchan Aruch, Orach Chaim* 608:2; and *Be'ur Halachah* there.

2. See Rashi, *Bereishis* 20:16; *tochachas* means clarification.

> wrongdoings. If the rebuker senses that his words are not accepted, the *mitzvah* of rebuke is not upon him. The *mitzvah* of rebuke is not for the sake of the rebuker, so that he can protest when he sees wrong being done, but for the sake of the recipient, so that he will change his ways (Rabbi Chaim Mordechai Katz, *Be'er Mechokek,* p. 257).

Rebuke is for the sake of the recipient. It is a form of *chesed* which aims to help others depart from their misdirected ways.[1]

A parent criticizing a child constructively is like a doctor performing surgery on a patient. While both are invasive and cause pain, they are also corrective. They are acts of love which consider the sensitivities of the recipients. They should leave the recipients appreciating the opportunity for an improved life.

Focus on the solution. To be corrective, parents cannot simply tell the child what he or she has done wrong; they also have to explain what the correct thing is and how to do it.[2] The major focus should be on the solution, not on the problem. This is the difference between criticizing and being critical.

Some parents, however, forget this obvious point. They get caught up in their feelings of anger or disappointment and criticize the child for the mistake without explaining how to correct it.

> Mayer, six years old, filled his cup to the brim with milk. When he lifted the cup to drink, he spilled some milk on his freshly laundered clothes. His mother was upset because the accident could easily have been avoided. She felt that Mayer was foolish for filling his cup so high, and she said in an excited tone, "Mayer, look what you did! You spilled the milk on your clean clothes! Can't you be more careful?"

Mayer's mother was not helpful. She focused on the problem, not on the solution. She offered no instruction, and as a result, Mayer had no idea how to improve.

Unless Mayer was trying to be mischievous, his mistake was innocent and unintentional. He is young and may not have asso-

---

1. Rabbi Aharon Kotler, *Mishnas Rabbi Aharon,* vol.1, p. 242:3.
2. *Mishlei* 12:18, following the Vilna Gaon.

ciated a full cup with the possibility of spilling. Or he simply forgot. Therefore, instead of condemning him, Mayer's mother should have taught him how to pour milk and motivated him to do it properly the next time. She should have said gently, "You spilled the milk because your cup was filled to the top. If you leave some room at the top, it won't spill as easily."

If she feels that Mayer would be open to another lesson, she may go one step further and relate his behavior to the *middos* of care and responsibility. She might add, "Pouring this way is a careful and responsible thing to do."

To highlight the solution, his mother could have Mayer practice pouring milk into a cup several times. This would also demonstrate her support and confidence in him.

In the revised scenario, Mayer's mother is *con*structive by being *in*structive. Mayer is now aware of the problem, and more importantly, he has a solution. Hopefully, he will do it correctly the next time.

Be specific. In the revised scenario, Mayer's mother was specific. She pointed to the exact problem and solution. There was no room for confusion.

Similarly, if a child is doing poorly in school, it is not a good idea to say, "I am not satisfied with your work. Please improve." This is not specific enough. Say instead, "I am not satisfied with the 65% you received on your last test. If you study ten minutes more every night, I'm sure you will do better." There is no room for confusion now. Specificity also shows the child that you are on top of the situation.

Focusing on the problem may create more problems. In Mayer's first scenario, his mother was non-corrective and problem-oriented. By highlighting the problem, she came across as critical and condemning. She offended Mayer and hurt his feelings, making him the victim of an attack rather than the recipient of constructive assistance. Focusing on problems usually has this kind of result, to some degree or another.

Now, even if someone offers Mayer a solution or he thinks of one himself, he may *choose* not to improve at this point. His mother offended him, and in retaliation, he may intentionally be uncooperative.

If Mayer, in addition, has an emotional need for control, especially if he and his mother already struggle for power, his resistance may be even sharper. To him, improving is synonymous with submission. It means surrendering his control to his mother, and he will certainly not do that.

Who knows? Mayer may not retaliate by spilling the milk again; he may choose to offend his mother in another way on another day. He may condemn her for one of her mistakes, just as she condemned him. He may fight with her about an unrelated issue. He may refuse to fulfill a responsibility or simply disregard one of her requests. Whatever it is, the intent is the same — retaliation.

An adult behaves the same way. When someone hurts him, he wants to "get back." Some people will take the aggressive path by being abusive to the offender. Others are more passive; they resist the offender by disregarding him and rejecting his leadership. And if they have an emotional need for control, especially if they already have a poor relationship with the offender, their reaction may be even more severe.

No matter what path Mayer chooses, one thing is certain; his self-esteem has been affected by his mother's reaction. Mayer looks up to his mother and takes her word seriously. When she implies that he is careless, he believes it. And if his mother continually treats him this way, Mayer may develop serious emotional problems.

Another thing is even more certain — Mayer's mother offended him, and he does not feel good about it. As a result, he probably has negative feelings toward her.

Some parents ignore this issue. They say, "What's the difference if he doesn't like me? My job is to instruct him and motivate him to be a responsible human being. I'm not competing in a popularity contest." These parents do not realize that a poor relationship impairs their ability to instruct and motivate. Later in the chapter we will discuss this point.

There may be one more consequence. Because Mayer has seen his mother react strongly to a minor mishap, he will not learn to distinguish between the value of minor and major mishaps. As he matures, he too will react strongly to minor mishaps.

We have mentioned a number of consequences brought about by Mayer's mother. Certainly, one critical remark is not going to create *all* these problems; however, it will create *some* problems, to *some* degree. If Mayer's mother becomes more positive — and the sooner, the better — he will bounce back. But if she continues in a negative pattern, especially if she begins to criticize more severely, the general atmosphere will deteriorate and these problems will become a realistic threat.

Let's analyze what happened. Mayer made a mistake; he spilled a few cents' worth of milk. His mother hurt him by being critical and condemning. Depending on the frequency and severity of her remarks — past, current and future — she may have caused one or all of the following: resentment, retaliation, lowered self-esteem, distorted judgment of the severity of mishaps, a weakened relationship, and a more intense power struggle. All of these will continually reduce her ability to be effective with Mayer in the future. And after all this trouble, Mayer may still not pour his milk properly!

Focusing on the problem doesn't help. It is a negative action and has negative results. It may cause more problems than there were in the first place.

Be corrective and sensitive. What if Mayer's mother corrected him, but in the same condemning tone? "Mayer," she might say, "Look what you did! You spilled milk on your clean clothes! Can't you be more careful? You know, if you leave some room at the top of the cup, it won't spill as easily." Now that she has attached a correction to her condemnation, will Mayer be more receptive?

No one can predict. If Mayer's threshold of sensitivity is high, he may brush off the condemnation and accept the suggestion. But if his threshold is low, he may still resent the implication that he is careless. Although his mother is giving him a solution, she is still attacking him and hurting his pride. After being put down, he may not even *hear* the solution; and if he does, he may reject it.

Constructive criticism means not only telling the child about his mistake and how to correct it — it means getting through to him. And the way to get through is to be sensitive to his feelings. Make him feel good about himself and about you, and the scene will be set for acceptance — which is the end goal of constructive criticism.

Earlier we asked, "How can parents minimize resistance and maximize cooperation?" The first element of the strategy is to be corrective. The second is to be sensitive to the child's feelings.

Sensitivity to the Child's Feelings

Criticism does not have to be a devastating experience for either the parents or the child. Parents can reduce the sting by adopting the proper attitude and choosing the right words and the right time and place. This means that they cannot say *what* they want *whenever* they want. Rather, they have to be aligned with their children's personalities and sensitive to their needs and emotions.

Parents have to be careful not to say anything that will reduce morale or hinder motivation. Therefore, before speaking, they should consider these points:

Does the action warrant my response?

Will my response help or hinder?

Should I respond verbally or non-verbally?

Exactly what should I say?

When should I say it?

What tone of voice should I use?

How can I offer the correction and let the child save face at the same time?

Children should walk away from criticism with their self-confidence intact, motivated to improve. If they walk away feeling defensive, condemned, violated, broken spirited, unmotivated to improve or unsure of their parents' support, it is an indication that the parents may have been insensitive to their feelings.

Your goal is to motivate your child to improve, but you must overcome some obstacles first. These consist of the natural resistances your child has, even before you begin to speak. You can bypass the obstacles by being sensitive to his or her needs and feelings, or you can create more obstacles by being insensitive. Obviously, you want to do it right. Following are some guidelines.

Criticize the action, not the person. Every human being is comprised of his or her *person* and *actions.* The *person* includes the ego, emotions, tendencies, capabilities, sensitivities, innate talents, etc. The *actions* include performances and behaviors, past and present.

Don't target a child's *person* in a negative way; that would be an unnecessary put-down. Rather, target the child's *action,* which is the object of your disapproval, and let him or her save face. You are unhappy with the *action*, not the *person*. Separating them will save the child unnecessary pain. For example:

Don't say: Peninah, you failed another test. I know the reason. You don't study. You are so lazy! What are we going to do with you?

Say instead: Peninah, I see that you received another failing grade. You are smart and capable of passing. If you study harder, you will do well.

The first approach targets Peninah's *person* in a negative way. She does not appreciate being devalued and will feel a need to defend herself. She may oppose her parents and reject their criticism.

In the second approach, her parents also talk about Peninah's person, but they do so positively and non-offensively. They say that she is capable and will do better with more studying. The second approach targets Peninah's *action*. She will feel better about herself because her parents have confirmed her value as a person. They are focused on improving the performance, not the *person*, which will enable her to respond with less resistance. Although she may defend herself, she has less of a need to do so since her parents have let her save face and have left her personal value intact.

For the parents, targeting the *person* reduces the effectiveness of their admonition. But for the child, the negative effects are even greater. First of all, it reduces her self-esteem. A child looks up to her parents and believes what they say. If they tell her that she is lazy, she will believe them and will begin to have less respect for herself. The damaging effects of a negative self-concept are innumerable.

Putting a negative focus on the person has another contrary effect: the child begins to live up to the label. When parents tell a child she is lazy, she unconsciously becomes lazier and lazier. Haim Ginott, a popular child psychologist, said that a parent who attaches labels disables.

Children are whole people. They don't consist only of their current actions. Effective parents manage their children as whole beings by keeping their total welfare in mind. This means that they consider both the *action* and the *person* whenever they address a child. There is a big difference between saying, "You have failed three times" and "You are a failure."

In a previous chapter, we mentioned a successful business manager who imagines signs on the foreheads of her employees that read, "Make Me Feel Important." In an effort to do so, she carefully thinks through everything she says before beginning to speak. Even when she gives criticism, she makes sure to address the employees' performances, not their persons. Her employees appreciate her style and respond with increased productivity.

You can use this strategy, too. Picture your children with signs on their foreheads that read, "Make Me Feel Important." Let them save face and make them feel important by being sensitive to their feelings and giving them value. Remind them of all their wonderful traits and abilities. Tell them how much they can improve if they only try. Yes, show them their mistake; but be clear and specific about the errors, and show them how to improve. Maintain the children's value by talking positively about each one's *person.* They will feel assured of your support, knowing that you still value them as people, and they will reciprocate by being more cooperative.

Consider each child's individual personality. You can neither change a child's nature — the *person* — nor break it. A child's nature remains with him or her permanently. The Vilna Gaon put it succinctly:

> "Train a child according to his way, and it will not depart from him when he becomes old" (*Mishlei* 22:6) ... It is impossible for a person to break his way, i.e., his *mazal* ... but he is given the choice to hold onto his *mazal* and maintain it as he wants. He can be a righteous person, an evil person or a person in between ... "Train a child according to his way" means: train him and guide him to do *mitzvos* according to his *mazal* and nature, so then "when he becomes old, your instruction will not depart from him." But when you force him against his nature, he will listen to you now out of fear, but afterwards when your yoke is removed from his neck, he will break away from it, because it is impossible for him to break his *mazal* (Vilna Gaon, ad loc.).

Rabbi Shlomo Wolbe commented on this:

> These words are amazingly clear, that we may not go against the nature and character of children. The work of training children is to preserve their nature and character for the good. It is obligatory on parents to understand the character of their children so that they will know how to direct their training, because it is impossible to train all children with one method (*Alai Shur*, p. 263).

Rabbi Wolbe's words are also amazingly clear. When you criticize children, be sensitive to their individual natures. Tailor your comments for each one's personality.[1] You may even decide that criticism is inappropriate for a particular child or event. Become acquainted and align yourself with each child. Don't ignore his nature or say that it is *his* problem. Let's illustrate this point.

> Yanki H., nine years old, is independent and likes to be in control. His parents get the feeling that he wants to be "king of the world." Yanki's father is a tough disciplinarian, and they have been locked in a power struggle for a long time. When Yanki misbehaves, Mr. H. forcefully reprimands him. Yanki yells back and is sent to his room. Although Yanki's behavior does not change, Mr. H. is convinced that his approach is correct.
>
> Mrs. H. has tried to convince her husband to change styles by explaining that Yanki does not respond to reprimand. He has a need to be in control, and when criticized, he becomes agitated and disregards the reproof altogether.
>
> Mr. H., however, is adamant and justifies himself: "In this family, misbehavior is not tolerated. Yanki knows what is expected, and he has no reason not to comply. If he wants to control this family by disregarding me, that's *his* problem. As his father, I *must* do the right thing and correct him."

---

1. See Rabbi Yeruchom Levovitz, *Daas Torah, Shemos* 19:3. See also Vilna Gaon on *Mishlei* 16:4; *Midrash Rabbah, Bamidbar* 21:15; and Rabbi S. R. Hirsch, *Yesodos HaChinuch*, pp. 55-56.

Indeed, Yanki's need for control is his problem. However, it is also his father's. It is causing them to "lock horns," and as long as it does, Mr. H. will be doing his job ineffectively. One of them has to take the initiative to change his style — and it won't be nine-year-old Yanki.

Mr. H. should begin to consider Yanki's personality. He should realize that he cannot treat him the same way that other parents treat their children or even the same way he treats his other children. Yanki is different. He has his own personality and his own emotional needs.

Mr. H. should first recognize Yanki's need for control. Then he should plan a way to correct Yanki without stripping him of all control. He should stop reprimanding Yanki and begin to use a lighter form of criticism, speaking to his son with more respect and letting him do more talking. He should encourage Yanki to explain why he misbehaves and invite him to devise a solution. He should also give him choices. Giving choices is especially useful with children such as Yanki.[1]

Once Mr. H. begins working *with* Yanki, rather than *against* him, the tension will probably ease. Yanki will feel respected and more in control. And if Mr. H. really changes his style, he will start to be more positive by praising, rewarding and treating Yanki as a winner.

Yanki would definitely appreciate this. He would not feel violated, and even more important, he would feel valued. The relationship would improve and Yanki would become more cooperative. By being sensitive to Yanki's individual personality, Mr. H. could minimize resistance and maximize cooperation.

For various reasons, many children do not respond well to criticism. Some are extremely sensitive; they are easily insulted and cry at the slightest criticism. If you severely reprimand such children, you lose them. Instead, use a light form of rebuke and emphasize all that you appreciate about them.

Some children are stubborn. They have no interest in changing and disregard any attempt to bring about change. You cannot coerce these children to accept your "edicts" because, as the Vilna Gaon

---

1. See the fifth chapter for a full discussion on the topic of choices.

said, they will break away as soon as they can. Instead, use persuasion and salesmanship to make an impression. See the chapter on persuasion for strategies.

Some children are argumentative. They argue with anyone who tries to influence them to change. Don't become offended, and don't punish them for being so difficult. Give them all the time they need to say what they want. Show sympathy and respect. Assure them that you are on their side. Let the argument pass.

Some children have low self-esteem. They protect their tender emotions by justifying all their actions. Be especially careful not to put these children down; not only does a put-down intensify resistance, it constitutes real emotional abuse. Demonstrate your support and confidence in them by smothering them with love and emphasizing their attributes.

How can you discover each child's character? By observing them involved in independent activities.[1] Watch how they approach their goals and deal with challenges. After learning about them, you can decide on the strategy most suitable to each child.

You can also read Miriam Adahan's book, *Appreciating People — Including Yourself,* which categorizes and describes common personalities. Knowing which category your child falls into can be very useful in dealing with him or her.

Treat the child with respect. Treating children with respect makes them feel important. To be a successful motivator, you have to make children feel important. Therefore, you have to respect children before you can motivate them.

The *Sh'lah* explained a point in *Mishlei* with this concept:

> "Do not rebuke a scorner lest he hate you; rebuke a wise person and he will love you" (*Mishlei* 9:8). When you rebuke another person, do not degrade or insult him by saying, "You are a scorner," because he will hate you and will not listen to you. But "rebuke a wise person" and say to him, "You are so wise. Why are you doing this?" and he will love you and listen to you (*Sh'lah,* cited in *Chovas HaTalmidim,* ch. 1).

---

1. Rabbi S. R. Hirsch, *Yesodos HaChinuch,* p. 55.

The *Sh'lah* is telling us that we have to treat all children with respect. Even if you think a particular child is "difficult" and does not deserve it, respect him anyway. Relate to him as a wise person, as if he is already on the level you want him to reach. He will like you and will cooperate with you. But if you treat him disrespectfully, he will hate you and reject everything you say.

Giving respect is functional and utilitarian. It is at the core of any good strategy, the key that unlocks the doors of cooperation and receptivity. Everything else is "just commentary."

But giving respect is more than that. Even if parents have nothing to gain in return, they should respect their children at least as much as they would any other deserving human being. Here is a story that illustrates the point:

Rabbi Isser Zalman Meltzer, a brilliant Torah scholar and the venerable Rosh Yeshiva of the Eitz Chaim Yeshiva in Jerusalem, was testing a group of thirteen-year-old students on their Talmudic studies. He asked one student to explain a certain *Tosafos*, but the student gave the wrong answer. Rabbi Meltzer did not want to embarrass the boy by telling him directly that he made a mistake, so he asked him, "Maybe this is what you meant?" and proceeded to give the proper explanation. The boy answered, "No, that is not what I meant," and repeated his wrong explanation. Rabbi Meltzer then explained the *Tosafos* in an easier way and said to the boy, "Maybe this is what you meant?" But the boy insisted on his own explanation. For ten minutes Rabbi Meltzer patiently explained the correct explanation, but the boy kept repeating his mistake.

Rabbi Meltzer then excused himself and went into another room. He said to himself, "Showing respect to other people also applies to children. Showing respect to other people also applies to children." After repeating this several times to himself, he returned to the students. He sat down, turned to the boy with amazing gentleness, and said once again, "Please tell me how you will now explain the *Tosafos.*" He reopened the conversation, hoping to help the boy understand the *Tosafos* properly.[1]

---

1. *Bederech Eitz HaChayim*, vol. 1, p. 211, cited in Rabbi Z. Pliskin, *Growth Through Torah*, p. 34.

When *Chazal* talk about the importance of honoring others, they certainly do not exclude children:

> Honor others the way you honor yourself (*Avos* 2:10).
>
> The honor you have for others should be the same as the fear you have of your Rebbe (*Avos* 4:12).
>
> Having a "good eye" means that one is not jealous of his friend, and his friend's honor is as dear to him as his own (Rashi, *Avos* 5:19).

The Rambam wrote that a person is not permitted to degrade his gentile slave with gestures or words. He may not yell at the slave too much or become excessively angry with him. He must speak gently with him and listen to all his complaints.[1] Certainly, our own children should not be treated with any less respect!

Yet many parents feel comfortable talking to their children without respect or sensitivity. They growl and yell at their children. They put their children down or treat them like babies. They would never dream of talking to neighbors or guests in the same way. These parents are making a grave (both meanings intended) mistake, because the prohibition of hurting others with words[2] applies to children, too.[3]

Don't overpreach, overlecture or overadvise. Some parents make every occasion an opportunity to moralize and teach a lesson. They elaborate on their message until they feel it has been thoroughly exhausted.

> Mrs. S. is a very dedicated parent. She wants her children to learn responsibility and develop good attitudes.
>
> When her daughter Nechama accidently spilled a bucket of mop water, she told her how to avoid it the next time and gave her a speech about the importance of being careful. When Nechama came home from school late, Mrs. S. reminded her that she must come home on time

1. *Yad HaChazakah*, Laws of Servants 9:8.
2. *Vayikra* 25:17.
3. Rabbi S. Wagschal, *Successful Chinuch*, Feldheim Publishers, p. 41.

> and then lectured her on the importance of responsibility. Whenever Nechama made a mistake, she was in for a lesson and a speech.
>
> After a while, Mrs. S. sensed that Nechama was not listening to her lectures. She realized there was a problem when Nechama began to argue with her. Mrs. S. could not understand why Nechama, who had never been a difficult child, was being so unreasonable.

At first, Nechama was able to tolerate the speeches, but as time went on she began to feel "preached at." She didn't want to be lectured every time she made a mistake, and she took offense at the unspoken message her mother was sending each time: "Listen to me. I am much more experienced than you. I know something you don't know." Nechama felt that her mother was looking down on her. She felt insulted and devalued, and she became resistant. She thought, "I'm not a baby. She has no right to put me down that way." The normally cooperative Nechama had become "difficult."

Although Mrs. S. was correct in everything she said, the cost of saying it was too great. She caused resentment and created a new obstacle to her daughter's cooperation. She ruined a healthy relationship and reduced the chances of being effective in all her future motivational attempts.

While preaching and moralizing is instructional and has a benefit, using it excessively is unproductive. Had Mrs. S. simply mentioned the problem and solution and left it at that, she would have been more effective.

Don't criticize in public. Public embarrassment is a profound violation of a person's pride. It is the most insensitive thing one can do to another human being. Public embarrassment is so severe that *Chazal* compare it to murder.[1]

While the Torah requires us to give *tochachah*, it categorically forbids public *tochachah*.[2] This means that parents should not hit, yell, admonish or criticize their children in any form when they are outside the house or in view of other people. If you are on the

1. Talmud *Bava Metziah* 58b.
2. Talmud *Arachin* 16b and Rashi there.

street, on a bus, in a store, or in the house when guests are present — use gestures to convey disapproval. But save the reproof for a private setting.

Some experts even recommend removing a child from his siblings before admonishing him. This will save him from being embarrassed in front of them.

Don't use fear tactics. Fear, which serves as a natural barrier between parents and children, is an important element in any healthy parent/child relationship. In fact, children are required to fear their parents.[1] Furthermore, parents may use the fear of a penalty to motivate children to improve.[2]

All this is true as long as it is not in excess. Excessive fear is neither required nor healthy. It is abusive, and in the long run ineffective.

> Mr. L. drives his children to do their best in household chores, school work and personal conduct. If they perform poorly, he punishes them and threatens more of the same. While they are performing, he reminds them of the consequences of failure.
>
> Lately, the children have been defiant. They say, "We don't care. You can punish us." They also avoid Mr. L.'s company; when he is in the house, they find a reason to leave. In school they are developing behavior problems, too.
>
> Mr. L. believes he is performing his duties appropriately. His job is to motivate his children. This is the way his father motivated him, and he believes that the same treatment is effective with his children, too. He is aware of the recent developments but he does not associate them with his own behavior.

The children resent their father's fear tactics. They see it as manipulation and have decided not to tolerate it any longer. They have also lost respect for him. They are unhappy at home and unhappy with themselves, so it is no wonder that they misbehave in school.

---

1. *Vayikra* 19:3.
2. Rabbi Eliyahu Dessler, *Michtav M'Eliyahu*, vol. 4, p. 228.

Too much fear is detrimental. It ruins relationships and causes rebellion[1] and emotional maladjustment. For this reason, parents are forbidden to create a home atmosphere permeated with fear.[2]

Avoid anger. Anger is one of the most disdained traits in the gamut of human characteristics. It is equated with idol worship[3] and is cited as a cause of Torah scholars losing their knowledge.[4] Articles, chapters and even entire books have been written on this subject.[5]

Halachah forbids parents to motivate their children while angry, but they are permitted to put on a *show* of anger.

The Rambam suggests a method. First, remove all emotions of anger from your system. Then enter into a relaxed state of mind. After you feel relaxed and in control, put an angry expression on your face and say what needs to be said.[6]

But if you feel angry — even a little — don't say anything, because while angry, you are emotional and not in control. Stop immediately. Wait until you feel relaxed and in control. Otherwise, your words and actions will flow from your negative emotion and will lose their greatest effect.

"But," you say, "how can I just say nothing? The child misbehaved and must be reprimanded." Yes, he must be reprimanded, and he will be. But not now.

Try to look at the "big picture." The life span of a person is about eighty years, and one delayed reaction will not have a devastating effect. However, one angry outburst *can* cause great damage to the child and to your relationship with him — damage so severe that it is very difficult to repair.

Consider the loss against the gain. When it comes to criticism, open your heart and close your mouth. Tell the child, "We will talk

---

1. Rabbi Shlomo Wolbe, *Alai Shur*, p. 261.

2. Talmud *Gittin* 6b: "A person is forbidden to put too much fear into his home, because there are many damaging effects from too much fear."

3. Talmud *Shabbos* 105b.

4. Talmud *Pesachim* 66b.

5. See *Sefer Erech Apayim* by Rabbi Avraham Yellin. See also Rambam, *De'os* 2:3; *Mishlei* 19:19; *Mesilas Yesharim*, ch. 11; *Orchos Tzadikim*, ch. 12; and *Alai Shur*, p. 260.

6. Rambam, *De'os* 2:3.

about this later." The child senses your concern and will know that the issue is not yet closed.

Give reasons. Children, like all people, want to know the reasons for the things they have to do and the benefit they will receive. With the information, they become motivated to fulfill those responsibilities. When they are not given the information, they may feel coerced. They may resent the parents' autocratic style and may even rebel.

Parents should not be autocratic, and children should have no reason to think they are. Everything parents expect their children to do should have a stated reason and value.[1] The children will then know that their parents are not acting out of whim or autocracy, and they will be more cooperative.

Five Reactions to Poor Behavior

The ideal way to handle the hurt and resistance associated with criticism is not to criticize at all. We cannot do that because it is often appropriate. But we can do the next best thing — criticize in a way that reduces the hurt *as much as possible.* Following are five approaches to reducing the negative impact of criticism.

The problem/solution approach. We discussed this approach earlier, the one where the parent addresses both the problem and the solution. The child is reminded of the problem and is told how to correct it. The parent is solution-oriented and sensitive to the feelings of the child.

The advantage of this approach is that it is corrective and focuses on the solution. However, it still contains a sting because it calls attention to the problem, and if the child's threshold of sensitivity is low, he may feel hurt. He may also become defensive. Rabbi Eliyahu Dessler suggests a solution to this problem:

> Do not criticize your friend in an open manner because he will become very defensive. All wrongdoers, even the worst murderers, in their hearts do not admit to their misdeeds (*Michtav M'Eliyahu,* vol. 4, p. 244).

---

1. Rabbi S. R. Hirsch, *Judaism Eternal,* vol. 1, p. 230.

When Moshe Rabbeinu rebuked the Jewish people, he did not talk about their mistakes in clear, specific terms; rather, he hinted at them indirectly, avoiding the embarrassment and other negative effects that ordinarily accompany rebuke.[1]

Be indirect. It sidesteps the resentment and defensiveness that direct criticism evokes. There are four ways of reacting indirectly. These approaches do not remove the sting totally — they reduce it *as much as possible.* We will now list the four approaches, in order of more direct to less direct.

Responding in the positive. In this approach, phrase everything in the positive. Mention *only* the solution and make no reference to the problem. Let us illustrate with the case of Mayer, the little boy who spilled the milk after filling his cup too high.

Using this approach, Mayer's mother would say, "When you leave some room at the top of the cup, you will be able to drink from it like a real professional." With this response she completely sidesteps the spilling issue by making no mention of the incident or its consequences. She doesn't even use the word, "spill." She is completely positive and solution-oriented.

She does *not* say, "If you leave room at the top, you won't spill any milk." While this comment is solution-oriented, it still alludes to the problem and retains a sting. But by phrasing everything in the positive, she reduces this sting.

It works best when the child does not already feel bad about a mistake he has previously made. For example:

> Pinchas finished his breakfast and announced that he was ready to go to school. His father noticed that his shirt was not tucked in and his shoelaces were not tied. He said, "Pinchas, you are looking great this morning. If you tuck your shirt in and tie your shoelaces, you will be fit for a wedding." Pinchas looked at himself, smiled and quickly put himself together.

Yes, Pinchas senses the problem. But up until now he was not aware of it and has not suffered a consequence for it. When his

---

1. Rashi, *Devarim* 1:1.

father suggests that he straighten himself out, he is not reminded of a hurtful event. He feels less of a sting and does not resist.

Refer to the problem indirectly. Once again, the parent sidesteps the problem by referring to it indirectly. Let's illustrate:

> Beresh is a sociable twelve-year-old boy. He likes to spend as much time as he can with his friends. Like most children, though, he sometimes makes fun of his friends and laughs at their mistakes.
>
> One day, Beresh made fun of another boy who could not answer a homework question. This was not an ordinary homework question; it was a point the teacher had discussed at great length that morning. Beresh said to the boy, "We spent all morning on this and you can't remember it! Where are your brains?"
>
> Beresh's father was standing nearby and heard this. He did not want to embarrass Beresh by taking him aside and talking to him right then. Later, at home, he sat down with Beresh and said, "I heard the conversation you had with your friend about the homework. I just want to tell you that the Torah forbids us to hurt people, even with words."
>
> Beresh quickly associated this with his earlier comment and put his head down in remorse. His father gave him an encouraging touch, reminded him that he loved him and walked away.

Had Beresh's father talked openly about the mistake, Beresh would have been more hurt. He may have even defended himself by saying, "It's not so bad. All the other kids do it." Since his father sidestepped the problem and referred to it indirectly, he weakened the sting and reduced the hurt.

Another way of reacting indirectly is to say, *"Es past nisht."* It means, "This is not for you. You are better than that. You are expected to live up to the high standards which you already have." It emphasizes that the behavior is not befitting a child of such high caliber.[1]

The "I feel" message is also indirect. When the child behaves inappropriately, you respond by discussing your *feelings,* not the

---

1. Rabbi Abraham Twerski, M.D., *Generation to Generation,* vol. 1, p. 15.

action or even the solution. Say, for example, "When you don't do as I ask, I feel that I am being ignored." The finger is pointed directly at your own feelings, not at the child.

The "and" message is another way of calling attention to a mistake indirectly. Let's illustrate.

> Duvi was doing poorly in school because of his careless attitude. When he finally passed a test, his parents encouraged him to do the same in all his subjects. They said, "You passed this test — you are obviously very capable, *and* by continuing your efforts you will do really well in all subjects."
>
> Duvi asked, "Do you really mean it? Do you really think I could do well in the other subjects, too?" They assured him that they were serious. He felt encouraged, and together with his parents, he worked out a program of improvement.

By telling Duvi that he could improve in the other subjects, his parents indirectly referred to the problem he was having in those subjects. They did this by using the "and" message; they attached words of encouragement to the original praise. With the "and" message, they built Duvi up and encouraged him to continue his progress.

We are all very familiar with the "but" message. This is where parents say, "You passed this one, but you are still failing in your other subjects. Now let's see you improve in those subjects, too." The "but" qualifies the praise. It directly calls attention to the problem and detracts from the original praise. The child may even doubt the credibility of the praise and think that it was only used as a lead-in to the criticism. As a result, he will not be as responsive. The "and" message, however, avoids this problem.

Here is another illustration of the "and" message:

> A student submits an assignment with pictures drawn on it. The teacher says in a friendly tone, "This picture is beautiful. Nobody could have done a better job. And if we were in art class, you certainly would be expected to submit such work."

The teacher then hands the assignment back to the student, who understands the message and returns to his seat to clean up his paper.

The positive comment that the teacher attached to the original praise sends an indirect message to the student: "Don't ever do this again." The teacher accomplishes this without reprimanding, and the student gets the hint and responds appropriately.

Reacting with gestures. A gesture, such as a "dirty" look, can convey a message of reproof without mentioning the problem or even the solution. The child understands the meaning of the gesture and will respond less defensively.

King Shlomo said that parents should not withhold the "rod of discipline" from their children.[1] Rabbi Shlomo Wolbe explained that there are two kinds of rods — harsh and gentle. A "harsh rod" refers to reprimand and physical punishment. A "gentle rod" refers to giving a look of anger or disappointment. Rabbi Wolbe prefers the "gentle rod" because it is the most effective.[2]

Successful teachers can attest to the effectiveness of the "gentle rod." Using it, they are able to control an entire class of children who want nothing more than to take all the control for themselves.

There are various forms of the "gentle rod." They include a severe look, an angry stare, a look of disappointment, a sigh, a tap on the desk, a snap of the fingers, raising the eyebrows, placing the hands on the hips, walking toward a child and standing in place, and placing a hand on the child's shoulder. Without uttering a word, a competent teacher is able to take control and avoid confrontations.

Avoid confrontations: that is the key. The reason the "gentle rod" is so effective is that it avoids confrontation. When a teacher orders or asks a child to be quiet, the dialogue frequently goes like this:

Student: Why are you picking on me? Chaim is also talking.

Teacher: You *were* talking, and I am *not* picking on you.

---

1. *Mishlei* 13:24: "The one who withholds his rod hates his son."
2. *Alai Shur*, p. 261.

Student: It's not fair. You're not being fair.

Teacher: It doesn't have to be fair. Now I don't want to hear you talking again.

What just happened? The teacher tried exercising control and unintentionally created a confrontation. It happens all the time, and each time, a little of the teacher's stature and control is lost. How can teachers avoid confrontations? How can they exercise a dignified control?

By using a "gentle rod." The teacher gives the student a look of anger or disappointment. If the student becomes defensive and says, "I didn't do anything," the teacher has no need to respond — she never said the student *did* do anything. If the student asks, "Why are you looking at me?" the teacher can simply reply, "You know the reason." There is no dialogue and no confrontation.

An angry look says, "You and I both know you are wrong. There will be no discussion about it, and it better stop *now.* A disappointed look says, "I am disappointed in you because I care about you, and I wish you would do better." Both responses are quiet and inoffensive, yet forceful; both enhance cooperation. All gestures share these qualities.

Both teachers and parents can apply the "gentle rod" of gestures. One word of caution: keep a straight face. One smile or giggle, and the child will sense that you are not completely sincere. He will not relate the gesture to its intended meaning, and you will never be able to use it again. If you are new at gesturing, make sure you can do it before you "perform." Practice first with someone else or in front of a mirror.

Reacting by saying nothing. Sometimes, the most sensitive and effective reaction is to say nothing at all. Of all our approaches, it is the most indirect. Let's call on Mayer, the boy who spilled the milk, to illustrate the approach — but first we will modify his story. After he spilled the milk, this is what happened:

> Mayer looked at the spill with a distressed look on his face. Noticing his reaction, his mother gently gave him a sponge to wipe up the milk and checked to see if he needed clean clothes. Mayer cleaned up the spill and refilled his

> cup properly. He looked at his mother and smiled. His eyes said, "Thank you for not saying anything." She softly smiled back and continued her work.

Noticing Mayer's reaction, his mother surmised that he was also upset and would do whatever he could to avoid a recurrence. If so, why say anything? Mayer is already aware of the problem and the solution. Any remark at this time would come across as critical, rather than constructive.

Mayer's mother sidestepped the problem by not talking about the incident altogether. What a relief this was to Mayer! A reprimand, an angry look or even a short statement would constitute useless punishment at this time. Instead, Mayer's mother earned his trust and love by *expressing* trust and love.

The effect of saying nothing is powerful. Mayer now has no reason to feel hurt or to retaliate. His relationship with his mother is enriched, and her ability to motivate him in the future is also enhanced. Such treatment may even boost Mayer's self-esteem.

This approach is especially beneficial when you are using praise to motivate a child to improve a performance. When using praise as a *motivational technique,* according to the principles laid down in the first chapter, criticism of any form must be minimized.

So far, we know how to be corrective, sensitive and respectful. We have a choice of five reactions, and depending on the case, we will be as indirect as necessary. But before delivering the message we must consider two more points: goals and timing.

Review Your Goals

Set clear goals. Before calling attention to a mistake, make sure the child understands the expectations.

> At bedtime, when Mrs. Kaufman's children took baths, they always left their dirty towels and clothing on the bathroom floor. Mrs. Kaufman instructed her maid to collect the dirty items every morning.
>
> Once or twice a week, when Mrs. Kaufman had time to be with her children at bedtime, she called attention to their routine and told them that they should

collect their dirty things rather than expect the maid to do it.

This had been going on for the last four weeks, and she was ready to reprimand them for their behavior. As she was preparing her remarks she asked herself, "Is the goal clear to the children?" This was a real eye-opener. She realized that it wasn't. On one hand she had been telling them to collect their own dirty things, but on the other hand, she was also telling the maid to do it. Who was supposed to do it? What were the children to think? In effect, they were being rewarded for leaving their clothes on the floor.

Mrs. Kaufman decided that she had no right to reprimand the children because she had never made her expectation clear. Instead, she reviewed the rule with them and told them that the maid would no longer collect their dirty things.

After clarifying the goal, Mrs. Kaufman made it a point to check the bathrooms more frequently. When she found dirty things on the floor, she asked the children to collect them. After a few weeks the problem was solved, without a single reprimand.

Mrs. Kaufman did the fair thing — she analyzed the situation to determine if the children deserved a reprimand. She realized that the goal had been vague and that she was not justified in scolding her children. She clarified the goal and maintained its clarity by enforcing it.

One time, a novice first-grade teacher asked me, the principal, to reprimand her students. They were constantly calling out and interrupting her lessons, and it had to be stopped once and for all. I asked her if she had clarified the goal — that is, did the students understand that they must raise their hands and wait to be called on before talking? The teacher said that she had mentioned the rule, but she felt that it was not yet clear to the students.

We went into the classroom and reviewed the rule with the students. Then we had them practice raising their hands and waiting quietly to be called on. From then on, the teacher enforced the rule with no problem — all without a single reprimand.

Are your goals attainable? Just as parents do not have a right to criticize their children for not reaching an unclear goal, they have no right to criticize them for not reaching an unattainable goal.

> Kalman's parents told him that he must sit nicely at the dinner table, but Kalman was hyperactive and unable to sit quietly for more than ten minutes. Day after day, he either squirmed, got out of his seat or put his feet up on another chair. His parents could not tolerate it any longer and decided to reprimand him for his poor behavior.
>
> As they were preparing their remarks, they asked themselves if the goal had been made clear. It had. Then they asked themselves if the goal was reasonable. They realized that it was — for any other child, but not for Kalman.
>
> They decided not to reprimand Kalman. Instead, they made some rules which allowed him some freedom to move. They even thought of ways to keep him occupied and seated. After a week, the table atmosphere became more relaxed.

Pick the Opportune Time

If you try to criticize people while they are angry, depressed or totally absorbed in another activity, they will not be receptive. If you try to change people's opinions or moods while they are intensely engaged in them, you will accomplish exactly the opposite of what you want — they will dig in and intensify their original feelings.[1]

Timing is important. Yaakov, our forefather, knew this. He waited until he was close to death to reprimand his children. He did not do it earlier for fear that his oldest son would leave him and go to Esav. Moshe Rabbeinu also waited until he was close to death to reprimand the Jewish nation. He felt that the people would not be receptive at any other time.[2]

Chazal tell us that an angry person cannot be appeased.[3] If a

---

1. Maharal, *Derech Chaim, Avos* 4:19.
2. See Rashi and Sifri, *Devorim* 1:3.
3. *Avos* 4:9.

person, while angry, does not respond to soft, appeasing words, he certainly will not respond to criticism or rebuke! Timing is critical.

You may have to delay a criticism. Before criticizing a child, ask yourself, "What is the child's mood now? What other things are on his mind? How intense is he about the issue at hand?" After answering these questions you may decide that anything you say at this time will not be constructive. The child may just not be in a receptive frame of mind and will either reject it, ignore it or argue about it. The best thing is to wait for a more opportune moment. Let's illustrate this point.

> Ariella's mother was upset about two things: Ariella's messy room and her misbehavior in school. She was waiting for Ariella to return from a friend's house so that they could talk about it.
>
> When Ariella arrived home, she was upset about a fight she had just had with her friend. She quietly walked in and flopped down on a chair to sulk.
>
> At first her mother thought that she was relaxed, and approached her to begin the discussion. When she saw Ariella's sad face, she quickly decided to delay her remarks. Instead, she asked Ariella what the problem was and talked with her about it. The next day she brought up her two points.

Sometimes the child may be in the proper frame of mind, but you aren't. For example, you are too busy to give the child your full attention or you are in a bad mood and unable to be as sensitive as you should. Ask yourself, "What kind of mood am I in? Will I be sensitive and corrective?" If you decide that you are not in a proper frame of mind, delay the criticism. There is no sense trying to correct a problem now that can be corrected more effectively at another time.

But if you and the child are both in the position for an immediate reaction, the issue should be given immediate attention. This applies especially in a situation of impending danger.

Reprimand immediately if you can. Some parents wait to criticize their children until they can "give them the goods." This means they don't call attention to mistakes as they occur, but instead take mental notes of the mistakes and call attention to a number of them at once. They feel that this has a stronger impact.

The problem with this approach is that when children are walloped with numerous citations at once, they become overwhelmed. They intensify their natural resistance in order to defend themselves. They will argue with their parents and are sure to be left with hurt feelings.

Parents who call attention to mistakes immediately, however, create less hostility. They have more control over their emotions and the children will react less defensively. Additionally, the children see that the parents are on top of the situation and consistent in their expectations.

Now that we have reviewed our goals and picked the opportune time, we are ready to deliver the message.

Delivering the Message

Use soft words and a gentle manner. Just as our choice of words can be sensitive or offensive, our manner of delivery can go either way, too. The delivery can make the difference between acceptance or rejection, between hostility or placation.

You can pacify angry people by responding to them in a soft, friendly tone of voice. But you can create new hostility by speaking in a harsh, unfriendly tone.[1]

The *way* we present a point is as important as the point itself. Therefore, tone of voice and choice of words should be warm, sweet, pleasant, friendly and positive.

> Pleasant words are like a honeycomb, sweet to the soul and healing to the bones (*Mishlei* 16:24).
>
> Points presented in a very pleasant way are sweet as honeycombs to the listener, and they help the soul and body. This is the way to draw the hearts of people to one's opinion, whether it is related to an ethical matter or a physical necessity (*Metzudas Dovid,* ad loc.).

We mentioned earlier that the *mitzvah* of *tochachah* requires a receptive party. If you speak angrily or impatiently, the child will sense an attack and raise his guard, and you will not be able to

---

1. *Mishlei* 15:1, following Vilna Gaon and Rabbeinu Yonah.

fulfill the *mitzvah.* But if you use soft words and a gentle approach, the child will be receptive, and you will be able to reach him.[1]

When a child makes a mistake, don't say, "You are wrong" or "You made a mistake." This is vindictive and causes pain — even if he *did* make a mistake. Instead, if you see that the child is holding on to his position, say, "You may want to consider ..." or "It seems to me that ..." In this way, you are not pointing your finger at the child or attacking him. You are showing respect, and the child will reciprocate in kind.

You can create an air of gentleness by holding a child's hand lovingly during a criticism. Deliver your message with a smile. Gesture in a slow, calm manner. Make friendly, supportive eye contact. All of this will reinforce your soft words.

Add some words of praise and encouragement. A child is made up of more than his recent behavior. He has many attributes which add to his total personality and which are worthy of recognition. There is no better time to recall those virtues than now — while you are in the midst of criticism.

When a child is criticized, he may feel devastated and inferior. He may feel that he is incapable of improving or that his parents do not love him. As a result, he may not even try to improve. Therefore, he needs to be motivated, made to feel that he is capable of achieving the goal you have set for him. He also needs to know that you still love him and support him.

For this reason, show him how positively you feel toward him. Remind him of his attributes. During the admonition, tell him that you know he is capable of excellence.[2] After the admonition, make him confident of your love and help him feel good about himself.[3]

Sometimes, it is advantageous to show the child how easy it is to correct the mistake. At the time of criticism, he may feel incapable, but if he realizes that the task is not so difficult, he will be more comfortable tackling it.

Chazal tell us to bring a child close with the right hand and to

---

1. Talmud *Shabbos* 34a: "One must say it gently so that they will accept it." See also Rabbi Shlomo Wolbe, *Alai Shur,* p. 261, and Vilna Gaon, *Even Shlaimah* 6:5.

2. Rabbi Eliyahu Dessler, *Michtav M'Eliyahu,* vol. 3, pp. 21-23.

3. *Mishlei* 3:12, following Rashi, Vilna Gaon and Rabbeinu Yonah.

push him away with the left hand.[1] This is not a casual arrangement. We are instructed to use the *weaker* hand to criticize and push the child away, and the *stronger* hand to bring him close with kind, positive words.

This is what Moshe Rabbeinu did when he rebuked the Jewish nation in the desert, calling them to task for their mistakes and at the very same time giving them a blessing that there should be a thousand times more like them — the same people he was rebuking.[2]

Talk about your own mistakes. People find it much easier to hear about their faults if the criticizer humbles himself and admits that he also has faults. Using this principle, you can soften the blow of a criticism by telling the child about the mistakes you once made and the knowledge you did not have when you were her age.

> Chaya often left her closet disorganized, with her clothes hanging awkwardly or thrown on the shelves. Her mother wanted her to become more organized. She knew she had to talk with Chaya about it but did not want to hurt her feelings.
>
> She decided to weaken the blow by talking about her own mistakes also. She said, "Chaya, I noticed that some of your clothes are hung awkwardly or left unfolded on the shelves. I can understand how that happens. When I was your age, I sometimes did the same. I had a hard time reaching the hangers and the high shelves. But as I grew older, I began to understand the value of keeping a neat closet. You might want to get a stool to help you reach the high spots or ask me for help when you need it."
>
> After the discussion, the subject was dropped. But an interesting thing happened. Chaya began keeping her closet more organized. And when she needed help, she even asked her mother for it.

Chaya's mother did not judge her by adult standards, but by the standards she had when she was Chaya's age. Then she reduced the sting by talking about her own mistakes. Chaya did not feel put down and was more receptive.

---

1. Talmud *Sanhedrin* 107b.
2. Rabbi Leibel Eiger, cited in Rabbi Z. Pliskin, *Growth Through Torah*, p. 380.

When you are about to criticize a child, ask yourself if you ever had similar deficiencies. The fact that you are more knowledgeable now or have stronger values now is irrelevant. You have been shaped by your experiences, and you have had a thousand times more experience than the child. Therefore, you cannot expect the child to have the same knowledge, values and skills that you have now.

What is relevant now is the knowledge, value and skills you had when you were the child's age, when you did not have much experience. If you really think about it, you may even realize that you had *more* deficiencies then than she has now, and that she is far ahead of where you were at that time. How humbling! Now tell her, and make her feel better.

Even if you still make the same mistakes as an adult, talk about it.[1] Tell the child about your current challenges and how you overcome them. Once again, she will not feel put down because she will see that you have similar problems.

Be persuasive. Constructive criticism is corrective. The child is supposed to accept your points and improve. But what if he is not convinced that there is a problem? What if he disagrees with your solution?

Children sometimes have to be *persuaded* to change their ways. This is not unreasonable. Children, like all people, have their own ideas and may need to be shown the best way.

There are many ways to persuade a child. Please refer to the chapter on motivating through persuasion, which is dedicated to this topic.

Be a good role model. The message parents give is not conveyed only by their words, it is also conveyed by their actions. As the saying goes, "Actions speak louder than words." Even the most thought-out and constructive message loses its full impact if the parents' actions do not support it.[2]

Being a good role model is the best *tochachah* because it shows what you want and demonstrates your values, while avoiding the

---

1. Rabbi Eliyahu Dessler, *Michtav M'Eliyahu*, vol. 4, p. 245. See also *Ruach Chaim* on *Avos* 2:1.
2. Chazon Ish, *Emunah U'Bitachon* 4:16.

sting and resentment that ordinarily accompany criticism. The children get the message and make the necessary improvements — exactly what *tochachah* is supposed to accomplish — without the negative side effects.[1]

A parent once asked me how to stop her child from saying "shut up." As we talked, she admitted that when she loses patience and becomes exasperated she also says "shut up." She began to realize that she was actually teaching her child to say it, even though she had often told him how terrible it was. She also realized that there was no motivational technique that could cure the child until she herself stopped doing it.

Parents have to "walk their talk." They cannot say, "Do as I say, not as I do." When the child sees a parent doing something, he believes it is the right thing even if the parent tells him otherwise.

A parent who always talks about the difficulty of Judaism, who says, *"Es iz shver tzu zein a yid* (It is hard to be a Jew)," cannot expect his child to love Judaism. A parent who says, "You have to make many sacrifices to keep Shabbos" sends a negative message about Shabbos and cannot expect his child to love Shabbos.[2] A father who socializes in *shul* cannot expect his son to sit quietly, even after lecturing him on the importance of sitting quietly in *shul.*

The *way* that parents criticize their children is also a model for *middos.* Parents who criticize with anger and impatience teach these *middos* to their children. Even if the children accept the criticism and improve, they have learned that anger and impatience are valid reactions to disagreeable events. They in turn will act the same way with their children[3] — and parents. But if they are treated with love and patience, they will learn these *middos* and will probably treat their children — and parents — the same way.

Delivering a Reprimand

Of all the levels of criticism, a reprimand is the most severe and causes the most pain. Because of its strength, some experts

---

1. *Mishnas Rabbi Aharon,* vol. I, pp. 244-245.
2. Rabbi Moshe Feinstein was known to make these comments.
3. Chazon Ish, ibid.

have devised additional guidelines for delivering a reprimand.[1]

First, tell the child about the problem and the solution. Although a reprimand is a severe form of criticism, the rules of correction and sensitivity still apply, as we discussed earlier.

Tell the child how you feel about his performance. If you are disappointed, for example, tell him. If you are extremely upset, tell him. Say, "Your grades have dropped by five points, and I am very disappointed." Say it with feeling. This conveys sincerity and creates a strong impression.

Then stop for a few moments of uncomfortable silence. Let the child get a sense of how you feel, and let him feel it, too. This reinforces the impression.

After the silence, offer words of praise and encouragement. Say how much you value the child and reaffirm your high expectations and your confidence in him. The need to add positive words of praise and encouragement is the same for a reprimand as for any other form of criticism.

Finally, make physical contact with the child, such as a handshake, a caring touch or an arm around the shoulder. The gesture reinforces your sincerity. One word of caution: some children dislike physical contact. If this is the case, don't do it.

There is no need to prolong the delivery. The entire message can be conveyed in a minute or less.

Praise before the reprimand? *Chazal* suggest that parents praise children following the reprimand because positive words help take away the sting.[2] However, these *chazal* do not talk about praising before the reprimand.

On this issue, there is a debate among successful business managers. Some use the "sandwiching method," praising before *and* after the reprimand. They believe that a person must be softened and prepared for uncomfortable words, and there is no better way of doing this than with sincere, honest praise. Others claim that this ruins the effect of the reprimand because the other person becomes suspicious of the motive and "waits for the other shoe to fall."

---

1. Adapted from *The One Minute Manager*, William Morrow and Co., 1982.
2. *Mishlei* 3:12 according to Rashi, Vilna Gaon and Rabbeinu Yonah.

Furthermore, it is easier to loosen up after the reprimand than to tighten up after the praise.

Develop a Healthy Relationship With the Child

The degree to which a child accepts your words is dependent on the kind of relationship you have with him:

> The wounds of a loving person are faithful and the kisses of a hater are a burden (*Mishlei* 27:6).

These words are the key to successful human relations. If you love a person and work for his benefit — and he knows it — he will accept the pain that you cause him. But if you dislike a person or do not care about his welfare — and he knows it — he will loath even the beneficial things you do for him.

The way you really feel about the other person is of paramount importance. For this reason, it is critical to develop a healthy relationship in which the child sees you as someone who loves him. He must know that you are dedicated to his welfare; then he will accept your reprimand. But if he sees you as an antagonist, or as someone who does not have his best interest at heart, he will want no part of you — not even your kisses and favors.

The Chazon Ish explained *Chazal's* statement, "Love people and bring them close to Torah,"[1] to mean that we *first* have to love people and through this we can bring them close to Torah.[2] Loving people is the prerequisite to influencing others. For this reason, a teacher must be firm and demanding — but never negative — in the beginning of the year. Otherwise, the students will get the idea that he is against them, even though he really isn't, and they will not respond to him throughout the year.

Children must know you love them. It is not enough to love your children. They have to *know* it. It is not enough to tell your children that you love them; you have to *show* them. You have to behave in a loving, caring way and *earn* their vote. Otherwise, your

---

1. *Avos* 1:12.

2. Cited by Rabbi Meir Munk in *S'char VeHa'anasha BeChinuch*, ch. 1. See the entire chapter for a discussion of this point.

constructive criticism will not be accepted, no matter how well you follow the "rules."[1]

Give the Child the Benefit of the Doubt

Children have their own perception of what is good for them, and it often differs from their parents'. So if children do not follow your instruction the first time around, or even the second or third, they may not be rebelling or challenging your authority; they may simply be trying to do what they consider best for themselves.

Sometimes they have no motive at all. They simply do not remember their responsibilities. It doesn't mean that they are negligent or do not care about the goals you have set for them; they simply get involved in other activities and forget.

Sometimes children do not comply because they do not understand what is expected of them. Either it was never explained clearly, or they never comprehended it to begin with. Once again, this is not an expression of defiance; it is truly excusable.

Some children do rebel, but for understandable reasons. Their parents do not treat them respectfully. They put them down, use fear tactics, apply undue pressure or treat them in other ways that precipitate rebellion. Their defiance indicates a bigger problem — unskilled parents.

If you don't know why a child is not reaching the goals you have set for him or her, ask yourself the following questions:

- ☐ Did I explain the goal clearly? Does the child understand it?
- ☐ Is the child forgetful?
- ☐ Is the child thinking about something else?
- ☐ Is my treatment of the child causing the problem?

If you have the answers to these questions, you are in a position to address the issues effectively. But if you do not have the answers, don't assume the worst. Give the child the benefit of the doubt.[2] Calmly and respectfully, ask him why he did not comply. You may discover that he has a legitimate reason; or you may discover an

---

1. See Rabbi Chaim Shmulevitz, *Sichos Mussar*, 5733:19, for a discussion on this point as it concerns leadership.

2. *Avos* 1:6.

extenuating factor that can be corrected; or, if he is defiant, you may discover the reason for it.

By giving the child the benefit of the doubt, you demonstrate your trust in him. The child will appreciate it and will reciprocate by trusting you, too.

Another benefit is that the child learns to trust people in general and to give them the benefit of the doubt. When he himself is trusted, he becomes familiar with the concept of trust and learns that others can also be trusted. As an adult, he will treat his wife, children and business associates with the same sense of trust, avoiding many potentially bitter disagreements, because he gives them the benefit of the doubt. His children will also become imbued with the same healthy attitude.

Be Patient

The *mitzvah* of *tochachah* requires parents to rebuke their children over and over again until they improve. If necessary, the parents must even repeat themselves one hundred times.[1] Obviously, the one-hundredth rebuke should be performed with the same skill and sensitivity as the first, and this undoubtedly requires a great deal of patience.

Parents often ask, even after three or four admonishments, "How can I be so patient? How many times can I keep repeating myself? I am not an angel — I don't have superhuman strength."

If you are one of these parents, you can motivate yourself to be patient by reminding yourself of this very basic truth: You are interested in your children in the first place because you love them. You want them to become responsible and successful because you love them. If you were dealing with any other child, you would walk away at the first sign of non-compliance. But because you love your children, you have decided to stay.[2]

Keep that feeling of love and devotion in front of you all the time, especially when you are challenged, and let it become your driving force. Let your words and actions flow from that love, and you will find yourself acting with renewed patience.

---

1. Talmud *Bava Metzia* 31.
2. Vilna Gaon, *Mishlei* 3:12.

Be Honest

Don't lighten the significance of a large mistake by saying, "Oh, it's not so bad." Similarly, don't inflate the significance of a small mistake by saying, "What you did is awful!" Whether the deed is large or small, tell the truth. Otherwise, the child will not improve.

> The one who rebukes his friend should reveal all hidden matters and avoid flattery. The rebuker should either justify or incriminate his friend according to his actions. This is the reason: a *tzaddik* (righteous person) and a *rasha* (evil person) are two opposite extremes. A person who does not act like a *rasha,* but also does not act like a *tzaddik,* is in between the two. Therefore, he cannot be called a *tzaddik* until he becomes one. Since the purpose of the rebuke is to make him a *tzaddik,* the rebuker should reveal every true matter (Rabbeinu Bachya, beginning of *Nitzavim,* commenting on *Mishlei* 27:5).[1]

Be Sincere

When presenting your point, make it clear that your only interest is the child's welfare and that you have nothing to gain personally. When children sense that you are sincere, they become receptive. As the well-known saying goes, "Words that leave the heart enter the heart."[2]

What Are Your Real Motives?

The Torah endorses criticism only when it is constructive and in the interest of the child's physical, emotional or spiritual welfare. Sometimes, however, parents are driven by other motives. Have you ever asked yourself what your motives are? Try it some time. Ask yourself, "Why am I criticizing my child? What is driving me to do it?"

If you find that you are motivated to help your child become a responsible human being and that you have nothing personal to gain

---

1. Translation from the original is modified.
2. Rabbi Moshe ibn Ezra, *Shiras Yisrael,* p. 156.

other than the resulting *nachas* — you can assume that your words will flow from love and sensitivity, and that they will make an impression on the child. But if you find that you are satisfying an emotional need of your own, you will not make a lasting impression. A child can sense your attitude and will resent it.

Many parents do not recognize the forces that work within them. Day after day they criticize their children, unknowingly hiding behind a mask of righteousness. They are not even aware of their real motives. For this reason, we will now present a list of motives that may lie behind a parent's drive to criticize.

Ask yourself if any of these motives applies to you. If you are not sure, listen to your own words and take notice of your thoughts the next time you criticize. Become aware of your tendencies, feelings and interests. Get to know yourself. If you discover that you are satisfying a personal need, come out from behind the mask. Delay your response until you feel your motive in rebuking the child is genuine. Rabbi Shlomo Wolbe wrote that parents may have to break or improve their own *middos* in order to be able to raise their children properly.[1]

Following are seven motives that drive parents to criticize their children:

1. It is easy, familiar and convenient. In our culture, people are generally quick to find fault. Parents pay little attention to children when they are playing nicely, but as soon as trouble starts they are quick to reprimand. We have all witnessed our parents and teachers criticizing others; sometimes we were the recipients.

Parents are very familiar with criticism; they have seen it and experienced it. For some parents, it is often the only approach they feel comfortable using. Best of all, it is convenient; they can just blurt it out without thinking too hard.

2. It is an effective form of retaliation. Why does a person take offense at another's insults? Because he feels that the offender has violated his honor. He then wants to "get back" at him. One way to "get back" is to humiliate him. His motivation in this case is retaliation, not concern for the offender's welfare.

---

1. *Alai Shur*, p. 260.

Many people are motivated to some degree by their hurt feelings and violated honor. Indeed, they may want to see the offender improve, but this motive is secondary to the real one, which is selfish and retaliatory. Such a person will be ineffective. Rabbi Shlomo Wolbe even calls this person's behavior "revenge."[1]

When your child misbehaves, disobeys or challenges your authority, your typical reaction is to punish or reprimand him. Why? Is it because you are concerned with his welfare and want to help him improve, or because he hurt your feelings by disobeying? If the second reason is driving you, even if it is in conjunction with the first, you may be acting out of revenge — and, as Rabbi Wolbe writes, the prohibition against revenge applies to parents, too.[2]

3. It gives a feeling of superiority. Some people derive a perverted satisfaction from putting others down. It gives them the illusion that they are superior.

Psychologists say that people with low self-confidence and feelings of inferiority often *act* superior and overconfident. They feel so awful about themselves that they look for artificial ways to build themselves up. One convenient way is to put their children down.

4. It satisfies a need for power and control. Some people have a need to control their lives and the people around them. They disguise their motive by saying they want to have *influence*, but what they really want is *power*. Finding fault with their children and telling them what to do is a way of getting it.

These people may have been spoiled as children and grew up thinking that everything has to go their way. Or perhaps their parents took all sense of control from them, and now, as adults, they are trying to compensate. It is also possible that they were simply born with this tendency.

Whatever the reason, for these people criticizing children is nothing more than a power-seeking tactic in disguise.

5. It is a way of expressing love. Some parents think that being critical, even when it is insensitive, is the loving thing to do. They feel it is the way to fulfill parental responsibilities and to show the children how much they care.

---

1. Ibid.
2. Ibid.

Some parents express their love with this attitude: "This child has to learn respect, even if I have to beat it into him." They think that their beatings — emotional and/or physical — are expressions of love and concern for the welfare of their children.

Their children, however, perceive the parents' behavior as an expression of brutality. They conclude, "There is no reason to be so harsh. If they really loved me, they would treat me more sensitively."

The children also learn a very negative lesson — that brutality is a permissible reaction to other people's wrongdoings.

6. It is a way of venting hostility. Everybody has a history of failures, misfortunes and resentments. They would like to release their hostilities in many ways, but social norms restrict them, so they target their children. Children are younger, smaller and weaker — and they are supposed to respect their parents. What more convenient target for disguised hostility is there?

7. It gives a feeling of intelligence. Some people think that finding fault in others proves that they are intelligent. They reason, "If I am able to catch someone's mistake, I must be bright."

If parents sense in themselves any of the above tendencies, it is time to reevaluate their treatment of their children.

Avoid Non-constructive and Excessive Criticism

At times, criticism is inappropriate. *Chazal* tell us that there are four times when we may not criticize:

1) The recipient will be so embarrassed that he will not look at us.

2) The recipient will have a complaint against us.

3) We will lose the recipient altogether because he will leave us.

4) The recipient will reject the rebuke.[1]

Halachah forbids us to say what we want, whenever we want. We mentioned earlier in the name of Rabbi Chaim Mordechai Katz that "the rebuker must sense that his words are accepted, and that his words will help the recipient do *teshuvah* for his wrongdoings." It is very clear, then, that there is a purpose in our efforts, and the

---

1. Sifri, *Devorim* 1:3.

only time we can fulfill the purpose is when the recipient is open. If he is not, we are required to be quiet.[1]

Avoid excessive criticism. Picture the typical morning routine before school:

> Dinah gets out of bed after being nudged four times by her mother. She picks socks that do not match her dress. She becomes angry when her mother reminds her to make her bed. She brushes her teeth too quickly and fails to part her hair properly. On her way to breakfast, she accidentally bumps her brother and sends him off in tears. At the breakfast table she slouches in her chair, spills milk and sugar on the table, and fails to finish her cereal. When her mother asks if she *davened,* she says that she had no time. Just then, the school bus arrives. On her way out, she remembers that she has to get a test signed and begins looking for it.

On and on, every day — before school, after school, and on long weekends. Each day holds numerous opportunities for mother and father to find fault with Dinah and to demand that she improve immediately.

How would *you* feel if you had to correct all your faults in a single day? Imagine trying to get out of bed on time, giving your spouse and children all the loving attention they deserve, refraining from becoming angry or impatient, *davening* with *kavanah,* refraining from *lashon hara,* and the dozen other things you know you are supposed to be doing. If you are already in the habit of not doing these things, it is probably too much to achieve so many goals in a single day.

Children are no different. Therefore, "pick your battles" very carefully. Focus on a few goals and let the other misdemeanors slide by. If you were to call attention to each and every problem, you would create more problems. We will discuss this next.

The effects of misused and excessive criticism. The most important people in the life of a child are his parents. His developing self-image depends on the messages he receives from them. If

---

1. Talmud *Yevamos* 65b.

the messages are positive, the child will believe them and feel positive about himself; if they are negative, he will internalize a negative self-concept. And it makes no difference if the messages are conveyed explicitly or implicitly — he can read between the lines quite well.

Parents often unknowingly destroy their children with critical remarks. They don't realize that the children look up to them and believe what they say. Although they may not say it explicitly, sometimes their criticism implies, "You are lacking. Your performance is not good. You are not a good person." The child hears this message between the lines and believes it. With enough repetition, the child will begin to believe that he is unloved, unworthy and incompetent.

What else *should* he think? "If they really think I am a good person," he reasons, "why are they always attacking me?" He has no idea that his parents really love him but simply do not know how to criticize constructively — or that their approach springs from their own maladjustments. All he knows is what he hears and perceives.

Miriam Adahan calls non-constructive criticism a "death wish." It is another way of saying, "You are not the kind of person I want in this family. I wish you were not alive and could be replaced by somebody who meets my standards."[1]

Children are very susceptible to the destructive effects of criticism because they are young and impressionable, and because their self-images are undeveloped. Attacks on their efficacy deeply influence their developing self-concepts and lead them to make damaging conclusions about themselves.

Thus, they become negatively programmed as children; and these feelings will carry over into their adult lives, preventing them from reaching their potential in life. Their intellectual, emotional and social development will be stunted by haunting feelings of inferiority.

Some parents and teachers think that too much success egotizes and spoils, so they take children who appear high, even if they do not display any sort of conceit, and knock them down a few pegs. They may even put the children down as a preventative measure. These people are making a big mistake. Success energizes, propels

---

1. *Living With Difficult People,* Feldheim Publishers, 1991, p. 143. This book addresses the topic of destructive criticism.

and encourages growth. Failure, on the other hand, results in bitterness and low self-esteem.

Periodic criticism has its negative effects, but continual criticism chips away at the self-concept of the child and constitutes bona fide *child abuse.* The spilled milk, the unfinished dinner and the awkwardly rolled toothpaste tube pale in significance to the damage wrought by criticism for these events.

One of the major causes of emotional maladjustment and misbehavior in children is chronic criticism. Children who are criticized improperly feel rejected. They will either respond with active hostility, such as more disobedience, anger or disrespect, or with passive aggression, such as carelessness, slow movements or withdrawal. They may also develop other stress-related symptoms such as bed-wetting, psychosomatic illness or sleep and eating disorders.[1]

Misused criticism can be counterproductive. The parents of a five-year-old boy once asked me how they could stop their son from hitting his baby brother, throwing toys at family members, hitting his mother and calling her names, and running across the street unattended.

As we talked, it became clear that they responded harshly and critically to all their son's actions. They began to realize that they were part of a vicious cycle of negative behavior: the child misbehaves, they respond with a harsh reprimand or punishment, things calm down for a few hours, then the cycle begins again. The couple decided to take less severe and less frequent measures against the child, and to begin praising him for the things he did right.

After one month, they reported a significant improvement in their relationship. They were so impressed with the change that they asked their son why he thought he was behaving better. He told them, "Because you stopped hitting me and yelling at me." What an insight — from a five-year-old child! He clearly associated his behavior with theirs.

This child's actions were deplorable and *deserved* a severe response. But because he was hostile to all his parents' actions, their treatment was not bringing about the desired improvement. Only

1. Miriam Adahan, *Raising Children to Care,* Feldheim Publishers, 1988, p. 219.

after the parents eliminated a major cause of the child's hostility — their harsh style — did the situation improve.

The parents' original treatment *was* effective, to a small degree. As Miriam Adahan wrote, "Because humiliation is so painful, it is successful, and therefore it is the most frequently used method of getting children to conform and cooperate in the home and in the classroom."[1] But their son's insight taught them something new. They learned that humiliation works in the short-term but does not have a long-lasting effect.

Criticizing Properly Is Not Easy

When the Torah presented the *mitzvah* of *tochachah*, it added a warning: "Do not bear a sin with it."[2] The sin refers to embarrassing the recipient.[3] This *mitzvah* in particular has a warning attached to it because no other *mitzvah* has the potential to be so sinful. It is so easy to rebuke improperly and embarrass the recipient that we are specifically warned to proceed with caution.

There is another reason to be careful: we are forbidden to hurt others with words or gestures.[4] If so, how are we permitted to criticize on *any* level? Again, the answer is — be careful. Giving criticism is the healthy thing to do if it causes as little pain as possible.[5]

Rebuking properly is not easy. Nowadays, we have to be especially careful; in our culture, people are quick to recognize less-than-perfect performance and slow to recognize good performance. People are very busy catching others doing things wrong. When children perform well, they seem to think there is no need to recognize it — "After all," people say, "they did what they are supposed to do anyway." But if the children perform poorly, they quickly call attention to it and offer correction. Parents have the tendency to notice the one "C" on the report card but not the two "A's." Our culture is negative, and we are constantly influenced by it. We have to resist the pull and try to act positively and constructively. This is the Torah way.

---

1. *Living with Difficult People*, p. 20.
2. *Vayikra* 19:17.
3. Talmud *Arachin* 16b.
4. *Vayikra* 25:17; also see *Sefer HaChinuch, mitzvah* 338.
5. Rabbi Yeruchom Levovitz, *Daas Torah, Shemos* 18:14.

We have many forces working against us. The child's natural resistance is one barrier. Then, we create defensiveness when we point out the problem. Influenced by our culture and our own emotional maladjustments, we often tend to do it negatively. Yet, we have to restrain ourselves from hurting or embarrassing the child, and we have to resist our own negative inclinations.

It is easier to understand now why *Chazal* say that there is nobody who can rebuke properly.[1] It is a difficult task. Nevertheless, we are required to give constructive criticism whenever appropriate. We have to deal positively and constructively with our children, in a way that will leave their self-concept healthy and intact.

---

4. Talmud *Arachin* 16b.

Chapter Eight

Support the Child's Interests and Natural Talents

Why do we motivate our children? Is it only to help them reach a particular goal? Or is there more?

Certainly, we want to help our children *reach* goals. But we also have a long-term objective — to infuse them with an *inner drive* to reach those goals. We want our children to perform well and reach their goals *independently and free of external stimulation.* Then they will produce even when we are not standing over them.

Children do not usually start with this attitude. They need prodding and motivation to acquire an inner drive — and our job is to provide it. Afterward, we let them go on "automatic pilot."

Connect With Your Children's Interests and Talents

Did your children ever express a voluntary interest in a particular goal? To what extent did you have to motivate them? You probably did not have to prod them very much, if at all, because their "automatic pilot" was already activated to some degree. Because of their pre-existing attitude, your workload was lightened and they were probably more successful.

This is the ideal situation, and you may be able to capitalize on it more often than you already do. How? By discovering your children's interests and innate talents. If those interests and abilities are worthwhile, encourage them. By connecting with your children in this way, they will become more agreeable and your job will become less challenging. Let's illustrate.

> Ilan's parents wanted him to have a hobby. Ilan had an interest in chess; however, his parents felt it would be more valuable to be able to play a musical instrument. They tried to convince Ilan of the value of music and explained the benefits of having a musical talent. Then they hired a piano teacher for him.
>
> Ilan was not happy with the piano, and he made very slow progress. On the days he had lessons, he became subdued. Ilan's unhappiness disturbed his parents. They also feared that he would develop such a distaste for the piano that he would quit and never want to try again.
>
> Ilan's parents decided to stop for a moment and take a look at *Ilan's* interests. They knew that he liked chess, so they gave him the option of stopping piano lessons and joining a chess club. He jumped at the offer, and the next day they enrolled him in a chess club.
>
> Lately, Ilan's overall disposition has improved. He is more relaxed and has even become more cooperative at home. His parents know they did the proper thing and are hopeful that Ilan will want to take up the piano again some time in the future.

At first, Ilan's parents subordinated his interest to theirs. They felt that their goal was more worthy, so they made arrangements for him to reach it and pushed him in that direction. But when they realized that he would not develop an inner drive for something he naturally disliked, they conformed to his interests. They encouraged him to go in his own direction and he continued improving his chess game. He felt fulfilled and no longer had to be pushed and nagged.

True, Ilan was not reaching the exact goal that his parents had set for him, but he was still reaching their general goal — to have a hobby. After all, the skill of playing chess has its merits, too. Recognizing the value of good chess skills, his parents began to support Ilan in that direction. And who knows — sometime in the future, his interest in the piano may be rekindled.

Typically, when parents want their children to improve performance or to take on new goals, they coax and cajole them to comply, or they put an idea into their heads and try to make them think it is theirs. These tactics require skill and cunning — and often do not work. When you connect with the child's own interests, though, there is less need to use strategies that enhance cooperation because the child is already motivated.

This does not mean that parents should always subordinate their priorities to the child's. Rather, they should consider the nature of their goals before enforcing them, determining first if the goals are optional or mandatory. Let's explain.

Mandatory and optional goals. There are two kinds of goals: mandatory and optional. Mandatory goals pertain to morals, ethics, religious commitments and the pursuit of knowledge. Their worth is indisputable, and all respectable parents support them. Optional goals, however, pertain to such things as the hobbies a child adopts, the kind of *seforim* he learns and the kind of books he reads. Optional goals are elective and are based on personal interest. Parents should not force optional goals on children; rather, they should encourage their children's natural interests.

Chazal tell us that a person only learns — that is, really connects with — Torah topics which he desires to learn.[1] Therefore, a teacher should teach topics that interest the student. The reason is that "a

---

1. Talmud *Avodah Zarah* 19a.

person's heart follows his desire."[1] We can apply this principle to other areas of life as well.

This means that if the optional goals you have set for the child do not agree with his own interests, don't require him to subordinate himself to you. If his interests are legitimate, support them. In other words — be a coach, not a reformer.

Sometimes, parents and teachers take the attitude that children have to cooperate with them, and not the other way around. Some of the more insistent among them think that conforming to children is tantamount to relinquishing control. This is not true. Parents and teachers can assume all the authority in the world, but if a child is not reaching the goals they have set for him, they are ineffective motivators and their authority becomes meaningless.

However, when parents and teachers consider the child's interests and encourage him to pursue them, they are not relinquishing control; they are helping the child to succeed in a cooperative atmosphere. Rabbi Eliyahu Dessler said that people should always see things from the other person's point of view.[2] There is no reason to differentiate between adults and children.

Continue praising good performances. Encouragement does not stop when the child has reached his goal. It continues beyond this point, with praise and more encouragement. The child appreciates the praise and becomes motivated to repeat the performance. Hopefully, he will develop inner pride for the performance and will become self-motivated to repeat it in the future.

Encourage Children to Persist

Encouraging children to pursue their interests is important but is not always enough. Parents can offer their support and encouragement, but if the children are unwilling to persist when challenges arise, they will not reach their goals. At this point, parents can play an important role. Let's illustrate.

---

1. Rashi, ad loc.
2. *Michtav M'Eliyahu*, vol. 4, p. 243.

Yoni always wanted to play an electronic keyboard. He was looking forward to playing at *simchas* and family affairs, so he joined the after-school music club.

He had two lessons per week. This meant less time for his favorite activities — reading and playing with friends. He considered quitting, but his parents encouraged him to continue. They also suggested some time-management strategies and monitored his routines.

By the end of the year, Yoni was able to play the electronic keyboard. And as a bonus, he had learned how to manage his time effectively.

Yoni's parents did not watch their son fail; they became involved and helped him succeed.

Under similar circumstances, however, some parents may very well consider their children lost causes and allow them to fail. These parents may not know how to encourage their children to persist through adversity, or they may feel it is not their job. "If a child makes up his mind to reach a goal," they say, "it is *his* job to find ways of overcoming the obstacles." Let's illustrate this attitude.

Moshe, twelve years old, is a bright child with many interests. He wanted to learn about flight and space travel, so he purchased a hobby rocket kit. He looked forward to building his rocket and shooting it skyward.

He began assembling the rocket and discovered he needed special glue. He did not feel like returning to the hobby shop, but after several days, he forced himself to go back and purchase the glue. As he continued working, one of the pieces chipped, which meant he would need more materials to correct the flaw. Things were not going as smoothly as he had anticipated, and he slowly lost interest in the project.

Moshe's parents saw his excitement wane but did not want to get involved. They felt that he had committed himself to the project and was old enough to see it through, so they said nothing.

Moshe's parents were correct — he had committed himself to the project and was old enough to see it through. But they were incorrect in leaving him to his own devices and letting him fail. He had to learn how to *persist,* and his parents could have taught him, thus equipping him with the ability to persist in other challenging situations as well. Instead, Moshe will go on to another project, and if he is faced with a challenge he will probably give up again.

Moshe's parents could have provided suggestions and encouragement. They could have said, "This is a very interesting project. You can get the supplies tomorrow on your way to your friend's house. It may be a little inconvenient, but once you get the material you need and complete your project, you'll be happy you did it. You'll do a job that all of us will be proud of."

If their suggestion was not sufficiently motivating, they might even drive him to the hobby shop. Some traditional parents may protest this idea and say, "Now Moshe will learn that when things get rough, there is no need to persist. His parents will be available to do his work for him." This is a valid point and should be considered. Indeed, parents should not do the work of their children; however, it is appropriate for them to offer their services *infrequently* if they see that their efforts have positive effects.

Create a Cycle of Success

Educators use this approach with learning-disabled students who have strengths in non-academic areas. For example, they may create goals for their students in art or music. When the children succeed, they feel productive and their self-confidence is boosted. The successful experience in art or music also has a ripple effect. The children will feel better about themselves in general and will improve in other areas as well.

This approach is also useful for mainstream children. For example, a child may not be performing well in school due to lack of motivation. The child finds some subjects somewhat interesting, but because her parents and teachers are pressuring her to perform well in *all* areas, she has lost all incentive.

Instead of locking horns with the child by maintaining their pressure, the adults should create a cycle of success. They should ask the child which subjects she finds most interesting. Then they should negotiate with her and encourage her to perform well in those areas only, with the understanding that they will not pressure her to perform to the same extent across the curriculum.

The parents and teachers are not asking the child to make any sort of major change or to pursue uninteresting goals. They are asking her only to perform well in the areas of her natural interest. Since she already has *some* motivation in those areas, she may begin to improve in them, especially now that she feels less overall pressure. As she improves, she will begin to feel better about herself, and she may become encouraged to extend her efforts to other areas, too. The nature of success is that it breeds more success. This is what we mean by creating a cycle of success.

Discuss Interests, Talents and Goals With Your Children

People often have a pool of untapped interests and natural talents of which they are not aware. If they were aware, they would think about these new topics, talk about them and maybe even act on them. They would have a broader perspective on life and the advantage of new opportunities.

You can help your children develop a broad perspective on life by engaging them in conversation about the things that interest them. Talk with them about their dreams and aspirations, about hobbies, projects or anything else worth doing. Encourage your children to aim high and to pursue their interests. And, as we said earlier, offer your assistance if needed.

Suppose a child has an ambition and you are not certain she will succeed. If there is a reasonable chance of some sort of success, don't share your opinion. By protecting her from possible disappointment, you are also protecting her from dreaming, hoping and striving to reach her goals.

For example, let's say your daughter tells you she wants to begin a babysitting service, but because she is young, you are not sure if people will use her. Don't share your apprehension. Let her explore the idea and attempt to put it into practice. She may just do it! And even if she does not succeed, she will benefit; she will have opened her mind, dreamed and reached for the dream. Yes, she failed — but there was reason to believe that she would succeed, and with proper encouragement, she will go on to other challenges.

The Benefits of Connecting With the Child's Interests

Connecting with the child reduces resistance. People — children included — do not like to change. They have pride and resent being told that their performances are lacking. But if they already have an interest in a particular goal, there is no reason for them to resent encouragement in that direction. They will respond more openly to motivation attempts, and because there is less resistance, the parents' job is less difficult.

Connection creates inner drive quickly. As we mentioned earlier, our long-term objective is to help the child build an inner drive to achieve the goal, independently and without external motivation. When an interest already exists, the strong inner drive needed to achieve the goal is off to a head start.

You've heard the expression, "When the cat's away, the mice will play." This is an apt way of saying that if a child's motivation to perform comes from external sources, she will revert to her original unmotivated state when those sources are removed. We do not want that to happen; we want our children to perform well even when we are not around. When we connect with their interests and share their goals, we enable them to achieve with fewer external incentives.

Connection improves relationships. You know from your own experiences that when adults work together, cooperatively and without tension, their relationship is enhanced. When parents connect with their children and work cooperatively with them, the same holds true.

Furthermore, when parents consider their children's interests, they are showing concern and respect for them, and the children will reciprocate in kind. An atmosphere of cooperation is created, and fewer power struggles arise.

Connection creates independence. Sharing children's interests gives them the feeling that they have some control over their lives. It helps them learn to be independent and creates an atmosphere conducive to success.

Connection builds self-confidence. When parents connect with a child, they are conveying the unspoken message that the child's feelings and opinions are important. This is a boost to the child's ego and self-confidence.

Additionally, the child's chances of success are enhanced since he is doing something in which he already has an interest. With each success, he will be able to say to himself, "I am a capable person" — another boost to his self-confidence.

Chapter Nine

Quick Strategies to Enhance Cooperation

There are many ways to gain cooperation. Sometimes the easiest and quickest way is to give an order, and maybe even to mention the consequence for not complying. The problem with this approach, though, is that it is forceful and creates resentment. If the child is not happy to conform, he will not have a healthy attitude and will not perform to his potential. For this reason, it is best to gain cooperation without resentment.

You may ask, "Why should we tiptoe around children? We should expect them to be obedient." Yes, they *should* be; however, we are now concerned with children who are not obedient or who have a low threshold of sensitivity. In these cases, resentment can be detrimental and should therefore be avoided. In the long-term, forcing obedience may produce the opposite effect of what you want.

In earlier chapters, we described techniques that minimize resentment and maximize cooperation. While these techniques are effective, they require a considerable amount of thought, planning and understanding, and they often show their results only after a period of time. What if you cannot wait? How can you influence your children to cooperate immediately?

There are a number of quick strategies which are generally effective. The strategies presented here share common principles: give the child respect; make him feel important; understand his individuality; see the issue from his viewpoint; align yourself with his priorities; and avoid coercion. Rabbi Eliyahu Dessler encapsulated all these principles in one rule: Create a perception of the other person that matches the way he perceives himself.[1]

Not all strategies work for all children or for all situations. Everything depends on each individual personality and event. If you know your child's personality, you will be able to choose the best strategy. If you do not know his personality, you can experiment to discover the most effective strategy.

Some of the following strategies have already been presented as elements of broader motivational techniques. They are repeated here to show how they can be used independently to get quick results.

Ask Questions Instead of Giving Orders

People like to be in control of their lives. They like to do what they want, when they want it. For this reason, a child may resent being ordered to do a task, even if he is ordered in a respectful manner. He may perceive the demand as invasive and may not cooperate.

The problem can be circumvented by asking questions such as "Do you think this will work?" or "What do you think about this idea?" Questioning is an indirect way of telling the child what you want, and at the same time it preserves his pride. It allows the child to choose if and how he will perform, and as a result, he will be less resentful and more cooperative.

Halachah validates this point. A child may not directly correct a parent and say, "You made a mistake." Rather, he must be indirect and ask, "Isn't it this way?"[2] Both statements convey the same message,

---

1. *Michtav M'Eliyahu*, vol. 4, pp. 243-244.
2. *Shulchan Aruch, Yoreh Deah* 240:11.

but the second is more respectful. We see that asking questions is a more respectful approach than making direct demands.

Although parents are not required to respect their children in the way that children must respect them, they are not excused from showing respect. And if they want to have an influence over their children, giving respect and developing a good relationship are the keys to success.[1]

Let's illustrate this strategy.

> Rivki, eleven years old, is independent and prefers to make her own decisions. She has always resented her parents telling her what to do.
>
> Her parents came to understand Rivki's nature after several years of arguments and hurt feelings. As a result, they have decided to reduce the number of orders they give her.
>
> For example, when she makes her bed awkwardly, her mother says, "Rivki, do you think it would be easier to do it like this?" and describes a different way. When she forgets her books in school, her father says, "Rivki, what do you think of this idea?" and offers a suggestion to help her remember in the future. If Rivki rejects the idea, her parents drop the subject and do not persist.
>
> Since Rivki's parents implemented their new strategy, their relationship with their daughter has improved. They still make demands when necessary, but since they have converted many of their orders to questions, Rivki has been more cooperative.

When a child has a way of doing something and you feel that it is not to her benefit, questioning is a better technique than ordering. Rather than saying, "Don't do it that way" or "Do it this way," try, "Do you think this would work?" or "What do you think about this?" Asking questions encourages cooperation because it shows the child respect, considers her pride and allows her to act independently.

---

1. See the seventh chapter for a discussion on the topic of respecting children and developing a healthy relationship with them.

There is another type of question which enhances cooperation. We call it the "Don't-you-want-to-prove-how-good-you-are" request. If you want the child to perform a task, say:

"Would you be so kind as to do ...?"
"Can you find it in your heart to ...?"

These requests imply that the child is kind or has a caring heart. It sets the child up to prove that she is, in fact, kind. The child will feel compelled to comply just to prove that she is a person of virtue.

Give Choices

When a child does not want to comply with a parent's order or request, the typical parent says, "I asked you once to do it. You'd better do it or you'll receive such-and-such a punishment." The child is not given a choice and has no control. He may continue to defy his parent by disregarding the threat. The parent then becomes angry and raises her voice, frightening the child into compliance. If that doesn't work, she resorts to physical force.

A parent can break this vicious cycle by giving the child choices. She can say, "You have a choice. You may do as I ask or stay inside the house. Whichever you choose is okay with me." The parent must remain unemotional and show no vested interest, leaving the child with the control to choose which action to take. Because the child really does not want the consequence, he will probably cooperate. Why not? He has been given control and independence, and he has nothing to gain by not cooperating.

We described this strategy in the fifth chapter. To illustrate its effectiveness, we told the story of Tzvi, the little boy who stripped his bed every night at bedtime. At first, his mother yelled at him and remade the bed herself. He persisted in his routine, so she decided to use a different strategy. She gave him the choice of leaving the bed made or sleeping in it unmade. She made it clear that she would accept whatever decision he made. Tzvi immediately stopped his power-seeking routine.

Everyone wants to feel in control of his or her life. When a parent orders a child to perform a task, the child's first reaction may be, "You can't tell me what to do." However, when you give him several options, the control is in his hands. The parent is sending the unspoken message, "I do not want to control your life. I am not interested in taking your power."

Let the Child Suggest a Consequence

This variation of the choice-giving strategy leaves a little more control in the child's hands. Instead of the parent naming the consequence, the child suggests it.

> Shifra and her friends were playing in the house. At first, they were playing quietly, but after a while they began jumping on the furniture and throwing things around.
>
> Shifra's mother asked her to settle down, but she continued being rowdy. Her mother called her into the kitchen and said, "We have a rule about being wild in the house, and you have chosen not to follow it. I want you to have fun with your friends, but wild play is not allowed. If you continue, there will have to be a consequence. You may not like the one I choose, so I am going to let you suggest one. If I agree to it, you can decide if you want to continue being wild and receive the consequence."
>
> Shifra said, "You can send us outside if we become wild." Her mother agreed.
>
> Shifra quickly told her friends that they would have to settle down or go outside. They finished their game quietly and went outside on their own.

Shifra's mother did not scold or humiliate her. She simply reminded Shifra of a rule and let her suggest the consequence for not complying. She transferred control to her daughter and made her feel important, so Shifra became cooperative. Shifra was also more committed to the plan because she had developed it and was close to it.

Let the Child Find a Solution

When people play a role in developing a plan, they become committed to it because they feel a sense of ownership. Children are no different. If a child has a problem and finds the solution himself, he will be more committed to it than if the parents had suggested it.[1] Letting the child find the solution also stimulates creativity and problem-solving skills. Let's illustrate.

> For two weeks, Raphael had been failing in school. His parents suspected that he was playing with his friends too much and not studying enough. They knew that if they would order him to improve or forbid him to play with his friends, he would resent it, so they used another strategy.
>
> They asked Raphael what *he* thought he should do. They said, "Raphael, do you think you can get better grades?" He agreed that he could do better. Then they asked him, "What do you think could be done to help improve your grades?" Raphael thought about this for several minutes and then suggested of his own accord that he spend less time with his friends and more time studying.

Because it was *his* idea, Raphael was more committed to it than if his parents had ordered him to do it. By asking Raphael to think of a solution, his parents also stimulated his creativity and enhanced cooperation.

G-d used this strategy before He created man. He sensed that the angels would not agree to His plan, so He brought them into the decision-making process. Having played a role in the decision, they would feel better about the plan.[2]

Let the child suggest a solution and a consequence. Sometimes, you can combine two strategies by asking the child to find both the solution and the consequence. Take, for example, the previous story of Shifra. Her mother could have asked her to suggest a solution along with a consequence. Here is how that scenario might look:

---

1. See Talmud *Bava Metziah*, 38a: "A person prefers one share of his own possession to nine identical shares of his friend's." Rashi explains that a person cherishes that which he works to get. We are extending this concept to a person's ideas. See also *Mishlei* 21:2: "The way of a man is straight in his eyes."

2. Rashi, *Bereishis* 1:26.

"We have a rule about being wild in the house, and you have chosen not to follow it. I understand that you have your own interests, so I am going to let you suggest a solution. You can find a way of enjoying your friends without being wild, or if you choose to be wild, you can suggest a consequence for it. If I agree to it, you may choose to do as you wish."

Shifra suggests that they go outside to play as soon as they finish their game. Her mother asks, "That is a good idea. But what will be the consequence if you are wild *before* you go outside?" Shifra answers, "You can send us outside as soon as that happens." Her mother agrees.

Make the Child Happy About Following Your Suggestion

People have different priorities. What interests one person may not interest another. Children too have their priorities and will probably not be very interested in yours. Therefore, when you want to gain cooperation and commitment, show the child the benefit of following your request.

> Every person is interested in his own needs more than yours; therefore, show him how your needs agree with his. Do not try to influence the other person just to do the new thing, but to want to do it. Then he will be happy doing it ... Do not talk too much about yourself; talk with the other person about himself, and he will have an interest in listening (Rabbi Eliyahu Dessler, *Michtav M'Eliyahu,* vol. 4, p. 244).

Sometimes, the benefit is the natural result of the activity. Other times, you have to create the benefit. Let's illustrate.

It was a hectic day at the Rosen residence. Cousins were about to arrive for a visit, and the house was a mess. Mrs. Rosen looked at the clock and realized that she would not be able to straighten up in time. She knew she would need her children's help.

Mrs. Rosen also knew that interrupting their game to request help in the house was asking for arguments, and she did not have the time or patience to deal with that. So she planned a strategy. She asked herself, "How can I make them happy to follow my request?" She thought of a benefit for each child, and then she called them in from outside.

She said, "Your cousins are coming to visit us soon. The house is a disaster. Just look at it. What do you think?"

They looked around and emphatically agreed. She continued, "I think that we would all be embarrassed if they saw this mess. If you help straighten up, you will be doing your share to make the house a place we can all be proud of."

This was enough to convince her oldest daughter. She was accustomed to housework and took pride in a neat home. She said, "Okay, I'll start in the kitchen," and walked off to the kitchen.

The two boys, however, were not convinced. They said, "But we're in the middle of our game. It's not fair." Mrs. Rosen was expecting this and already had a plan. She said to the older one, "Yesterday you asked if you could go to the concert. I told you that it depends on how you behave in the next few days. Well, this is part of it." He thought about it and agreed to help.

Her youngest son was five years old and had no interest in the concert or in a neat house. She wanted him to clean his room and told him, "You are going to be the 'Chief Inspector of the Rosen Residence.' After you clean your room, you will be able to inspect the other parts of the house and tell me whatever has to be done." This son loved titles and the feeling of importance that came along with them, so he agreed to help.

Mrs. Rosen's children were not thrilled about helping. They still would have preferred to play outside, but they saw the benefits and cooperated.

As we mentioned, different people appreciate different benefits. Mrs. Rosen's daughter appreciated the natural benefit of a neat home. The boys appreciated the reward and the title that were created for them. All the benefits had a common purpose — to make the children happy about following their mother's suggestion. More on this topic can be found in the fourth chapter.

Get Involved With the Task

> Esther was asked to walk her little brother to the park. She usually liked this job but today she dawdled. First, she stopped to look at an interesting book. When her mother gently reminded her to take her brother out, she went to get him but stopped on the way to play with an interesting toy.
>
> Esther's mother did not want to scold her or create a confrontation, so she quietly took her son to the door and said to Esther in a friendly tone, "I am going to take your brother out to the sidewalk. Would you meet us there and walk him to the park?"
>
> In less than a minute, Esther finished her activity and went outside. She happily took her brother's hand and walked him to the park.

Esther's mother could have reprimanded her for dawdling, but that would have hurt her feelings and caused resentment. Esther would then be unhappy about the job and might even have refused to do it altogether.

Esther's mother used patience and wisdom. She did not take offense at Esther's behavior, nor scold her for being negligent. She knew that her daughter was not being uncooperative; she was just dawdling — a very normal human practice. So, instead of making problems worse, she got involved in the task and sparked Esther to take over. Esther appreciated this relaxed approach and became more than cooperative — she was happy to do the job. With only a minute of her time, Esther's mother maintained harmony and avoided the friction that so often accompanies criticism.

Use the Inertia of an Agreeable Mood

Our mood tends to determine our outlook. When we are in an agreeable mood, we behave in a spirit of approval and compromise, but when we are in a disagreeable mood, we act in a contrary and difficult manner. This is the law of inertia.

We can use the inertia of a child's agreeable mood to gain cooperation. For example, the time to ask a child to perform an undesirable task is when he is in a happy and positive frame of mind. He does not necessarily have to *do* the task now, he only has to *agree* to do it. Because you've made your request at an opportune time, he may cooperate.

But how can we gain cooperation when the child is in a *dis*-agreeable mood? By setting up his psychological process in an affirmative direction. In other words, make him agreeable by *creating* an agreeable mood.

You can create an agreeable mood by asking questions that you know will receive a "Yes" response. Responding "Yes" several times creates a receptive, positive atmosphere. Once the child's mood is headed in an agreeable direction, present the new idea. Let's illustrate.

> Bentzi was not doing well in school. After his parents met with his teachers, they decided that he should be tutored.
>
> The problem was — Bentzi. He was feeling negative about himself. He told his teachers that he was the "class dummy." He was afraid that he would feel even more inferior with a tutor.
>
> His parents wisely decided not to force the issue. They had to show him how a tutor would be beneficial, but they first had to put him into a more agreeable mood. This was their dialogue:
>
> **Parents:** You haven't been feeling good about your progress in school, is that right?
>
> **Bentzi:** Yes, that's right.
>
> **Parents:** And you would like to do better, is that right?

Bentzi: Yes, that's right. But I'm not so smart, so what can you expect?

Parents: If we could think of a way to improve your grades, would you be willing to try it?

Bentzi: Yes, if it works.

(This is the third "Yes" response the parents have evoked. Bentzi is becoming relaxed and receptive. The dialogue is productive, and he is bonding with his parents.)

Parents: We think a tutor will help you improve. Now, consider this before you decide: You are not feeling very happy and you want to do better. So why not give it a try? If you don't like it, we won't force it on you.

(They were prepared for a negative response. Before he could give it, they responded to it.)

Bentzi: I'm not so sure this will help, but I'll try it — if I can stop any time I want.

After enough "Yes" responses, Bentzi's mindset became more positive, which made him more agreeable. Had Bentzi not been in an agreeable mood, he might have resisted the idea without even considering its benefit.

Pay attention to children's moods. If they are in a disagreeable mood, turn it around. Then use the inertia of the new mood to gain cooperation. If they are already agreeable, grab the opportunity and make the request. You can even go one step further — if they are in an agreeable frame of mind, create *more* agreeability by evoking some "Yes" responses.

Sympathize With the Child

Sometimes a child avoids an assignment — not out of rebellion or opposition, but because he just doesn't feel comfortable doing it. He really would do it, but some emotion within him is holding him back. Giving sympathy can soften that emotion and motivate him to cooperate. Let's illustrate.

The Weinbergs were invited to eat a Shabbos meal

with some friends. Their son Yechiel was not happy about it because he didn't like one of the hosts' children. They never argued or fought; he just didn't care for him.

When it was time to go, Yechiel dilly-dallied. His father nudged him to hurry, but he still delayed. Then his father gently asked, "Yechiel, is there a problem?"

Trying to avoid eye contact, Yechiel put his head down. His father sat down near him and said quietly, "Let's talk about it." Yechiel told him that he did not want to go because he did not care for one of the children.

His father said, "I understand now why you don't want to go. It makes you feel uncomfortable to sit at a table together with somebody you don't care for. Sometimes I get that feeling, too. (long pause) But Yechiel, we were invited there for the Shabbos meal and we agreed to go. So I'll let you sit here for another minute to get your courage together, and then we'll go."

After a minute Yechiel got up, took his father's hand, and left the house.

Yechiel's father could have scolded him for delaying without even trying to discover what the problem was. Or he could have denied Yechiel's feelings by saying, "Don't be so silly. He is a nice boy." But neither approach would have generated cooperation.

His father could also have said, "Sometimes you have to break your *middos* and do things even though you don't want to." But what would that have accomplished? Yechiel was not interested in a sermon; he knew it already. He just wanted his feelings to be understood.

And that is exactly what his father did. Using the "mirroring" method of sympathizing, he neither agreed nor disagreed with Yechiel; he just repeated what Yechiel was feeling. He gave value to Yechiel's feelings and showed that he understood. This was enough to ease Yechiel and gain his cooperation.

Redirect Inappropriate Activities

If a child is acting inappropriately, he should be stopped — especially if he is being hostile or destructive. If you slap him or yell at him, he will probably stop, but at the expense of resentment and hurt feelings.

You can get immediate cooperation without resentment by redirecting the child's activities. Let's illustrate.

> At the Shabbos table, a child is playing with a piece of your good china. Say to her, "The china is not for playing. Here is a book to keep you occupied." Gently give her the book and take the china piece.
>
> A child is about to throw a rock at another person. Tell him, "Rocks are not for throwing at people. You can throw the rock at the tree over there." Point to the tree and gently turn the child's arm in that direction.

When you redirect the child's activities, you recognize his need for the activity but show that you disapprove of his method. You do not confront or scold the child; rather, you find a substitute outlet for the activity. Because he is satisfied with the substitute and his pride remains intact, he cooperates.

Such events occur all the time. One sibling teases another because he can't find anything else to do. A child swings a baseball bat inside the house as a way of releasing energy. There are endless activities in a child's life of which parents disapprove. The resulting collisions often end in tears, hurt feelings, punishment and weakened relationships. Instead of colliding, give the children something else to do. The home will be a calmer place and everyone will be happier.

Make the Goal Seem Easy to Reach

How do people decide if they are capable of reaching a particular goal? They refer to their past experiences and to the general perceptions they have of themselves. The problem with this method, though, is that they may come up with a wrong conclusion — and they won't even know it.

People often have misconceptions about themselves; they mistakenly think they are incapable of certain tasks. As a result, they impose limitations on themselves.

Parents can help children get through the self-doubt routine by making the goal seem easy to reach.[1] They can demonstrate that the goal is less difficult than it appears. They can also show the child that he has the ability to reach the goal. Once the child believes it and is confident enough to perform, the task becomes more manageable.

If a child is having a hard time reaching a goal, don't say, "Sure it's hard but that's what life is all about. You have to try anyway, and with enough hard work you will succeed." This only serves to confirm the difficulty of the task and may cause the child to lose interest.

Say instead, "You are smart and capable of doing a good job. It really is not as hard as it appears. You just think you are incapable, but you really have a hidden flair for it. I know that with a little more effort you will excel." Let him know that he can do it and that you have faith in him. Now he has two incentives — his new belief in himself and the desire not to disappoint you.

If the child still hesitates, shrink the goal by asking him to do it just this once or, if appropriate, to do only part of it. Assure the child that you do not want him to do something he is incapable of doing. Reducing the goal removes some of the difficulty and may enhance cooperation.[2]

Call Attention to a Mistake Indirectly

Sometimes a child makes a mistake and needs immediate correction. We can call attention to the mistake in either a direct or an indirect manner. Because the indirect manner is less offensive, it gains cooperation more quickly.

In the chapter on criticism, we presented several indirect approaches. Some examples include: responding in the positive; the "I feel" message; the "and" message; and reacting with gestures. Because they are inoffensive, they can be used as quick strategies to gain cooperation.

Are These Strategies Manipulative?

You may ask, "Isn't all this manipulative and dishonest? If we want our children to change, we should do the straightforward

---

1. Rabbi Eliyahu Dessler, *Michtav M'Eliyahu*, vol. 3, p. 293.
2. Ibid.

thing and tell them exactly what we want them to do. Plotting all these strategies is nothing more than playing mind games with the child. Shouldn't we be honest and avoid all these manipulative tactics?"

This question can be answered with another question. When you give orders to your children or criticize them, aren't you also trying to influence them to change? If so, why are those methods any less manipulative than the strategies we have just presented? No matter what you do, the goal is the same — to help the child change.

When our desire to change a child's behavior is for *our* benefit, our actions can be called manipulative. But if the change is good for the child, that label doesn't apply. And if our actions consider the feelings of the child and enhance cooperation, we will have done more for his welfare and our relationship with him than giving orders or criticism could ever accomplish.

And if you are ever unsure of the appropriateness of an action or reaction, ask yourself how you would like to be treated if you were in the child's place. How would it feel to be *your* child in *your* home? If you are a teacher, how would *you* like to be *your* student? The answers to these questions often indicate the feasibility of a particular strategy.

You Can Do It

A mother once shared with me her view of the ideas presented in this book. She said, "These ideas are good, but they're not practical. When my little one spills something or doesn't do as I want, it's nice to be able to stop and respond in a relaxed, loving, respectful manner. But that's not the way it works."

This mother decided on her own that she was incapable of applying these methods. Because they represent a style with which she was not familiar or comfortable, she imposed a limitation on herself. She felt she was stuck with her own style and habits. But she was mistaken. No one is stuck with their style or habits. Everyone is capable of change.

When it comes to *middos,* we are born with some and we acquire others through habit. We can still acquire new *middos* through practice, just as we did in the past. All we have to do is act as if we *have* that *middah* and it will soon become second nature.[1]

The mother in the above story can adapt herself to a new style by applying this concept. First she can get the necessary training by reading up on books about parenting. She can seek out other parents who have used positive motivational techniques successfully and ask them for advice. Then she can commit herself to one or two methods and *act* as if they were her style. With practice, effort and determination, they will soon come naturally. She will begin to say, "These ideas are good — and they're practical, too."

If you have any doubt about it, review the concepts presented here and research their sources in *Chazal* or in modern psychology. Make the commitment to try at least one or two new approaches. Do your best, and leave the rest up to the One Above. Be sincere and He will help you.

The strongest reason to make the commitment is the knowledge that it will produce children capable of living up to their potential. Your children are a piece of you; they are your link to the future. You want them to succeed, and by applying the ideas presented here you can make them, not break them.

---

1. Vilna Gaon, *Mishlei* 4:26; *Sefer HaChinuch, mitzvah* 16.

Glossary

Glossary

Abba	father
Aharon HaKohen	Aaron, the High Priest, brother of Moses
Amalek	a nation whose enmity to the Jews dates to Biblical times
Aveirah	sin
Avos	Pirke Avos, Ethics of our Fathers, section of the Mishnah dealing with ethical behavior
Bamidbar	Book of Numbers
Berachah/Berachos	(a) blessing/s; (b) a Talmudic tractate
Bereishis	Book of Genesis
Chazal	Torah sages
Chesed	kindness
Chumash	Five Books of Moses
Chutzpah	audacity
Daven	pray
Devorim	Book of Deuteronomy
Gan Eden	Garden of Eden, Paradise
Gemara	see Talmud
Halachah	normative Jewish law
Hashem	G-d

Ima	mother
Kavanah	concentration, intent
King Dovid	King David
King Shlomo	King Solomon
Kollel	institute of higher Torah learning, usually for married men
K'rias Shema	beginning with the words, Shema Yisrael, these three paragraphs of the Torah are recited twice daily, in the morning and evening prayers
Lashon Hara	disparaging remarks concerning another person
L'Chaim	a wish for life
Mazal	"Fortune"; astrological sign
Middah/Middos	character trait/s
Midrash	collection of interpetations on Scripture, often containing a moral
Minchah	afternoon prayers
Mishlei	Book of Proverbs
Mishnah	early codification of Jewish law
Mitzvah/Mitzvos	Torah commandment/s
Moshe Rabbeinu	Moses, our teacher
Nachas	pride and joy
Oneg Shabbos	party in honor of Shabbos
Parashah	weekly Torah portion
Rebbe	teacher; Chassidic Rabbi
Reuven	oldest son of Jacob
Rosh Yeshiva	head of a yeshiva
Sefer/Seforim	book/s
Shabbos	Sabbath, Saturday
Shacharis	morning prayers

Shemos	Book of Exodus
Shmuel	the prophet Samuel
Shul	synagogue
Shulchan Aruch	Code of Jewish Law
Siddurim	prayer books
Simchah/s	festive occasion/s
Succah	a temporary dwelling used during the holiday of Succos
Talmid Chochom	Torah scholar
Talmud	compendium of discussions on the Mishnah. The basis for Jewish law, as practiced.
Tehillim	Book of Psalms
Teshuvah	repentance
Torah	the entire body of Jewish learning. Sometimes it refers to the Five Books of Moses.
Tosafos	a commentary on the Talmud
Vayikra	Book of Leviticus
Yaakov	the Patriarch Jacob
Yeshiva	institute of Torah learning
Yosef	Joseph, son of Jacob

Biographical Notes

Biographical Notes

Baal Shem Tov — Rabbi Israel Baal Shem Tov (c. 1700-1760) founded the school of service of G-d known as Chassidus. By translating deep kabbalistic ideas into a practical approach to life and people, the movement and its philosophy motivated scholars and masses of ordinary Jews to strive for higher levels of learning and service.

Chazon Ish — Title of the works of Rabbi Avraham Yeshaya Karelitz (1878-1953), a Lithuanian scholar who spent his last twenty years in Bnei Brak. He held no official position, but was acknowledged as a foremost leader of Jewry. His works cover all aspects of Talmud and *halachah*.

Chofetz Chaim — Rabbi Yisroel Meir Kagan (1839-1933). He was known by the title of his book, *Chofetz Chaim*, which details the laws of *lashon hara* (forbidden speech). Renowned for his piety, humility and scholarship, he authored many books covering the gamut of Torah and Jewish life. Recognized as a worldwide leader and *halachic* authority in his generation.

Dessler, Rabbi Eliyahu — (1891-1954). One of the outstanding personalities of the mussar movement. Held leadership positions in Russia and England before settling in Israel, where he served as the *menahel ruchni* (spiritual supervisor) of the Ponevezh Yeshiva. His teachings were published posthumously in the four-volume *Michtav M'Eliyahu*.

Dubno Magid — Rabbi Yaakov Kranz (1741-1804). Became a *darshan* (preacher) at the age of twenty. Served in Dubno for eighteen years, where he became famous for his insightful stories and allegories. His works were published posthumously by his son and a disciple.

Feinstein, Rabbi Moshe — (1895-1986). Born in Russia, he settled in New York in 1937, where he became the *Rosh Yeshiva* of Mesivta Tifereth Jerusalem. Reverently known around the world as "Reb Moshe," he was respected as the greatest *halachic* authority of his time. His responsa, collected in *Igros Moshe,* deal with every facet of contemporary life.

Hirsch, Rabbi Shamshon Raphael — (1808-1888). Rabbinic leader of the Orthodox community of Germany; a fiery leader, brilliant writer and profound educator. Served as Rabbi in Frankfurt-am-Main for 37 years, where he vociferously opposed the growing Reform movement and virtually created the new German Orthodoxy.

Kamenetsky, Rabbi Yaakov — (1891-1986). Rav in Tzitevian, Lithuania and in Toronto, and *Rosh Yeshiva* of Mesivta Torah Vodaath; a foremost thinker and leader of Jewry. Famous for his encyclopedic knowledge, expertise in *halachah*, and for the sound advice he offered those seeking his counsel.

Katz, Rabbi Chaim Mordechai — (1894-1964). Born in Europe, he came to the United States in 1941, and with his brother-in-law Rabbi Eliyahu Meir Bloch, re-established the famous Telshe Yeshiva in Cleveland, Ohio. His lectures on mussar were published under the title, *Be'er Mechokek.*

Kotler, Rabbi Aharon — (1892-1962). Founder and *Rosh Yeshiva* of the Yeshivos of Kletzk, Poland and Beth Medrash Govoha of Lakewood, New Jersey. A pioneer in the American yeshiva movement, he was the foremost proponent of the *kollel* concept and revolutionized Torah life in America. He championed the cause of dedication to non-vocational Torah scholarship.

Levovitz, Rabbi Yeruchom — (1874-1936). A prominent mussar personality, best known as the *Mashgiach* (spiritual supervisor) of the Mirrer Yeshiva in Poland; he was famous for his profound insights into human character. A disciple of Rabbi Simcha Zissel Ziv of Kelm, he authored the *Daas Chochmah U'Mussar.*

Lopian, Rabbi Eliyahu — (1876-1970). A prominent mussar personality in Kelm and London, he began a new career when he settled in Israel in his eighties. His lectures were published posthumously under the title, *Lev Eliyahu.*

Luzzato, Rabbi Moshe Chaim — (1707-1746). Renowned for his works on ethics, philosophy and kabbalah. His most famous book was *Mesilas Yesharim,* which remains a basic mussar text to this day. In addition, he wrote many other seminal works.

Maharal — Acronym for Rabbi Yehudah Loewe ben Bezalel (1526-1609), one of the seminal figures in Jewish thought in the last five centuries. Chief Rabbi in Moravia, Posen, and Prague. Author of numerous works in all fields of Torah, in most of which he presented the concepts of kabbalistic mysticism in terms comprehensible to most scholars.

Maharsha — Acronym for Moreinu HaRav Shlomo Eidel's of Ostroah, Poland (1555-1632). *Rosh Yeshiva* and rabbi in a number of the leading communities of Poland. Author of monumental commentaries on the *halachic* and *aggadic* sections of the Babylonian Talmud. In the *aggadic* commentary he formulated many basic ideas of Torah and its philosophy of life.

Malbim — Rabbi Meir Leibish ben Yechiel Michel (1809-1879), Rabbi in Germany, Romania, and Russia, leading Torah scholar and one of the pre-eminent Bible commentators of modern times. He was vociferously opposed to the new "enlightenment" movement which was sweeping through Europe and influencing thousands of Jews.

Meltzer, Rabbi Isser Zalman — (1870-1953). Respected leader of world Jewry, who served as *Rosh Yeshiva* of the Slutsk Yeshiva in Russia, and later of Yeshiva Eitz Chaim in Jerusalem, where he was one of the primary leaders of Torah Jewry. He was the author of the classic commentary *Even Ha'Azel* on Rambam's *Yad HaChazakah.*

Munk, Rabbi Meir — Contemporary Israeli educator, author of *Schar VeHaanasha BeChinuch,* later translated as *Sparing the Rod,* an incisive guide for Jewish educators.

Netziv — Rabbi Naftali Tzvi Yehudah Berlin (1817-1893). Headed the yeshiva in Volozhin for some forty years. Was one of the wisest leaders of Jewry, especially in formulating responses to czarist persecution. Authored a commentary on Torah, talmudic novella and *halachic* responsa.

Rabbeinu Bachya — (1263-1340). Torah commentator and kabbalist who wrote an encyclopedic Torah commentary which considers the plain meaning, along with Midrashic, philosophical and kabbalistic exegesis. He also wrote on a broad range of topics.

Rabbeinu Yonah — (1180-1263). Rav and moralist of thirteenth century Gerona, Spain. Rabbeinu Yonah wrote commentaries on portions of Scripture, Avos, and several tractates of the Talmud. Among his mussar works, *Shaarei Teshuvah* has been a basic text for the last seven centuries.

Ralbag — Rabbi Levi ben Gershon (1288-1344). Best known for his commentary on Bible, he was also a talmudist, philosopher and astronomer. Wrote a book on astronomy and invented an instrument for precise measurement of heavenly bodies.

Rambam — Acronym for Rabbi Moshe ben Maimon ["Maimonides"] (1135-1204), a pre-eminent Torah scholar of the Middle Ages. His three major works are: *Commentary to the Mishnah*; *Mishneh Torah,* a comprehensive code of Jewish law; and *Moreh Nevuchim* ("Guide for the Perplexed"), a major work of Jewish philosophy. He was also royal physician in Egypt, where he influenced thousands of people through his writings and teachings.

Ran — Acronym for Rabbeinu Nissim (c. 1290- c. 1375). He was a Spanish talmudic commentator and wrote *Derashos HaRan,* a classic exposition of many fundamental subjects of Judaism.

Rashi — Rabbi Shlomo ben Yitzchok (1040-1105). Known as the "father of commentators" because of his clarity, brevity and profundity of understanding. His commentaries on the Bible and Talmud have been the basic tools for all scholars, from his time until today. Lived in France, where by the age of twenty-five he was considered one of the leading talmudists of his day.

Schwab, Rabbi Shimon — Contemporary rabbi and thinker, who has served for over sixty years in the rabbinate on two continents. He climaxed his distinguished career as spiritual leader of the Hirschian Khal Adath Yeshurun community in Washington Heights, N.Y.

Schwartz, Rabbi Yoel — A contemporary Torah scholar and educator, living in Israel. He has written over twenty books, and is widely acclaimed for his vast knowledge of Torah thought.

Shapira, Rabbi Klonimus Kalmish — (1889-1943). Chassidic Rebbe of Piaseczna and martyr in the Warsaw ghetto. Author of *Chovas HaTalmidim* and *Hach'sharas Ha'Avreichim*, works that guide youngsters and adults into the realms of Torah life and kabbalah. As an educator he put his ideas into practice and left an indelible impression on his students and followers.

Sh'lah — Rabbi Yeshaya Horowitz (1560-1630). Known by the abbreviated title of his monumental work on Talmud, law, ethics and kabbalah, *Shnei Luchos HaBris.* Rabbi in Poland, Frankfurt, Prague, and Jerusalem; one of the leading Torah scholars of the early-seventeenth century.

Shmulevitz, Rabbi Chaim — (1902-1979). Born in Lithuania, he was considered a master educator at the age of only twenty-two. After the German onslaught of World War II, he traveled with the Mirrer Yeshiva to Shanghai, China, where he led the yeshiva during its five-year exile. Later became the head of the Mirrer Yeshiva in Jerusalem, where he was famous for his mussar talks.

Twerski, Rabbi Abraham, M.D. — A contemporary Torah scholar and psychiatrist, considered one of America's leading experts in the field of substance abuse rehabilitation. Famous for his lectures and books, which combine Torah knowledge with modern psychology.

Twerski, Rabbi Michel — A contemporary rabbi, living in Milwaukee, Wisconsin, well known for his outreach work to both observant and non-observant Jews throughout the world.

Vilna Gaon — Rabbi Eliyahu ben Shlomo Zalman of Vilna (1720-1797), is referred to simply as "The Gaon," in recognition of his peerless genius. Considered the greatest Torah scholar in many centuries; acknowledged leader of non-Chassidic Jewry of Eastern Europe and spiritual father of the Yeshiva Movement.

Wagschal, Rabbi S. — Contemporary *halachic* authority and author of works dealing primarily with laws relating to the care and rearing of children.

Wolbe, Rabbi Shlomo — A disciple of Rabbi Yeruchom Levovitz, he is a contemporary mussar personality and one of its most influential teachers. Author of *Alai Shur*, he established the Bais HaMussar in Jerusalem, where he has initiated a renaissance of mussar study and its application to daily life.

Ziv, Rabbi Simcha Zissel (of Kelm) — (1824-1898). One of the primary disciples of Rabbi Yisrael Salanter, he founded the Yeshiva of Kelm. A leader in the Mussar Movement, and mentor of its next generation of teachers, his thoughts on various topics of mussar were later collected in the book, *Chochmah U'Mussar*.

Index

Index